Rescue 177

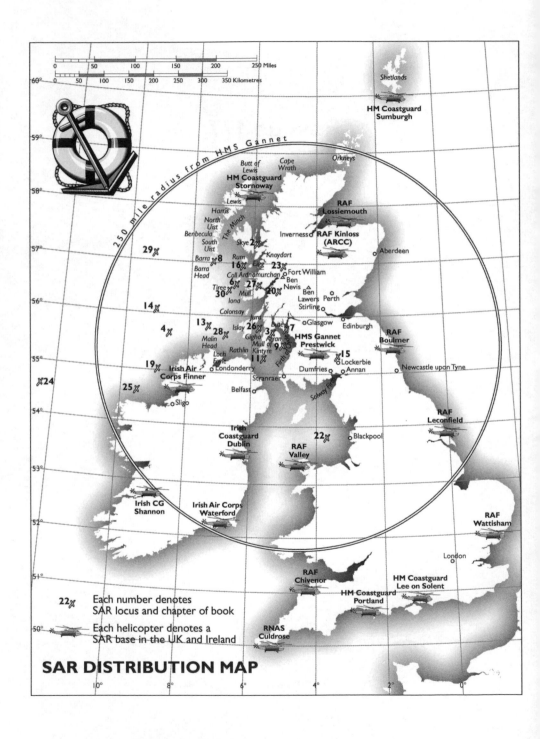

SAR DISTRIBUTION MAP

22✗ Each number denotes
SAR locus and chapter of book

Each helicopter denotes a
SAR base in the UK and Ireland

RESCUE 177

A Scots GP
Flies Search and Rescue
with the Royal Navy

JAMES A. BEGG

mercatpress
www.mercatpress.com

First published in 2003 by
Mercat Press, 10 Coates Crescent, Edinburgh EH3 7AL
www.mercatpress.com

ISBN: 184183 0542

Dedication

For Helen, Colin and Fiona, and all those engaged in Search and Rescue,
by air, land or sea

Set in Arial and Italian Garamond BT at Mercat Press

Printed and bound in Great Britain by Antony Rowe Ltd

Contents

Illustrations

PLATES BETWEEN PAGES 50 AND 51:

Mark 6 ASW Sea King near Ailsa Craig
Sick Bay Staff, HMS *Gannet* 1989
Mountain winching exercise, Isle of Arran
RNAS Prestwick, home to HMS *Gannet* and 819 Squadron
Sick Bay Staff, HMS *Gannet* 1991
Pool drills, Ayr Baths
One-man liferafts
Classic highline transfer from yacht
Winchman's view of highline transfer
Aircrewman going down the wire onto a motor cruiser
Aircrewman being lowered with strop to lift off casualty
Cockpit view of Highland glen on Navex
Heavy operational Mark 6 ASW Sea King

PLATES BETWEEN PAGES 82 AND 83:

The author in goonsuit with Sea King in background
First Pilot's view of approach to fishing vessel for stern transfer
Guiding highline being hauled in on vessel
Medics in transit to a 'job' in rear of Sea King
Monitoring and treating a stretchered casualty
Spacious cabin of the future
Night-time medevac, loading a heavy patient on a stretcher
All Scottish crew, 1992
SAR Sea King in aft deck transfer from nuclear submarine
The view from a two-man strop lift aboard a SAR Sea King

Foreword

Search and Rescue is a hazardous task. By definition it takes place when the weather is normally at its worst and when all other avenues have been explored and discarded. Military personnel accept these risks as part of their role; they lighten the darker moments with humour, content in the knowledge that their training, skill and teamwork will carry them through. That a civilian doctor should thrust himself into this often hostile environment with willingness, enthusiasm and boundless energy is testament to his dedication to deliver medical expertise wherever and whenever required. Doctor 'Jimmy' Begg is just such a civilian: successfully completing 64 missions in 11 years, he has been an integral part of the vital service provided to the people of the West of Scotland, the Highlands and Islands where the regular sight of the red and grey Sea King 'Rescue 177' has become synonymous with all that is good about the UK's Rescue Services.

Jimmy Begg took over the role of SAR Doctor at HMS *Gannet*, Prestwick, in June 1986 at a time when the role of the military aircraft in Search and Rescue was developing. In those early days military aircrew did not hold any recognised medical qualifications and so it was essential that either a Doctor or Medic flew with the aircraft. Additionally, the aircraft's medical equipment was poor, and it was through Dr Begg's efforts that the aircraft's medical supplies and equipment were upgraded to the levels expected in frontline ambulances. This kit is now standard across the SAR community, constantly and consistently saving lives: many people owe their lives to the persistence and tenacity, in those early days, of Jimmy Begg.

This book contains the true stories of some of his rescues: it reads like an adventure novel. From the nightmare of the Lockerbie Disaster, being guarded by Irish Special Branch, the loss of a Chinook on Mull of Kintyre, the lone fisherman who lost his leg, the first UK SAR to a Russian nuclear submarine and a myriad of routine and unusual missions, Jimmy Begg has been witness to them all and relates these stories, giving a fascinating insight into the ways of military SAR. We in the military are always indebted to the civilians who work with us, whatever their role, and having served for over 30 years I am only too well aware of the vital part they play in our everyday life. Jimmy Begg is just such a character: a poet, painter, writer, sailor and angler, he was a pioneer in the development of military Search and Rescue and will be missed by the aircrew of 'Rescue 177'.

Rear Admiral Scott Lidbetter
Officer Commanding 3 Group/ Flag Officer Maritime Aviation
Headquarters Strike Command, High Wycombe

Acknowledgements

The inspiration for this book comes from many sources, not least the camaraderie, humour, support and professionalism of my Sick Bay Medics and all the Royal Navy aircrews with whom I flew SAR. As collected stories gradually assumed book form, I was greatly encouraged by the positive comments and helpful technical advice of Cdr Peter Galloway RN (Rtd), formerly Captain of HMS *Gannet*, and now my fishing and sailing companion, who took the time to read and annotate the early manuscript. Many thanks are also due to my former partners who tolerated my frequent 'death or glory' dashes from busy surgeries, picked up my extra appointments, and still allowed me the valuable use of the Practice photocopier.

At HMS *Gannet* SAR Flight, I must thank the CO, Lt Cdr Andy Watts, and the SARO, Lt Cdr Mark McDermott, for their support and their permission to use 'RESCUE 177', the call-sign of Gannet's Sea King helicopter, for the title of my book. The enthusiastic publicity input of Lt Cdr Robbie Burns PRO, and Neil Smith, Director of Corporate Communications, FOSNNI, Clyde, has been invaluable, and I am grateful to the Ministry of Defence (Navy) and HMS *Gannet* SAR Flight for permission to use their photographs. Navy slang and jargon can be a problem for those, like myself, unfamiliar with 'life in a blue suit', and I learned a lot from Surg Capt Rick Jolly's marvellous book collection of 'Jackspeak'—which has been the inspiration for an indispensable glossary, and a rich source of colourful and humorous language.

To Rear Admiral Scott Lidbetter, FOMA, I sincerely appreciate the sparing of some of his valuable time, in the busy run-up to a war in Iraq, to write such a complimentary Foreword.

For any would-be author, it is a great thrill to find a publisher who sees some merit in his or her work, and I must thank Tom Johnstone and Seán Costello of Mercat Press for their commitment, encouragement and guidance in taking *Rescue 177* forward to publication.

A book on Search and Rescue could not be written without 'The Rescued', and I must especially thank all those patients who endured with fortitude what must often have been terrifying journeys into the unknown, and who have kindly and unhesitatingly allowed their stories to be told; and also their doctors for assistance in helping me to trace them.

Finally, to my dear wife Helen, CINC HOME BEAT, thank you for letting me go off flying while you had to face the fear at home, alone.

Introduction

Search and Rescue—or SAR to those in the know—owes its origins to the fast RAF Air Sea Rescue launches of the Second World War, sent out to retrieve downed fliers from the seas around the British coast.

Post-war development of the helicopter—fast, extremely versatile, and with a much greater scanning horizon for visual searches at sea—quickly led to its adoption by the RAF and Fleet Air Arm as their ideal search and rescue asset for the recovery of aircrew. Strategically placed bases—from RAF Lossiemouth in the north of Scotland, to RNAS Culdrose in Cornwall—ensured that no part of the British coastline was outwith the range of Air Force or Navy helos. Early Whirlwinds were soon superseded by the agile Wessex which gave superb service for many years, till phased out over the past two decades by the Westland Sea King, with its superior attributes of twin engines, radar for night navigation, and a much greater radial range of 300 miles.

Though the rescue of merchant seamen, fishermen and yachtsmen had hitherto, for well over a hundred years, been the task of courageous RNLI Lifeboatmen and the Coastguards, gradually the unique capabilities of military helicopters, both on land and sea, led to their incorporation in a nation-wide search and rescue service.

Operations in coastal waters involving lifeboats, assisting vessels, and latterly its own four Sikorski 61 helicopters are controlled by HM Coastguard. Distant offshore, or maritime, rescues were initially controlled by two military Rescue Coordination Centres—the Northern RCC at Pitreavie Castle, Fife, for operations from Latitude 32 degrees 30 minutes North (The Wash) to the Faroes; and the Southern RCC at Mount Batten, Plymouth, Cornwall, covering incidents from The Wash south to the Bay of Biscay. With advances in global positioning satellite communications (GPS), these two centres have recently been replaced by a single centre—RCC Kinloss in Morayshire—which now coordinates rescues over this vast area of ocean, backed up by long-range Nimrod aircraft, tasked to locate distressed vessels, and provide top cover for any rescue helicopters involved.

On the not-infrequent occasion when there is an overlap of responsibility for a maritime incident, RCC and HM Coastguard operations dovetail very effectively, making maximum use of all assets: Lifeboat Stations; Royal Navy Sea Kings based at HMS *Gannet* SAR Flight, Prestwick, and RNAS Culdrose; and RAF Sea Kings from RAF Stations—Lossiemouth, Boulmer, Leconfield,

Chivenor, Wattisham and Valley—as well as Coastguard Sikorskis at Sumburgh, Stornoway, Lee-on-Solent and Portland. These SAR Stations all have a range overlap, allowing one unit to cover another if its helo is out of station on a mission.

Initially conceived as purely military assets, whose use for civilian purposes was frowned upon and resisted for many years by the MOD, the enlarged role of the SAR helicopter has evolved in response to public needs, and a political awakening to the public relations benefits and goodwill engendered by each high-profile dramatic rescue. Nowadays only 5% of SAR activity involves going to the assistance of endangered military personnel. In addition to PR, there were obvious, tangible benefits to be derived from the superb training offered, as motivated aircrews honed and perfected their flying and medical skills daily in extreme real-life situations rather than on simulated exercises.

On land, over the past thirty years, the soaring popularity of climbing and hillwalking has led to a huge rise in mountain incidents, and generated a demand for increased provision of rescue services. After the War, the RAF had formed and maintained its own Mountain Rescue Teams to handle any military air accidents on land, while Police MRTs, aided by local volunteers, formed the backbone of the civilian effort. Very quickly, however, the RAF Teams became heavily involved in climbing rescues, while at the same time, in all major UK climbing centres, local highly trained, superbly equipped MRTs were being formed from the nucleus of farmers, stalkers and shepherds previously called out for their local knowledge and stamina, rather than their rock-climbing expertise. As climbing became more technical, so MRT members had to be able to respond to any situation.

It was inevitable that rescue helicopters would soon become involved in this challenging environment. Despite the flying constraints frequently imposed by appalling mountain weather conditions, they have proved invaluable in cliff rescues, airlifting casualties and MRT members, and in conducting day-long searches for missing climbers.

At sea, there were two separate perceived needs. On the leisure side, as in climbing, there had been a similar explosion in the popularity of sailing, sea angling, sailboarding, and just messing about in boats, which had also led to greatly increased demands on rescue services.

There was also a serious gap in the provision of emergency transport to hospital for inhabitants of remote areas of Scotland, especially the island communities. This need had been identified as far back as 1933, when the Scottish Air Ambulance Service was born. Using small twin-engined aircraft able to land on short grass airstrips, or even island beaches, this unsung pioneering initiative has quietly continued to provide the primary, major lifeline service from the islands to mainland hospitals for over seventy years.

The service was greatly expanded by the Scottish Ambulance Service in 1992, with the introduction of three light helicopters and three fixed-wing aircraft, with the aim of reducing their budgetary expenditure and dependence on SAR helicopters. This has not happened, since fixed-wing aircraft and light helicopters are also affected by adverse weather conditions, unable to land on waterlogged grass runways, operate in severe gales, snow or fog, or attempt night landings on some airstrips. Some small inhabited islands have no airstrip. In such situations, SAR helicopters have still found themselves just as heavily involved in Medevacs of patients with serious medical problems as they were in the late 1970s and early 1980s.

In those early days, long distance helicopter transfers—except on occasions when the patient was accompanied by an island doctor—were often undertaken without the necessary medical skills, or even adequate medical equipment to deal with potential inflight emergencies, since the MOD's only contractual responsibility to Health Authorities was to provide a transport vehicle for the patient, not medical expertise or equipment.

This was the situation in which I found myself in June 1986, when I took over the role of SAR Doctor at HMS *Gannet*, Prestwick, from my illustrious predecessor and friend Dr S.Y. MacKechnie MBE. Suddie had been the Base Civilian Medical Practitioner for the previous fifteen years, and had been involved in around twenty SAR missions during this time. Search and Rescue was then only a relatively minor operational part of the work of 819 Squadron, Fleet Air Arm, whose primary role was anti-submarine warfare. Since Gannet was not then a designated SAR Station, callouts were infrequent, averaging around thirty a year, and the response time—at 45 minutes by day, and 90 minutes by night—was more leisurely than rapid.

Worldwide, the skills and protocols for Pre-Hospital Immediate Care were still in their formative stages, and many of our present-day standard procedures were as yet unknown. I had been fortunate in being asked to help establish an Immediate Care Scheme for Ayrshire and Arran Health Board in 1976, and my experience of dealing with road accidents and other pre-hospital emergencies, and awareness of the new techniques and equipment being developed by the British Association of Immediate Care Schemes (BASICS) and the Scottish Ambulance Service, quickly made me aware that a Royal Navy standard Ship's Doctor's white plastic box, containing a couple of drip sets, some drugs, a few field dressings—and a bottle of Smelling Salts!—fell far below the standard of equipment routinely available on our frontline ambulances.

Since Rescue 177, our SAR Sea King, was becoming increasingly employed as a 'frontline ambulance' for the islands, ships, fishing boats and mountains, I felt strongly that it should be equipped as such—and as soon as possible.

This book tells of early struggles to achieve simple objectives, like a second oxygen cylinder on board—'We've got to watch the weight, Doc!'—and the purchase of a set of cervical collars; and of the thrill of acquiring a thousand pounds-worth of surplus ambulance equipment.

It highlights the frustrations of dealing with Navy bureaucracy when trying to obtain 'non-standard' vital items of equipment such as a Heartstart defibrillator and a Propaq vital signs monitor, once HMS *Gannet* had become a designated SAR Station in 1989—with the take-off response time for Rescue 177 sharply reduced to only 15 minutes from dawn to dusk, and 30 minutes by night.

Between 1986 and 1995, annual SAR total callouts rose exponentially from 30 to 230 per year, making HMS *Gannet* the second busiest Search and Rescue unit in the UK after RAF Lossiemouth. Finally, with 274 callouts in the year 2000, Royal Navy Air Station Prestwick overtook 'The Crabs', and achieved the distinction of being the busiest SAR Base in the British Isles.

This book tells of the constant learning curve, and of lessons learned and applied after encountering unexpected problems during a mission; like the quiet satisfaction on hearing that a newly installed defibrillator had saved another premature baby.

The lessons learned, the availability of first-class monitoring and resuscitation equipment on board, and a more professionally structured Service programme of Advanced Pre-Hospital Care training, gradually produced a build-up of confidence and expertise among my Medical Assistants and backseat aircrew, to the extent eventually that they seldom felt the need to call in the Doc. By 1997, I was virtually—and happily—redundant, having participated in sixty-four SARs.

Most of these were Medevacs from the islands, inter-hospital transfers or Casevacs from vessels at sea. Due to the nature of mountain rescue work, often involving long, exhausting searches, I was seldom called out to witness superb flying skills in extreme weather conditions, or experience the naked fear of flying within a few feet of a thousand-foot cliff-face in blizzard conditions. Although unable to relate them first-hand, I have heard many tales, and can only marvel at the courage of those involved.

Despite the massive press coverage often given to those saved in major dramatic rescues, because of that self-effacing modesty which characterises the professional persona of aircrew (I'll say nothing about their Mess and Wardroom antics!), very little is usually learned by the general public about the background to each drama.

For eleven years, I was privileged to fly as a member of a SAR Aircrew with some great lads—and lasses—to observe, and participate in, many exciting, monotonous, humorous, tragic, challenging and mundane jobs. I was also (sorry lads!), in the words of Robert Burns—'*a chiel amang ye, takin notes*'—or at least, taking note and fascinated by all that happened.

The end result is intended to give a fly-on-the-bulkhead picture of the wise-cracking camaraderie of the SAR Aircrews, often used to lighten a hazardous moment or a harrowing experience; and also a personal tribute to the tremendous skill and team-work involved in getting there, doing a good job, and returning safely.

Because of the sensitive nature and tragic end to some of the tasks undertaken, and the need to preserve patient confidentiality, and where I have been unable to trace patients to obtain permission to describe their stories, I have in some instances used fictitious names and fictitious illnesses, and changed town or island names to protect individuals. At other times, especially where there was press publicity of an incident, and there was a happy outcome, I have not disguised identities—with the gracious permission of those involved. It was marvellous—and very touching—to speak again with many of these former patients, and learn of their progress and success over the intervening years. I hope that this format will offend no one, but in the unlikely event that it does, I apologise unreservedly for any intrusion of privacy.

Finally, there are two unwilling parties to this adventure, without whom it would never have been accomplished. Firstly, my partners who, under sufferance (but well-remunerated!) had to absorb my interrupted surgeries when I shot off up the bypass with green light flashing—and had occasionally to fly themselves in the early years—and secondly but most importantly, my dear wife Helen.

Helen's suffering was greater than any other, and probably shared stoically by most of the wives and partners of our SAR Aircrews nationwide. It is one thing to swan off on some 'Action Man' stunt on a horrible dark night, getting your 'Adrenalin fix' in the sure company of a bunch of guys you can trust. It is another to lie awake with a mind running wild, as an Atlantic winter gale batters against the bedroom windows, worried sick and agonising as to whether you will ever see your husband again. And sometimes, when carefully arranged social plans went 'oot the windae', she'd wish I'd join them!

Thank you, love, for putting up with my selfishness and 'Boy's Own' capers!

James A. Begg

1

June 1986

'Boy's Own Stuff...'

'It's Suddie MacKechnie for you.'—Helen handed me the phone with a puzzled look, and my heart leapt in guilty anticipation. Apart for looking for a reserve for the curling, and that was unlikely in midsummer, there was only one reason why Dr Sutherland Y. MacKechnie, MBE, would be ringing.

'Is that you, Jimmy, my boy?' His soft gravelly Highland voice was music to my ears. 'Are you still interested in Gannet?'

I hesitated for a moment, fearing Helen's predictable reaction, then, masking my excitement, replied in one word—'Yes!'

It was the realisation of a dream I had cherished for the past eighteen years, ever since joining the Cathcart Street practice as 'the boy doctor', when Alan Paterson, my senior partner, with a flourish like the Merry Monarch bestowing Dukedoms, had casually asked—'How would you like to become the Admiralty Surgeon and Agent for Ayr and District?'

One of my boyhood ambitions had been to join the Royal Navy. Here was a dream fulfilled, I had thought—with visions of scrambled egg on my bunnet, four rings on my sleeve, and visits to ships of the line and nuclear submarines. I was soon brought back to earth, or high tide mark at least, by the sad discovery that this grand Pooh-Bah title was worth a measly thirty quid a year—doing Entry Examinations on a brace of Royal Naval Auxiliary Service volunteers, or putting the kibosh on attempts by a few lead-swinging Jacks to extend their shore leave!

However, when 'The Troubles' broke out a few years later in Northern Ireland, and the MOD decided, for security reasons, to move HMS *Gannet* with its anti-submarine helicopter squadron, lock, stock and barrel from Ballykelly Airfield near Londonderry, to Prestwick, I wrote to the Admiralty volunteering my services (hopefully well-remunerated!) should they require a base doctor. I was bitterly disappointed when they replied informing me that the current CMO at RAF Prestwick, Dr S.Y. MacKechnie, Sqn Ldr (Rtd), had been appointed in a dual role to cover the Navy as well. Suddie was an old family friend of Helen's folks, and over the years we had talked of his work and of my interest in it, with always a promise that he'd keep me in mind when he eventually retired.

Unfortunately, as happens with so many of the 'best laid schemes o' mice and men', several young partners appeared on the scene who were able to stand in for Suddie during his annual leave, and who consequently became his heirs apparent as the years progressed. Suddie had been apologetic, but I could appreciate his predicament with regard to his practice loyalties, and quietly resigned myself to the fact that, from now on, parading the decks of a Mirror dinghy would probably be the pinnacle of my naval career.

What had happened? Why the sudden about-turn? I knew Suddie had not been seeing eye-to-eye with his former partners since his retirement from general practice, but this development was completely unexpected.

'I've been retired four years now, Jimmy, and have had fifteen years doing SARs. I've thoroughly enjoyed the experience, but I'm getting a wee bit too old now for jumping in and out of helicopters.' Suddie was always secretive about his age, and as even his best friends could get no closer than 'round about, or on the wrong side of seventy', I reckoned that his last remark was 'a wee bit' of an understatement. For a man of his age to have been winched on and off ships and mountainsides, in all sorts of weather, was a tribute to a sound constitution, bolstered by a lifetime of active participation in rugby, golf, curling and malt whisky.

'You'll maybe only get two or three trips a year out of it, mind you, for my Medical Assistants are very highly trained medics, and usually deal with the broken legs, appendicitis cases, and suchlike. Even so, I've had over twenty callouts for serious medical cases where a doctor was requested. I'll contact Captain Davis in London and arrange a meeting.'

At this meeting a few weeks later, I discovered that various differences of opinion between the Navy and Suddie's ex-partners had led Captain Davis to seek alternative SAR cover, and when he heard I was already a Navy appointee as Surgeon and Agent for Ayr, the matter was settled.

Helen, needless to say, was less than enamoured by the prospect of her dearly-beloved disappearing week after week into the teeth of storm and tempest to rescue mariners in distress, but when Suddie sweet-talked her and explained how seldom I would be called out, and that most cases would be hospital to hospital transfers, she relented, and slowly resigned herself to what she thereafter referred to disparagingly as my 'Boys' Own' capers and 'Action Man' stunts.

My partners were equally hesitant, and only the inducement of a substantial financial bung fired their mean and mercenary hearts to volunteer to a man to cover my absences. Paul 'I Love You, Mammon!' Stevens, who was once quoted as saying 'You'll never get me up in one of those machines!', found himself offering to be my Number Two—as a result of which he and I presented ourselves at HMS Gannet on a beautiful sunny sixteenth of September 1986, to be measured for our flying suits, and to undertake our first training flight and winching practice.

The pre-flight briefing was not new to me, as I had already flown in a Sea King ten years previously, on a practice flight as one of the Ayrshire Immediate Care Scheme doctors; so I watched with interest the alarmed expression on Big Paul's face as the Petty Officer Survival Equipment ran through the standard procedures for opening the emergency exits with the helicopter upside-down in the water.

He was white-knuckled as we were strapped into our seats for take-off, but once airborne he relaxed considerably, and even appeared to enjoy the flight over the beautiful Ayrshire countryside, with a bird's eye view of many of its well-known landmarks—from the stark modern Liquorice Allsort of Crosshouse Hospital with its designated helicopter landing site, to Culzean Castle, Robert Adam's magnificent eighteenth century masterpiece, crowded by its wooded policies to perch precariously on the edge of sheer sea cliffs rimming the Firth of Clyde twelve miles south of Ayr.

We even had time for a wee birl above our respective houses before arriving back at Prestwick for a winching session over the runway. The mysteries of the strop and the earthing cable were explained to us before I was lowered to the tarmac with the ominous and terrifying instruction to keep my feet up, or risk being fried by powerful static electricity from the Sea King flashing through me rather than the cable, should I be so stupid as to touch the ground before it did!

Needless to say, I obeyed, and survived intact, but had to watch in horror as Paul, all six foot four of him, barely made it with inches to spare, when the earthing cable curled up slightly at its tip, and only just touched the ground ahead of his big feet. Double-man winching followed, being lowered and hoisted along with the Winchman, before the session ended with a cup of coffee in the crew-room.

'That was great!' said the Big Man as we drove back into Ayr. 'When's the next practice?' The answer to that question came a few weeks later when I walked into the staff-room and announced Pool Drills—life-raft practice scheduled for the swimming baths. 'You'll never get me in one of these things!' cried Paul, aghast. 'I cannae swim!'

2

2 March 1987

First SAR

Forget all that nonsense about 'stuffed shirts and old fogeys' in Rotary Clubs. I'd just joined Ayr Rotary and was still reeling from the after-shock of their curling weekend at Kinross. We had wined, dined, danced and curled ourselves into such a state of exhaustion that on the drive home to Ayr through gale-driven squalls and spray-fog from heavy lorries, Helen fell fast asleep and left me nodding and frantically head-shaking to keep myself from doing likewise; so it was a pleasant feeling to crawl between the sheets—before midnight, for once in my life—and look forward to a long and unbroken slumber.

Then the phone rang.

'Is that you, Jimmy?' It was Paul.

'Aye. What's wrong?'

'This bloody bleep has just gone off! I've phoned Gannet, and they said something about Skye and needing oxygen!'

I'd been round to Paul's house to pick up the bleep shortly after we got home, but he was out and Frances had big-heartedly said he would just hold on to it till the morning… like a hot brick!

'It's OK, Paul. Leave it with me and I'll see what's happening.'

Ops Room could only tell me that there was a SAR on—a man in Skye with a head injury was to be transferred to the Southern General Neurosurgical Unit in Glasgow—and that a doctor had been requested to accompany him.

Helen was less than happy at the prospect, and I couldn't blame her. 'It's a terrible night with that gale. Do you really have to go? I won't sleep a wink till you get back!' With as much reassurance as I could muster, I kissed her goodbye and left.

At the base I was relieved to find I would be accompanied on the flight by one of the medical assistants. MA Paul Newton was a quiet, thoughtful, assured young medic who had been working with me over the past few weeks, upgrading and refurbishing the medical equipment carried on SARs. Up in Sick Bay, he helped me struggle into my 'Goon Suit' and flying boots, and I had only just time to phone Helen and tell her I would be away about four hours, before a staff car picked us up and whisked us down to the waiting helicopter.

Engines roaring, rotor-blades whirling, red lights flashing, the Sea King sat there like some great, black, hungry dragonfly, as we scrambled into the darkness of its belly with our gear. In the first-time confusion and excitement, I could make out dim figures here and there as I was pushed hurriedly forward and thrust into a seat just behind the Pilot and Co-Pilot. Seat-belts fastened, helmets plugged into the intercom, and dead on midnight we were airborne.

'Speak when you're spoken to, and shut up when you're told', are cardinal in-flight rules, so I sat obediently silent and listened, with a strange feeling of detachment, to the aircrew going professionally about their business of getting us to Skye.

'Fifty knot headwind... will give us a ground speed of sixty knots... should take about two hours... Stratus cloud-level around one thousand feet... heavy rain squalls... better fly low... up the coast to West Kilbride first...'

'Can Doc come up-front, Sir? It's his first SAR,' MA Newton addressed the Captain.

'OK, Doc. Unstrap and come forard.'

A few steps and I was standing behind and between the Pilots, peering through rain-lashed windows and flailing windscreen wipers as the orange lights of Ayrshire coastal towns slipped past, below and to starboard.

'Can you give me any details of the casualty?' I ventured cautiously, as I felt I should at least know something about the case I would be dealing with. In the rush to get on board, I had been told nothing.

'Don't know much, Doc,' came a non-committal reply. 'All we've got from Rescue Control in Edinburgh is a message to pick up a man with a head injury from a field near Broadford in Skye. We might get more details as we fly.'

A Scots voice broke in—'I think that's West Kilbride now... we'll head for the south end of Bute.' The Pilot was rustling away with a quarter-inch to the mile flight map of Scotland laid over his instrument panel, apparently identifying the landmarks.

Nice to know there's another Scotsman aboard, I thought.

The aircraft banked to port, and soon we could just make out a dull mass beneath, sparsely dotted with lights, some moving, which was firmly identified as the tail end of the island of Bute. Far to the left were the faint village lights of Corrie, on Arran, while here and there on the black void in between twinkled the navigation lights of a few hardy fishing boats. We headed north west up Loch Fyne, and faint, darkly ominous outlines of hills loomed high on either side. I only hoped the Pilot could see them as well as I could... Should I tap him on the shoulder and tell him? With a supreme effort of will I restrained myself.

Far away and dead ahead, a string of orange street lights flickered on the horizon as a squall cleared.

'What are these lights?' I asked.

'Ardrishaig,' the Scots voice replied.

'How far?' I queried.

'Thirteen and a half miles,' came the prompt reply.

These guys must have dead reckoning down to a fine art, I thought, most impressed by such a precise estimation—I would have guessed about ten miles.

A few minutes later, and we were over Ardrishaig.

'Now where's the bloody Crinan Canal?' said the Co-Pilot.

'Should be somewhere down to your left,' the Scots lad informed him, and simultaneously two brilliant beams of light shot out from the underside of the aircraft, as its searchlights played over rooftops and fields and we waltzed over the village, trying to locate the elusive waterway. 'There it is… No! It's just the bloody road.'

Just to the left of the road, we eventually locked on to and followed a black ribbon of water snaking through the flat countryside towards Crinan, illuminating, as we went, the masts and rigging of yachts fast asleep at their moorings.

Beyond Crinan we passed low between the islands of Scarpa and Luing into the Firth of Lorne, and soon the lights of Craignure on Mull were visible away to port. Then into the Sound of Mull, and there, in the farthest distance, a single light flashed a faint message.

'That's Ardnamurchan Lighthouse dead ahead. We'll head for it.' We did just that, then turned right up the coast and into the Sound of Sleat. By this time I was becoming more and more impressed by the Pilots' navigational skills in foul weather and in pitch darkness, as they regularly checked the maps on their laps. Once through the Kyles, and we were virtually at Broadford.

'Where's the landing site?'

'I don't know. The map shows an airfield just to the east of Broadford. We'll make for there.' Almost immediately, a windsock was picked up in our landing lights, and we dropped down on to the airstrip. It was deserted.

'Don't see any flashing blue lights. Do you?'

We all peered out into the inky blackness, and a searchlight was trained on the airfield buildings. Nothing.

'This could be most embarrassing, chaps, if we've landed at the wrong place,' cracked our Pilot.

'Most embarrassing!' echoed the others.

'I… think there's a hospital at Broadford,' I chipped in hesitantly, mindful of old press reports of climbing accidents on the Cuillin.

'Is there, Doc? We'll try there.' We took off towards the lights of Broadford just across the bay and, quickly spotting a single flashing blue light, landed on a gently sloping field beside a low white building—the hospital.

'Right, Doc,' said Paul Newton. 'It's our turn now!'

We disembarked and were, to my surprise, joined by two other crew members from the back of the aircraft—not just the Winchman I had expected to be there.

A bustle of nurses met us and our Stokes Litter stretcher, and guided us to a sideroom where a young white-coated doctor hovered over a deeply comatose man, all dripped and catheterised, and ready for transportation.

'A climbing accident?' I asked.

'No. He was working up a ladder and fell eight feet on to concrete. He has been in here with a badly fractured skull for the past forty-eight hours, but his condition has started to deteriorate, and the Southern advised shipping him out.'

Sister, who obviously recognised MA Newton's worth more than mine, by the red cross on his helmet, ignored me completely and buttonholed him with the nursing details, after which we gently transferred the patient onto our stretcher and carefully loaded him on board the Sea King.

'How high can we fly, Doc? The weather is clearing and we have a tailwind.'

The question was unexpected, and before I could reply, the MA interjected 'About three thousand maximum, Sir,' thus saving me a moment of minor embarrassment, for although I knew it would be unsafe to fly high with a head injury, I wasn't yet familiar with the various 'ceilings'. I had a lot to learn.

This height allowed us to fly overland most of the way back, and I was amazed to find us over Glasgow Airport only forty-five minutes later, having reaped the benefit of a fifty knot tailwind. The outward journey to Skye had taken over two hours!

I also discovered quickly that monitoring a patient's condition in the dark, noisy, vibrating environment of a helicopter posed unique problems, for it was impossible to check blood pressure, and almost impossible to check anything but the strongest pulse. It was obvious that one could only rely on instinct and basic observation to sense if something was going wrong, but fortunately, in this case, the poor man's condition remained stable till we handed him over to Glasgow ambulancemen for the last leg of his long trip to the Neurosurgical Unit. Sadly however, medical expertise was not able to save him and he died three days later.

Our task done, we lifted off, and within ten minutes were back at Prestwick. The crew alighted and promptly vanished. It was four o'clock, and time for kip!

'Well, did you enjoy your first SAR, Doc?' Paul Newton asked me as we struggled out of our flying gear.

I affirmed, and mentioned how impressed I had been with the crew's piloting and navigational skills under such adverse weather conditions, before asking curiously who the fourth crew member had been.

The MA grinned. 'Oh, that was Lt Fraser Anderson, the Observer. He's a Scotchman, like yourself and the Pilot, Lt Barrett.'

'So that's why he knew Ardrishaig was thirteen and a half miles ahead. It was his Scots voice, and not the Pilot's!'

'Yeah. He has transparent plastic charts that fit over his radar screen, and by pressing a few buttons he can tell the Pilot exactly where his position is, to within a few yards, anywhere in the West of Scotland... And any hills or electric pylons up ahead of him.'

So much for 'dead-reckoning'—I needn't have worried—but come to think of it, I didn't much anyway.

And neither, apparently, did Helen, for when I phoned home she was sound asleep!

3

11 March 1987

'When Eight Bells Toll!'

Be-e-ep! Be-e-ep! Be-e-ep! Be-e-ep!

I surfaced in a panic from a deep, deep, sleep—a rare enough occurrence at the best of times—wondering what the hell the noise was. Then it dawned, and I cursed the timing—four o'clock on a March morning was, to say the least, inconsiderate, given that Helen had only just stopped twitching following my first SAR to Skye ten days previously—and here was the possibility of another. So much for Suddy MacKechnie's 'two or three a year'!

I groped for the telephone and dialled Gannet.

'Hello, Doc. MA Stephenson here. We've a submarine with a case of peritonitis on board… West of Arran… the Captain has requested a doctor… Shouldn't be a long trip… Can you come in?'

Winched down to a sub! That'll be a novel experience, I thought, as I simultaneously placated an angry, agitated wife and struggled into my trousers.

We took off over the Firth of Clyde into the inky blackness of a cold, clear, moonless night, skirted the northern ridges of the Arran Hills, and soon were dropping down on to the Kilbrannan Sound. The submarine was quickly located, distinguished from a scattering of fishing boats by its bow, stern and conning-tower lights.

As we approached and illuminated the vessel with our powerful searchlights, a strange feeling of total incredulity possessed me. I was utterly calm. No nerves, no palpitations, no sweaty palms. The scene below was too unreal. The long, matt-black, sinister shape sat motionless on a flat sea, for all the world like one of those fake test-tank models we used to spot in war films as wee boys at the pictures; so artificial that they always destroyed any illusions of film-time reality. It was like a scene from an Alastair MacLean movie.

As we circled above the submarine, quiet voices over the intercom reminded me it was for real.

'What do you want done, Sir? Will the MA go down first?'

'No. I think we'll let Doc go down first. It'll be good practice for him… Is that OK with you, Doc?'

I was secretly chuffed to get the chance, for if the Medic had gone down first, as was customary, I might have been surplus to requirements. 'Yes. That's OK by me… What do you want me to do?'

'Go down below and assess the guy. He's got stomach pains, but if he's fit enough, I want him up in the harness. The stretcher can be a bit awkward and I'd prefer not to have to use it… The Aircrewman will follow you down later. OK?'

At that, another friendly voice chipped in—'Oh, and remember to keep your knees up—if you don't want your balls fried off!'

I remembered all right. Powerful aircraft static… earthing wire on to metal submarine… Knees up Brother Brown!

Raising my arms into the harness strop, I snuggled it under my armpits, pulled the toggle tight, then bum-shuffled my way across to the open door to sit, legs dangling over the edge.

Thumbs-up, a jerk, and I was launched into space. Below me, our down-draught sent a rosette of flying spray swirling over the three Ratings on the for'ard deck as they crouched for shelter behind the submarine's upraised diving vanes. For an interminable time I seemed to hang in mid-air, spinning round and round and round, before being brought down low enough to the narrow walkway to gain a footing, and be grasped by the waiting sailors.

I didn't see it—maybe my knees were up over my eyes—but they told me later there was an almighty blue flash as the earthing cable contacted the deck. Which is probably why one of the Ratings looked scared out of his wits as he tried to hook me on board with a large boat-hook, itself earthed to the deck with a wire cable and magnetic clamp!

Safely onboard, and with the helicopter circling at a distance, the Sub's First Lieutenant introduced himself and led me along the narrow walkway to the for'ard hatch. For several minutes the four of us stood gawking down this gaping black manhole like kids at a wishing well, while nothing happened.

Eventually I made a knocking gesture with my knuckles, and bawled in his ear—'Dae ye have tae chap doun?' I doubt if he understood the Scots idiom, but he got the message and promptly conducted us further along to the con-ning tower, where a door opened sesame—through which we gingerly entered to negotiate steel ladders and narrow hatches plunging down into the bowels of the sub. As I clambered down the vertical shaft, I mentally took my hat off to any submariners faced with the problem of getting out in a hurry… And how the hell would we get this guy out on a stretcher?

At the foot of the ladder, a mahogany plaque proclaimed *HMS Odin* in large brass letters, and I wondered where I had heard the name before. Then it clicked. This was the submarine used to train potential submariner captains, which I had seen prominently featured in the BBC 'Perishers' series only a few months previously. It was all I had ever imagined a submarine to be like, with pipes, valves, and cables lining a claustrophobic central passage running fore and aft, off which opened even more claustrophobic cabins—and right beside me, in the middle—a real up-periscope!

Ushered into one of these cabins, I was faced with as piratical a bunch of buccaneers ever seen this side of the Spanish Main. Close-cropped heads mirror-imaged the four-day stubble on their chins; grubby singlets exposed a gallery of tattooed arms and chests; half a dozen pairs of eyes stared unblinking from tiered bunks around a table cluttered with mugs, cigarette packets, and mounds of fag-ends; while on a bottom berth in the corner, a bulky sailor lay clutching his stomach and looking bloody miserable.

I knelt beside him and soon established, from its colicky nature, that his belly-ache was certainly not peritonitis. More like a surfeit. If he had been one of our Practice patients, I'd probably have suggested a couple of codeine tablets, a cosy cuddle with a hot-water bag and a good fart! But in this situation— what to do? The Sub had another twenty-four hours of its tour of duty still to run. The Captain—perhaps a trainee whose career was on the line—had requested a doctor, and several million pounds-worth of helicopter was hovering expectantly overhead at £2,000 an hour… To suggest a good fart would hardly be wise. Another form of evacuation was called for.

By this time, Steve Gardiner, the Aircrewman, had joined us, and we kitted out our patient with ear-muffs and life-jacket before helping him up on deck for winching by harness. Once on board, he was able to sit between us, and managed to 'Huey' a couple of times, but not before a NATO Issue Puke Bag was hurriedly produced and passed to him by the M.A.. Naval Air Command don't like their helicopters reeking of vomit, and traditional inter-branch Senior Service rivalries were soon manifest, with some choice, derogatory, slagging remarks over the intercom about the unpleasant, unhealthy, and unnatural habits of submariners in general—naturally unheard by our guest!

Within twenty minutes we had landed him safely at Crosshouse Hospital, near Kilmarnock, and a few minutes later were back at Prestwick. As we walked across the tarmac back to the Ops Room, Bill Barrett the Pilot was strangely apologetic: 'Sorry about that, Doc!'

'Sorry about what?' I asked curiously.

'That winching… the wire jammed when you were half-way down, and we had to hand-winch you the rest of the way!'

'So that's why I birled around so long!'

'Not to worry, Doc,' consoled Stevie later. 'It's always the same with Lt Barrett. Something always happens on his trips. They call him 'The Reaper'… but he always gets you back!' I recalled the Skye trip—when we had landed at the wrong place.

In the morning, curious to know if my diagnosis had been correct, I rang Crosshouse, only to find that our matelot had already been discharged.

11

'Just a case of gut-rot, Doctor!' confirmed the young resident, and added with a laugh, 'By the way, it was the Cook who diagnosed the Peritonitis!'

4

3 April 1987

Bandit Country!

'We're on stand-by at the moment, Doc,' the Duty Officer informed me as I hurried into the Ops Room to find assorted fully-kitted aircrew lounging around, feet up, drinking coffee, like latter-day Battle of Britain pilots.

'The information we've got so far from Edinburgh is that a Norwegian fishing boat somewhere west of Ireland has requested help to lift off a seaman with abdominal pain. She's heading for the Irish coast at present, and it all depends on her position as to whether it will be worth our while going.'

It was seven o'clock on a fine April morning, and I didn't relish the prospect of heading back home for breakfast and a dreich morning surgery, so when the go-ahead call came through from Edinburgh Rescue Centre a few minutes later, I was more than delighted.

Helped on by a thirty knot easterly tail-wind, we made good time over to the Mull of Kintyre and along the Antrim coast, then, keeping well outside the Irish Republic's twelve-mile limit, we skirted the distant, rugged coastline of Donegal, where long arcs of silver sand, fringing broad Atlantic bays, glinted and beckoned like sirens in the early morning sun.

Sitting aft in the helicopter, I found myself plugged into the main intercom, and was intrigued to learn that we had the support of a Nimrod reconnaissance aircraft, which was directing operations from six miles up, having probably flown down from RAF Kinloss in less time than it had taken us to come over from Prestwick.

'Rescue One Seven Seven... Nimrod. You are directly on course for Norwegian ship *Stalegg Senior* four miles dead ahead. You should have visual contact any time now.'

By this time I was up front, standing behind the Pilots, and unsuccessfully scanning the horizon for a glimpse of the ship, when Lt Moffat, our Captain, suddenly responded—'Nimrod... Rescue One Seven Seven. I have visual contact at one o'clock, and am now making my approach.'

I could still see nothing on the horizon, but on looking downwards and slightly to the right, I eventually spotted a small red-hulled vessel, apparently almost directly below us, but in fact still several miles ahead. I hadn't appreciated quite how much difference flying at four thousand feet could make to the visible horizon, and just how short a distance four miles was from that altitude.

We descended rapidly to inspect the craft. She turned out to be a big trawler, at least a hundred feet long, dipping and yawing in a heavy swell which made her mast and long twin radio antennae sway alarmingly, posing an obvious problem for the Winchman. So much so, that the Captain, in Emergency Channel Sixteen contact with the skipper of the *Stalegg Senior*, decided to lower 'Bing' Crosby, the Aircrewman, rather than POMA Wyle or myself, to assess the need for a stretcher or medical attention—and I didn't argue with him! Especially since it took two attempts with the high-line to get Crosby and the stretcher on board.

As we circled awaiting developments, it was fascinating to watch hundreds of fulmars and gannets feeding and gliding in the proximity of the vessel, and wonder just where their breeding cliffs might be, as by now we were about twenty miles west of Donegal—a long way from home.

The winch-up was uneventful, and a large broad-faced, blue-eyed, stoical Norwegian seaman was hauled swiftly inboard on the stretcher, and deposited uncomplaining, at my feet.

Examining a patient in the back of a lurching helicopter is fairly basic. Peeling through layers of blankets and clothing to reach bare skin, a little prodding here and there, and a lot of sign language, soon established that his left-sided abdominal pain was most probably due to renal colic. Initially he declined help, but as the vibrating aircraft juddered towards Ireland, he eventually signalled acceptance of an injection of Pethidine to relieve his pain.

Then the radio crackled into life again—the Nimrod was talking to a ship, but we couldn't quite make out the call-sign. 'There is a Sea King with a doctor on board on its way to you now, and should be overhead soon.'

We looked at each other in puzzlement. We were already there. We had our casualty on board... surely the silly buggers knew that much—even allowing for the RAF! Then Dusty Miller, our Observer, contacted the Nimrod for clarification—and all was made clear. As well as our SAR, the Nimrod was now coordinating another rescue several hundred miles away in the south Irish Sea, involving a Sea King from RAF Brawdy in Wales which was flying a doctor out to a ship with a badly burned seaman on board—most impressive.

Leaving them to their task, we retraced our route outwith the twelve-mile limit, rounded Malin Head, and flew along the coast to the mouth of Lough Foyle, where we encountered possibly the most hazardous part of our entire trip. On the flight charts, on either side of the entrance to the lough, were drawn large red circles, ominously marked 'Danger Zone'.

At once, the reality of 'The Irish Problem' hit me with a jolt—no longer simply the remoteness of a TV news report—we were now part of the action.

We marked time for a long ten minutes, well offshore, before Air Traffic Control announced—'Rescue One Seven Seven... Sandpiper... you now have clearance to proceed to Ballykelly'.

As we sped low up the lough, the long narrow strips of cultivated land running directly downhill from a row of whitewashed crofts scattered along the Donegal hillside contrasted sharply with the large patchwork fields of prosperous looking farms on the flat and fertile Ulster shore. There was a sense of being in a time warp.

It was not the time warp, but the *mind* warp, which bothered me. The sad fact that this beautiful, tranquil landscape could spawn such twisted and evil minds, and so much murderous hatred, bigotry and bloodshed. There was a certain tension as we made our approach. Nothing was said, but I'm sure we all had the same mental picture of IRA terrorists reaching into the thatch of isolated farm steadings for their SAM missiles and M16 machine-guns, in readiness for our return trip down Lough Foyle!

Ballykelly Airfield, just a few miles east of Londonderry, had been home to HMS *Gannet* till it moved, lock, stock, and barrel, to Prestwick in 1971 when terrorist activity began to escalate. It was still used by the Army Air Corps and as a transport depot, and was well guarded. Nevertheless, we touched down and took off again with a minimum of fuss and maximum of speed—our feet only hitting Irish concrete long enough to carry our patient to the waiting ambulance, and hand over a hastily scribbled note to the driver.

Sensibly, Lt Moffat did not retrace our flight path down the lough, but instead headed across country past McGillicuddy Prison towards Portrush, and as we flew, relaxed banter once more crackled over the intercom.

'You know, it's hard to believe there are places down there where you'd be shot if you had to make a forced landing.'

'Even on a SAR?'

'Yeah, even on a bloody SAR! There are no big RESCUE signs on the sides of this beast—like the RAF have on their 'Crabs'... we'd just be another military chopper and fair game for these bastards. The RAF and Air Corps boys have been trained to go to ground if they have to abandon their aircraft during operations, and must sit tight till reinforcements arrive.'

'IRA, INLA, UVF—they're all the bloody same—you'd never know what tribe of savages you'd landed among.'

'Whose tribal territory is that over there, then?' someone asked.

'Oh, that's Walli Jumblatt land! and yon hilly bit is ETA country... there are a lot of bad Basques over there!'

'And I suppose Ghaddafi's gorillas run that town!' quipped another as we passed Portrush.

'Yeah!... and the Ayatollah's Martyrs are holed up in Kharg Island over there,'—pointing to distant Rathlin Island.

15

Typically, only a few days after our flight over Antrim, there were violent Protestant terrorist riots at McGillicuddy Prison, and in another incident, two policemen were murdered by the IRA in Portrush.

'I wouldn't mind a look at the Giant's Causeway,' broke in Dusty Miller—our Aussie Observer on a two year secondment to 819 Squadron—who had been quietly poring over his charts during this repartee. 'It's a shame coming twelve thousand miles and not having a look… might not get another chance before I go home.'

'No problem. I see you've plotted a heading that'll take us right past it anyhow, you crafty bugger!'

Within minutes, off our starboard quarter, we had a marvellous and unusual aerial view of the strange basalt columns—some long and some short, like organ-pipes and horizontal honeycombs—which make up the seacliffs and rock steps of this famous natural curiosity. Then we banked on another heading towards Sanda, Pladda and home.

'I'm back, dear! Guess where I've been?'

'Away off the west coast of Ireland picking up a man from a Norwegian fishing boat!'

My jaw dropped, and Helen laughed.

'I heard it all on the Scottish news—about a Sea King with a doctor on board. It was great… On one bulletin you were on your way out, and on the next one you had picked up your casualty and were heading for Ireland. Nice to be able to keep tabs on you for once. Wish it was like that all the time! Oh, and it also mentioned another SAR off the Welsh coast—a badly burned man on a ship.'

She knew more about that incident than did the Ops Room at Gannet!

5

26 April 1987

'Ferrex'

The broad concrete apron in front of the Gannet Ops Building was crawling with 'Crabs'—the Navy's descriptive and derogatory slang for the RAF and their helicopters. As well as their bright yellow Rescue Sea Kings, several long-nosed camouflaged Wessex helos—which always reminded me of some weird, sad, wedge-faced tropical fish from a coral reef—had been flown in from Northern Ireland.

The Briefing Room was packed with Aircrew listening to a boyish Sub-Lieutenant—who looked even younger than the proverbial policeman—presenting the weather report in acronyms, abbreviations and figures which seemed to make sense to Pilots scribbling on their knee-pads, but which were totally lost on me. By and large, most airmen looked only marginally older than the boy, but here and there a grizzled head or huge handle-bar moustache identified the veterans, the Alpha males, old hands who proclaimed their experience with a nonchalant air of casual detachment.

There seemed to me to be little rapport between Navy and RAF—inter-Service rivalry can be intense—and the whole scene was reminiscent of one of those awful weddings with the groom's lot down one side of the kirk, and the bride's lot down the other. Soon, however, bored resignation suddenly snapped to attention when Lt Roy Lewis, the Officer of the Day, entered and began his briefing.

'Good morning, Gentlemen. We are taking part today in a major maritime exercise in conjunction with the Coastguards and Lifeboat Service, the object of which is to test our ability to cope with a major disaster at sea where hundreds of passengers and crew have to be evacuated from a ship... In this case the Islay ferry *Iona*, with three hundred passengers on board, has been crippled by an engine room fire and is drifting in the Sound of Jura.

'The passengers are all volunteers from Territorial Units and Naval Auxiliary Service, and among them will be a number of casualties... Oh, and because of the recent *Herald of Free Enterprise* disaster, there will be a lot of pressmen taking pictures—although it should be made very clear to all that this show was planned many months before Zeebrugge.

'To make it as realistic as possible, your take-off times will be staggered at intervals based on the time it would have taken you to get there from Lossiemouth, Leuchars, Northern Ireland, or wherever... and there will be some surprise incidents tossed in for good measure!

'The first Sea King off from Prestwick will act as the command aircraft and will be piloted by Lt de La Fosse. His task will be to locate the ferry, assess the situation, and drop the Doctor and Aircrewman on board to arrange evacuation priorities. Thereafter he will direct in the other aircraft as they arrive, to lift off casualties and passengers. The Islay lifeboat will also be on station to take off survivors.

'The exercise will terminate at eleven thirty sharp to allow the *Iona* to prepare for her scheduled afternoon sailing to Islay... Any questions?'

'Sorry about yesterday, Doc.' Roy Lewis turned to me as we left the Briefing Room. 'We hadn't forgotten about you... just hadn't got round to telling you about it.'

Which, I suppose, amounted to the same thing! Helen had unthinkingly pointed out an article in the *Glasgow Herald* a few days previously about this imminent major exercise, and had lived to regret it. From that moment on, I had eagerly anticipated a call from Gannet, and when it hadn't materialised by Saturday morning, I had rung them to ask if the SAR Doctor was included in their planning—to assist with casualty evacuation.

From the pregnant pause at the other end of the phone, and the slightly embarrassed response, I got a wee niggly feeling they had overlooked this aspect of the exercise—but was assured I most certainly would be required.

Anyway, the question of whether I had been asked to the wedding officially, via a last minute 'Fiddler's Bid', or whether I was just here as a pushy gate-crasher, was now irrelevant. At eight-fifteen on a beautiful Sunday morning, I was well and truly embarked on Rescue 177, the first aircraft out to the 'stricken' ferry.

As we throbbed across the Firth of Clyde, I was keenly anticipating the marvellous views we would soon be having of Kintyre, Islay and the Paps of Jura... especially Islay, where we had spent so many idyllic, peaceful holidays with the kids. Maybe we'd even be landing our casualties there... maybe...

My reverie was interrupted, as the voice of Fraser Anderson, our Observer cut in over the intercom—'Shit! This bloody radar's gone on the blink again! How the hell do they expect us to act as command aircraft with a duff radar!'

'We'll have to hand over to Rescue One Seven Eight.' replied Tim de La Fosse. 'Bloody shame. I was looking forward to this. I'd better contact the Coordination Centre.'

Rescue 178, which had taken off ten minutes behind us, duly assumed command, and after a detour to Kennacraig, the Ferry Terminal on West Loch Tarbert, to pick up Dr Neil MacDonald, the Tarbert GP, whose remit it was to treat any genuine casualties resulting from the exercise, we proceeded on a radar-less heading to locate the *Iona*—a task which turned out to be by no means easy.

For the sea haze we encountered in the Sound of Jura had done an invisible mending job on the horizon, merging sky and sea into a shimmering, seamless, pale blue back-drop, on which was suspended like a surrealist painting, a tiny black and white ship with red funnels. My romantic aspiration to 'once more behold the Hebrides'—in the soft green slopes of gentle Islay, and thrusting Jura's gleaming, quartzite Paps—was sadly dashed. Visibility was no more than a mile, and my dream islands did not exist!

'God, no wonder some of these RAF Fighter Pilots get disorientated and fly straight into the sea at six hundred knots!' the Co-Pilot wryly observed, as we approached at a safe, sedate one hundred and ten, '...It's bad enough at this speed.'

Channel Sixteen was open and Tim de La Fosse cleared our winching approach with the *Iona*'s Captain. As we manoeuvred overhead, I was conscious of being watched by a host of upturned pink faces, garlanded with bright orange Board of Trade lifejackets like pilgrims at some Hindu festival, as the passengers below congregated at muster stations on the upper decks.

Lowered on to the crew cabin roof amidships with Bob Yeomans the Aircrewman, we then had to climb down a vertical ladder to reach the most seriously injured 'casualties' lying in various dramatic postures on a narrow deck section just aft of the port bridge. After prioritising the first half-dozen casualties, I quickly reported to the wheelhouse, from where the Captain transmitted to our aircraft the nature and severity of the injuries of those being winched up first.

One lad, beautifully splinted and strapped into a Neil-Robertson stretcher, looked more crestfallen than relieved when Yeomans informed him that for safety reasons we could only stretcher up real casualties! We kitted them all out with Navy lifejackets and ear-muffs, and up they went in the harness one by one, broken legs, spinal injuries, fractured skulls—and one guy with his broken arm still in a sling—which scared me shitless till I saw him safely grabbed on board the helicopter.

Because several were theoretical stretcher cases, taking up valuable cabin space, Rescue 177 departed with only five on board for the waiting ambulances back at Kennacraig. A second Sea King then lifted off the remaining 'walking wounded', leaving the way open for general evacuation of passengers.

By this time, helicopters were circling the ship like Indians round a waggon train, and would peel off and approach as the command aircraft directed them in one by one. With the casualty evacuation completed, my official role was at an end, but Rescue 177 had disappeared, leaving myself and the Aircrewman stranded. Bob Yeomans, however, still had plenty to do preparing passengers for winching to safety, so I buckled-to and gave him a hand—which was just as well, for the survivors all had to leave their bulky Board of Trade lifejackets behind, and be fitted with Navy ones, plus ear-muffs, before they could be hoisted on board the aircraft.

By now the RAF had arrived, and seemed rather diffident about getting too close to the ship. One bloke in a Wessex (obviously backward!) reversed into position overhead, which caused no end of consternation for those beneath him, while another Lulu tossed down rolled-up RAF lifejackets one by one on to the deck, resulting in a mad scramble to retrieve them before they were blown overboard!

Then there followed a bit of 'Anything you can do I can do better!' as ship-wise Navy Sea King cab-drivers hovered twenty feet above the deck while the 'Crabs' dared go no lower than forty. But the 'Crabs' always winched up two survivors at a time to the Navy's one, which evened the score a bit. This advanced winching, (or wenching!) technique was a source of much envious ribaldry from the assembled 'Terriers', depending on the pairings. Some really scored as they were winched up tightly hugging double-bumped bits of crumpet, while others had to settle for sweaty cuddles from their butch and hairy tattooed Oppos!

After ninety minutes buffeted by downdraughts, deafened by engine roar, suffocated by kerosene fumes, and nagged by the thought that another twenty feet lower and that beast would land on our heads, a welcome lull in the proceedings allowed us down to the crowded Bridge for a breather and a chance to look around. Assorted brass-hat observers from the Navy, RNLI, Coastguard and Fire Service, and their bowler-hatted counterparts from the Board of Trade, were making their contribution—to a growing pile of plastic coffee cups—while Captain Ferguson seemed to be the only man working, keeping the lines of communication open with the helicopters and Lifeboat. Neil MacDonald was having a pleasantly untroubled morning, a far cry, as he remarked, from the mountain rescues and ski injuries he used to have to cope with when he worked as a GP in Aviemore.

Eavesdropping the radio conversations, we discovered that the lull was due to two of the RAF helicopters being tactically withdrawn and grounded with 'engine trouble', which provoked some caustic comments later in the Crewroom at Gannet, when they learned that some of the 'Crabs' had spent the entire morning on their backsides, drinking tea at RAF Machrihanish.

Then, away to the east, a small shape slipped through the curtain of haze, and quickly materialised as the Islay Lifeboat *Helmut Schroder*, returning from Kennacraig after landing her first rake of fifty survivors. As she approached the *Iona*, two small craft, hired by newsmen, closed in for action photos of the Lifeboat and another Sea King, which had arrived and was in the hover over the ship, lifting off passengers. Sadly for the press, the helo's downdraught was too much for the Lifeboat to manoeuvre against, and she was swept away from the ship's side and had to stand off until the aircraft was loaded up and had departed—doubtless spoiling somebody's front page photo scoop!

'Thank God it's a flat calm.' was the dry comment from Captain Ferguson as we leant over the Bridge rail to watch as a batch of survivors, embarking on the *Helmut Schroder*, negotiated with some difficulty a two-foot gap between the vessels. 'Heaven help us if it was gusting Force Five, far less blowing a gale!'

These sentiments were echoed by everyone, for the complete evacuation of three hundred passengers, one hundred of whom went off by Lifeboat, took over three hours in perfect conditions and in broad daylight. However, the exercise had envisaged the worst possible scenario where none of the ship's lifeboats could be launched or liferafts used, and where casualties had to be transported fifteen miles to the nearest landfall, whereas in most circumstances at least some lifeboats would have been utilised, and other vessels, e.g. fishing boats, would have been in the neighbourhood to accept ferried survivors.

All said and done, it was an interesting experience and a most worthwhile exercise, which later that evening received prominent coverage on the national TV news. And, naturally, what did they show winching off survivors? True to form… A bright yellow RAF CRAB!

6

27 April 1987
'Much Ado...'

The day after 'Ferrex', believe it or not, I was airborne again, despite strenuous efforts to wriggle out of it in the interests of marital harmony.

'A toddler with gastro-enteritis on Coll? Surely you don't need a doctor for this one!' I argued with Gannet Control, fearful of Helen's wrath.

'I'm sorry, Doc. Edinburgh Centre have requested a doctor to accompany the child.'

Reluctantly I left the Surgery, stuck the flashing light on top of the car, and set off at a rate of knots through the evening rush-hour traffic. What a wonderful way to travel! The exhilarating feeling of naked power, as other drivers deferred to the green beacon and full-beam headlights and drew in to let me pass—except for a few mirror-shy morons who needed a raspberry from the horn to send them wobbling over to the kerb like dinghies in the wake of a speedboat. By the time I reached the bypass I was ready for Silverstone. And by the time I got myself kitted out at Sick Bay and rushed down to the main gate where Stevie the LMA was waiting for me, the helicopter was already burning and turning on the apron.

'You're going yourself, Doc! Won't need two of us. We're short-staffed here just now... all the gear is ready for you.'

I grabbed the heavy white plastic Ship's Doctor medical box and the Pneu-Pac resuscitator, which comprised two-thirds of our total—and pathetically inadequate—SAR equipment inventory, trotted out to the Sea King, heaved the gear on board and jumped in.

'Strapped in Doc? OK, we're off!'

Once airborne, with the mad rush over, I had time to take stock. If this kiddie was violently sick and inhaled vomit I'd need to suck him out... I'd seen a Laerdal Suction Pump somewhere among the gear before—where the hell was it?

Checking through the resuscitation pack and the big white box, all I could find was a suction catheter, but no sign of a pump. Brilliant! That bugger Stevie had forgotten to put it out with the rest of the equipment!

I voiced my predicament to Roy Lewis the Captain, and a message was relayed to Coll via Edinburgh to try and provide an aspirator. Availability confirmed, I was settling back to relax and enjoy a tantalisingly beautiful evening sky, when LACMN Bob Yeomans slapped a blind over the large cargo-door window opposite, blocking out the sunlight and any prospects I had of savouring the wonderful scenery of the Inner Hebrides en route to Coll. It was done with no evil intent, I realised, simply to give the Observer a better-shaded radar picture on his screen—and something which shortly turned out to be a lot more vital to our welfare than any gratification of my visual senses.

'Better climb to five thousand feet… on a heading of three thirty degrees.'

What on earth for, I wondered, then discovered that my Inner Hebrides were, in fact, under a vast blanket of sea-fog which began just beyond Arran. Such are the vagaries of West of Scotland weather. While we had been enjoying a lovely spell of brilliant warm spring sunshine, out to the west they had been smothered in a chill, dank sea mist for days.

The directional, running commentary from Fraser Anderson in the Observer's seat, as land masses appeared on his radar screen, made it even more frustrating.

'We are now two thousand feet above the Paps of Jura… heading towards the south west corner of Mull… just skirted Colonsay… now passing over Iona… Staffa is just below and to the right… now bring her down to four hundred feet and see if we can get below this fog… no joy… you have the southernmost tip of Coll four miles direct ahead… two miles… one mile… no obstructions to final approach… half mile…'

At this point a small islet appeared, followed shortly by the dark, low outline of a patch of land. Coll! We had arrived. The landing site was a small grass airstrip normally used by the Loganair Air Ambulance, which would routinely have done this job instead of a Sea King, had the weather conditions been more favourable. A couple of cars and a small knot of people were clustered by the gate at one end of the strip as we ducked the whirling rotors and ran towards them.

'Thank goodness you were able to find us!' exclaimed a small middle-aged woman—Dr de Mornay, the Island's GP. 'We've been lost under this fog for the past three days.'

'That's no problem,' I replied, cheerfully blasé about the navigational and flying skills which had got us there—'Coll still shows up on a radar screen.'

'This is Mrs Browne—a visitor to the island—and your wee patient.' She turned to a slim, attractive, anxious young woman in a Barbour jacket, standing with a rosy-cheeked, robust wee toddler wrapped in her arms—and sound asleep.

Doesn't look too ill to me, was my first, uncharitable thought—with all the cocksure smugness of a townie GP whose nearest Sick Kid's Hospital was less than a mile from his surgery. Then I viewed it from the other perspective—three days vomiting and diarrhoea, three days of dense fog… the fog could go on for another week, but the child couldn't… potential dehydration and sudden collapse.

It is difficult enough sometimes for GPs like myself, with all the facilities close at hand, to judge when to put a sick child into hospital—and there are no medals for making the wrong decision! Life on an island like Coll, with only one hundred and fifty patients, might seem idyllic, a dream come true for a stressed-out town doctor with two and a half thousand, but it obviously also had its drawbacks—with different clinical parameters having to be involved in decision-making.

'Oh, and here's the suction pump you radioed for.' Dr de Mornay proffered a small hand pump. 'I'd be grateful if you could send it back as soon as possible.'

I thankfully accepted the apparatus and promised its speedy return. Needless to say, after all the fuss, it was not required, for young Master Browne, insulated from the roar of the helicopter by a thick warm blanket and a sound sleep, did not blink an eyelid till he was loaded on to the ambulance at Glasgow Airport.

In the event, his medical condition was judged sufficiently serious on admission for Yorkhill Sick Kids Hospital to see fit to detain young Rodney, rosy cheeks and all, for four days, until they felt he was well enough to go home.

7

5 July 1987

'A Lovely End to a Lovely Day'

The old cherry tree cast a cool evening shadow over the groaning table as we made short work of heaped plates of succulent barbecued chops and Cumberland sausages, fluffy boiled rice and a green salad of chopped onions, peppers, tomatoes and lettuce, washed down thirstily with a couple of glasses of chilled Mosel wine.

Hot days had been few and far between, and five hours hard graft in the garden made it all the more pleasurable to sit and relax at Bob and Kate's, enjoying our first barbecue of the summer. The sun dipped further into the west.

'Well, Bob… It's either we chop down Kate's cherry tree or shift the table, otherwise we're going to be too cold to enjoy our strawberries and ice-cream!'

We shifted the table, and warmed to the last rays of the evening sun. Not only did I enjoy 'seconds', but so delicious were the rich crimson strawberries freshly picked from our own fruit-cage, that I went back like a glutton for thirds.

As the sun finally swung behind the tall beech trees bordering the garden, a freshening sea-breeze shepherded us indoors for coffee and biscuits. Bursting at the seams and thankful for the coffee to ward off a post-prandial snooze, I was easing myself comfortably into a soft lounge chair—when the bleep went.

'Oh, shit!' proclaimed Helen and I simultaneously, and I was conscious of Kate's kindly look of mixed curiosity and compassion, contrasting with Helen's—'There's another bloody good evening spoiled again!'—visual if not verbal expression of suppressed indignation.

With a casual, dismissive—'Don't worry—it'll be one of their "silly season" dinghy-adrift-off-Troon-type callouts and I won't be needed,'—I went to the phone.

'It's for real this time, Doc. Can you come in?' It was Stevie.

'OK. What's the score?'

'Someone on a yacht with a fractured skull—off Arran.'

With hurried apologies I left, to be met on arrival at Gannet by a worried-looking Stevie.

'You'll never believe it, Doc, but we've got two SARs on the go! There's another call in for a guy on Jura with chest pain. They're trying to sort it out in Ops which one to go to first. We might have to do both.'

Fortunately, common sense prevailed, and while a shout went out for a second Sea King crew to do the Jura job (It turned out to be nothing worse than a TA squaddie with heat exhaustion), we set off up the Firth towards the Cock of Arran to search for the yacht.

All around me, lobster-faced Aircrew were suffering—trying to cope with the impossible thermostatic feat of maintaining a normal body temperature in a flying helmet and rubberised immersion suit after a day's sunbathing. Rivers of sweat poured off our heads, failed to penetrate the watertight rubber neck-seals, and flowed, back and front, down the outside of our goon suits. Inside, something similar was happening, and I swear I could feel my toes squelching! I vaguely recalled an old Fifties-Sixties newspaper and magazine advert for something called the *Stephanie Bowman Slimming Garment*—'guaranteed to take pounds off you'—and my adolescent curiosity as to what it must feel like inside a plastic bag with knicker-elastic cuffs round arms and thighs. Now I knew.

It was only a short trip, and we soon located a thirty foot sloop with sails stowed, motoring north east on a gentle sea towards Inverkip Marina.

'We'll high-line the Aircrewman down first, Doc, and then yourself, followed by the stretcher,' instructed Lt Roger Stringer, our Pilot.

I watched with keen anticipation as Lt Tilley, the Observer, slowly inched Leading Aircrewman Bob Pheasant towards the dauntingly tiny cockpit of the yacht a hundred feet below, with all the concentrated precision of a boy fishing for plastic ducks at the fairground. The yacht had come alive by this time, its tall mast swaying and dipping in our downdraught, and its rubber dinghy, tethered by its painter, leapt and thrashed about in the air like a well-hooked seatrout.

Then it was my turn. As I dangled from the strop, the cockpit looked even smaller than it had done from the cab, as upturned faces gauged my progress, and outstretched hands strove to make contact. I was swung alongside initially, but as the yacht moved marginally ahead, I found myself hovering over the stern with my feet a few tantalising inches above the deck. Dropped another foot by the winch operator, and I was there… Oh, no I wasn't!

The helicopter had slipped a yard astern, and there I was, dangling horizontally with legs crooked over the transom rail like a trapeze artiste, while Bob Pheasant vainly reached out to grab me! Incongruously, I felt no fear, reasoning the worst I could get was a ducking, and I found myself with a grin rather than a grimace on my face, as the Sea King finally eased forward and Bob's outstretched hand grabbed mine and hauled me inboard.

Directed for'ard, past a petrified-looking chap in a peaked yachting cap grimly clutching the wheel, I was ushered into the cabin where an auburn-haired, ashen-faced young girl of thirteen was curled up under a sleeping bag on the starboard bunk. The frightened faces of two other wee girls peered anxiously through the half-open door leading to the for'ard cabin, while the skipper of the yacht, who turned out to be the girl's father, stood by the cockpit door, simultaneously keeping Channel Sixteen contact with the Sea King, and a weather eye on his novice helmsman.

He was marvellously cool, calm and collected under the circumstances, and gave an excellent and precise history of what had happened.

'Jane, my daughter, was up on deck about seven-thirty, when the boom swung across and hit her on the left side of the head. She was stunned, and momentarily lost the power of her right arm and leg, but this returned within a few minutes. She's been bleeding from her left ear and has felt a bit drowsy since... Oh, and tell them she's been sick a couple of times and got rid of her lunch. That might be useful if she needs an anaesthetic.'

I checked her over. Fortunately she was fully conscious and responsive, no signs now of her transient paralysis, her pupils equal and reacting—but ominously, blood was seeping from her left ear, indicating a possible basal skull fracture.

By this time the big metal-framed stretcher had been lowered on board, but was too narrow to get through the cabin door and had to be balanced on the transom rails to one side of the cockpit. We were now faced with a difficult problem—how to get Jane on to the stretcher. I could have done with a spinal board like the one we used on ambulances to extricate back and neck injury victims from crashed vehicles, and cursed the inadequacy of our equipment. Luckily, she didn't seem to have a neck injury to worry about and, having sat up of her own volition during our struggle with the stretcher, the three of us were able to manhandle her gently up three steps, through the cockpit door and on to the Stokes Litter, where she was wrapped in blankets and securely strapped in.

The helicopter closed in once more, with a sandbag swinging like a pendulum on the end of the high line, which I eventually managed to grab on board and hand to Bob to guide down the winch wire and hook. He deftly attached the stretcher then his own harness to the hook, gave a thumbs-up, and they were airborne, spinning slowly upwards till safely hauled on board the Sea King by Lt Tilley.

'Are you going with her to hospital?' I asked her father.

'No. I'm the only one able to skipper the yacht to Inverkip.' He nodded towards the helmsman. 'Her uncle will go with you.' I was then winched up to attend to the girl while Bob Pheasant went back down finally for her uncle.

The Stokes Litter had been loaded head-first, which meant that the patient's head was positioned right at the tail of the aircraft—where vibration was at its worst, and access pretty cramped. Crouched down uncomfortably on my knees to monitor her condition as we headed full-speed for the Southern General, I could feel every rev of the rotors shuddering upwards through my body, from my feet to just above my navel. Initially just a possibility, it swiftly passed through probability to inevitability—I was going to puke!

The hot sweats became cold sweats. I tried deep breathing, tugged in panic at my rubber neck-seal to let some air in, and shuffled round to a bulkhead seat, where waves of nausea surged in rhythm with the throbbing engines... What the hell could I do? I didn't have a puke-bag. I knew the Navy did not like dockyard omelettes all over their helicopters... and what I'd had for dinner would fill the bloody cabin!

I momentarily grabbed the neck of my suit ready to empty myself inside it, then... it came to me with the true inspiration born of desperation—Gloves! My flash gloves, worn by all aircrew and made of fine white kid-leather... I rummaged through several pockets, and finally whipped one up to my face at the precise instant my pork chops and green peppers got airborne.

The glove suddenly went very heavy, and bulged like an Ayrshire cow's udder as hot vomit gravitated down to the finger-tips. Relief was only momentary, as another 'technicolor yawn' became imminent—probably the second and third helpings!

Holding the steaming container in one hand, I fumbled frantically for the other glove, and managed to find it and fill it expertly in one single swift movement. This time, relief was instantaneous—and permanent. I felt alive again—but pretty stupid, sitting there with a bloated cow's udder in each hand, like an overworked milkmaid.

Carefully giving a twist to each wrist, haggis-like, and folding it over, I gingerly stowed the offending utensils under a seat and resumed my medical duties beside Stevie, who was kneeling by the young girl, grinning from ear to ear at my predicament.

'Glad you've recovered, Sir... Thought I was going to have two to look after!'

By this time we were descending over Glasgow, and the familiar grey stone-work and Victorian outline of the Southern General appeared suddenly, framed in the open doorway, as the Winchman leaned out to talk the Pilot down on to a small grassy area fringed by tall trees.

Police cars and fire engines ringed the landing site, and nurses and patients hung curiously over verandahs and balconies, as we transferred Jane to the safe care of the medical team from the Neurosurgical Unit, then rejoined the helicopter to await the return of our stretcher.

Lt Tilley was beside me by the open door, enjoying a breath of cool air, as I emptied the ballast from my gloves on to the grass below.

'Hope the "shit" doesn't hit the fan on take-off... and splatter these firemen!' I joked.

'Feeling all right now, Doc?' he enquired sympathetically.

'What's up, Doc?' came an eavesdropping voice from the front end.

'He's been sick,' cut in Stevie, gleefully.

In a desperate plea of mitigation, with my pride at stake, I described my over-indulgences.

'Oh, what a shame!'

'Serves you right for being such a porker, Doc!'

'Lucky you've had your dinner, Doc... We've still to get ours.'

'What are you having for dinner, Roger?'

'Oh... ehmm... I think fried steak and onions, loads of broccoli and roast potatoes... and then a huge hunk of Black Forest Gateau with lashings of cream... and you?'

'I'd like a really hot, smelly Madras Curry... mouth's watering already!'

'Pity about Doc—he's had his!'

'Yeah!'

And so it went on all the way back to Prestwick. Living it down was going to take a lot longer than bringing it up.

Jane had, as suspected, a nasty skull fracture, and spent almost two weeks in the Neurosurgical Unit before returning to her home in Wales. Several months later, she finally and happily made a full recovery.

8

11 August 1987

Barra Bound

It had been a long and depressing day. Just before lunch-time, I had been radioed by Ambulance Control to rendezvous with a vehicle carrying a desperately injured young boy, and had spent a frantic ten minutes performing cardiac massage in the back of a wildly swaying ambulance as the driver two-wheeled it through roundabouts on a hair-raising journey to hospital where, despite all our efforts, the youngster died shortly afterwards.

Surgeries had been fully booked. All emergency appointments were filled with the usual non-urgent rubbish. And to cap it all, when the evening surgery finally emptied at 7.15 pm, on my road home for tea I had to spend a further forty minutes attempting to unravel an angst-ridden teenager's emotional problems. This visit came to an abrupt and timely halt when the bleep went. My heart sank as I asked to use their phone.

'Can you come in, Doc? We've to medivac a girl with a fractured skull from Barra.'

'From Barra!' My heart sank even further. I phoned Helen. 'What about your meal?' she exclaimed. 'And who can I get to cover the Practice?'

Her concern about my nutritional state was echoed by the deep grumblings of an empty, aching stomach faced with the prospect of a four hour trip, and without a scrap of sustenance—not even a cup of coffee—since one o'clock! Even helicopters have to refuel. So I dashed into the local cafe for a couple of Mars Bars and some chocolate to eat on the flight, and had guzzled one of the choc bars by the time I reached Gannet. I was ravenous.

It was a miserable rainy evening, with low stratus masking the Carrick Hills—always a good height indicator: cloud level around five hundred feet. Rescue 177 was parked some distance from the Ops Building, so we all crowded into a minibus for the trip across the apron.

'We meet again, Doc. It's been a long time,' smiled the bearded crewman on my right. It was 'The Reaper' himself, Bill Barrett, who had piloted my first two SARs as a shadowy nocturnal figure whom I had never seen in daylight.

Oops! I wondered—what will go wrong tonight?

'One up for the Navy tonight, Bill.' Lt Lloyd our Observer chipped in. 'I hear the Crabs couldn't do this job 'cos the weather's too bad!'

'Wouldn't worry about that, Doc,' Stevie reassured me as we loaded the gear on board the Sea King. 'We've got a good pilot—Barrett's one of the best.'

We were airborne at 2000hrs and it was a race against time to get to Barra, one hundred and thirty miles away, before darkness closed in. Flying low up the Clyde through rain showers and patches of sea-fog, we made good time through the Crinan Gap and into the Sound of Jura. Then my ears pricked up as the Observer gave a heading for Scarpa and Corrievreckan.

'Corrievreckan!'—a word to conjure with—a place of fear and foreboding since my childhood—that mysterious, awesome whirlpool of West Highland legend, whose ferocious vortex had sucked down countless ships, and through which only the most foolhardy or most skilful of yachting skippers would dare make passage—and then only at slack tide.

'Can I come up front?' I asked eagerly.

'Better be quick, Doc! We're just about there!'

I scrambled for'ard, just as we entered the narrow strait between the north-ernmost tip of Jura and the island of Scarpa, where the flood-tide rushes over submerged reefs and rock sills, producing a maelstrom of surging, seething rip-tides, currents and undertows which are at their most spectacular when the flood tide is running against a strong westerly wind. Disappointingly, it was only half-tide as we overflew, but the dark menace of the swirling currents and boiling eddies below was only too apparent—as were the fog-enshrouded cliff-faces on either side of us!

I was relieved when we reached open water and headed towards Mull. The weather too, opened up for a spell, and we climbed to 4000 ft to take advantage of a thirty knot tailwind which boosted our groundspeed to one hundred and forty knots. This weather window allowed me a glimpse of some of the Hebridean treasures I'd missed on previous trips—the sacred island of Iona lay to port as we passed over Bunessan and the Ross of Mull, and a few miles away to the north west, a small insignificant knob was identified as Staffa. As we approached, POACMN McDougall, who had once paid a visit by sea, was able to point out for us a dark shadow in the basalt columns—the entrance to Fingal's Cave.

Beyond Staffa lay the Treshnish Isles, a group of small uninhabited islands, the largest of which, being flat, with a rounded, central rocky outcrop, has the intriguing name of The Dutchman's Cap. From the air, its even more intriguing configuration—elongated and tapered at both ends, with an oblong turret amidships—prompted me to remark:

'Better watch lads, you don't land in trouble some dark night—picking that up on your sonar and reporting it as a Russian sub!'

'We'd be in bigger trouble, Doc, if it was a Russian sub—that size.' came the laconic retort.

Overflying Coll and Tiree, we were complimented by Edinburgh Rescue for improving our ETA by at least twenty minutes, but no sooner had they done so than we hit fog again, and had to descend to 200ft to get below it for the last fifteen miles of our trip.

As we arrived off Barra in gathering gloom, the grey veil lifted enough to reveal the silhouette of Kisimul Castle, ancestral home of the MacNeils of Barra, brooding darkly on its rocky islet in the bay. Circling overhead, the crossed headlight beams of police and ambulance vehicles marked out for the Pilots a landing strip on the football field behind Castlebay village.

In the ambulance was a teenage holidaymaker, only just conscious enough to whisper her name was Linsey, who had fallen over some rocks on to the beach and had fractured her skull. The young GP attending her had been worried about her deteriorating condition and earlier loss of consciousness, but said that there had been an encouraging improvement in her conscious levels over the past half-hour. He pointed out an ominous leak of straw-coloured fluid from her left ear, a sign of a serious basal skull fracture, and as he did so, even more ominously, she began to vomit as we loaded her gently on to the helicopter. My heart sank at the awful prospect of having to aspirate or intubate her on the long trip back to Glasgow.

Heading back into the thirty knot wind dropped our groundspeed to eighty knots, and produced a lot of unwelcome turbulence which worried me considerably, as Linsey had been loaded head to the rear of the aircraft again, and I was concerned about the effect of vibration on her cerebro-spinal fluid leakage and the risk of further vomiting.

I needn't have worried, for she lay there stoically, eyes closed, flickering them open long enough during our quarter-hour conscious-level checks to let us know she was OK. It almost seemed a shame to keep waking her up! And it was me who had a momentary consultation with a NATO Puke Bag as my delicate stomach rebelled against the twin insults of an overload of Mars Bars and shuddering aircraft. Fortunately, a couple of dry retches were sufficient to restore me to normality.

'Told you you'd be sick eating Mars Bars,' smirked Stevie all-knowingly. 'You should stick to peppermints like me!' I think in future I will.

The race was now on to get to the mainland before daylight faded completely and left us relying completely on instruments—which would have necessitated a long detour round the Mull of Kintyre to avoid the more inhospitable sections of the return journey.

Sitting passively in the rear, Stevie and I could only listen intently to the two-way flow of directional information between Observer and Pilot, who were just as relieved as ourselves to get through Corrievreckan again, in the last glimmer of twilight. We relaxed too soon, for just as we passed over Crinan, the aircraft took a sudden violent dive which simultaneously left both our stomachs and hearts in our mouths, and us speechless. As the aircraft regained an even keel, Stevie breathed out slowly against pursed lips, looked at me, and wiped his brow in mock relief. Fortunately, Linsey was neither aware of, nor any the worse of the incident, and was safely transferred to the care of the Southern General twenty minutes later—where she remained for the next twelve days before being discharged home to Stirling, fully recovered.

'What the hell caused that sudden loss of height over Crinan?' I asked Bill Barrett as we were driven back to the Ops Room on our return from Glasgow to Prestwick.

'Oh, that. Sorry, Doc. We were flying clear when this bank of fog suddenly loomed up and I had to take avoiding action and dive under it to keep flying visual. Hope you didn't get too much of a fright.'

As Stevie once remarked—'Something always happens when you fly with The Reaper!'

9

27 August 1987

Fog Bound

The bleep went off at 0530. Helen swore volubly. 'What the hell is it this time?' she demanded sleepily as I got shakily out of bed.

'Shouldn't be very long, darling,' I soothed. 'Just a short trip. Another fractured skull… on Arran this time. Probably be back in time to run Fiona to school.'

It was unusual for me to be called to a medevac from Arran, since it was only a ten-minute flight across the Firth from Prestwick—less time than it would take me normally to drive to Gannet—and if the patient required medical supervision, the Arran doctors were usually only too happy to grab the chance of a trip over on the helicopter, and take the boat back later. But this was a serious head injury needing to be transferred to the Neurosurgical Unit in Glasgow rather than to the local District Hospital at Crosshouse, and the rules of the game were obviously different—hence the callout.

It was a funny, still morning, with a grey, overcast, dawn sky, and wispy hill-fog capping the Carrick and Dundonald hills. Arran was nowhere to be seen.

We took off at 0615 on a direct heading for Knockenkelly, near Whiting Bay, the designated landing site for medevacs from the island. Three miles out, we hit a dense bank of fog which exercised Lt Holman's navigational skills till we finally broke through it and found ourselves coming in over a caravan site, spot on for our landing on the football pitch where a police car and ambulance were waiting.

In the back of the ambulance lay an attractive young woman, deeply unconscious and unresponsive, with disturbing signs of severe brain damage, fixed pupils, shallow breathing, and now developing spasticity of her limbs. She had probably lain overnight, trapped and deeply unconscious in her car, till she had been found at daybreak, and was as yet unidentified. Her condition was deteriorating rapidly. Dr Alastair Grassie, one of the local GPs, handed me a batch of X-rays taken at the Arran War Memorial Hospital, which showed a nasty parietal skull fracture.

Loading her gently on board, head amidships this time—a policy I had introduced to reduce the harmful effects of vibration both for the patient and (with just a hint of self-interest!) myself—we headed smartly up-Firth towards Glasgow with the scheduled intention of transferring her at the Airport by 0730 and being back in Prestwick for breakfast by eight.

But, like 'The best-laid schemes o mice an men…', we went badly 'agley', and what began as a routine, quickie summer SAR became, within minutes, a severe test of the flying skills of the Aircrew as we once again hit fog, just off Ardrossan.

Though it was initially patchy, we were soon lured deeper and deeper into a dense, impenetrable white-out which quickly began to pose problems for Jeff Ainsworth, our Captain.

'Visibility's down to fifty yards!' he reported back to Holman; and simultaneously we felt the aircraft slow down appreciably. I glanced up at the array of instruments above the Observer's head. The speedometer was reading only sixty knots, about half our normal cruising speed, and the altimeter now registered less than one hundred feet.

'We'll have to go straight up the Clyde to Glasgow on radar.' he went on. 'I can't take the risk of going inland. This fog could be just as bad over the Largs hills.'

So began an hour-long, nerve-wracking exercise for both Pilots and the Observer, flying and relying solely on their instruments, while I sat in the back of the cab, worried sick about the effect the delay might have on my patient— but with complete faith in the crew's competence, and blissfully ignorant and totally unaware that they had never flown in such hostile conditions before. Holman, totally focussed, scrutinised his radar screen.

'Have a large object… ship… one and a half miles at eleven o'clock… and a smaller object… probably fishing boat… three quarters mile at two o'clock…'

Cautiously we proceeded, with an occasional acknowledgment from the Pilot of fleeting visual contacts, if we passed within a couple of hundred yards of the plotted vessels in thinning fog.

As Lt Holman talked us past the Cumbraes, Stevie, who was squatting on the floor by the patient's head, beckoned me over. As I did so, he slid aside the small lid covering a four-inch hole in the floor used to drop smoke flares, and pointed down. I peered down and couldn't believe my eyes—glassy grey water slid past, no more than an arm's length, it seemed, from the bottom of the aircraft.

Bloody hell—we were only flying five feet off the sea! I gulped and sat back in my seat, forcing myself to put even more trust in the obvious calm expertise of the crew—there was precious little else I could do. In actual fact, as it turned out, we were flying slightly higher—at forty feet.

'Can't go on like this!' exclaimed Jeff Ainsworth. 'Fog's getting worse. I'm going to climb to fifteen hundred feet and try to get above it. Is that OK with you, Doc?'

I acquiesced. The poor lass was deeply unconscious, and every minute was vital. Already we had been half-an-hour airborne.

'I'm above the cloud now… but it doesn't help us much… Glasgow's covered in fog.' Through the window opposite, I could see the top of Misty Law—highest of the Renfrewshire Hills—peeking above a sea of cloud which stretched to the farthest horizon.

Our intercom at the back was not connected to the Airport channel, so Stevie and I sat in tense silence for what seemed an interminable time as the aircraft made a Surveillance Radar Approach, being talked-down by Air Traffic Control slowly and carefully through the dense fog to an invisible Airport somewhere beneath us. Suddenly an elated voice broke the silence—'We're here!' And there, two hundred feet below, was a runway. 'I've just been congratulated by the Tower for my approach!' laughed Jeff, then added '…except they said I'd come in over the wrong bloody runway!'

Just as well it was a helo and not a fixed-wing aircraft they had been talking down, for we simply shifted sideways to starboard, lined up with the designated runway, and skimmed along to a vacant slot on the apron. Our patient, still deeply unconscious, was carefully transferred to the waiting ambulance which promptly sped off in a flash of blue lights for the Southern General. At the time, I had grave fears for her long-term survival.

We were left standing beside the Sea King to take stock of our situation. 'Well, that's us grounded till this fog clears,' Jeff Ainsworth declared. 'I broke all the bloody rules to get you down, and I'm not going to break them again to get us back to Prestwick. How do you get to the Control Tower?' He turned to a uniformed BAA employee standing nearby, who obliged by smartly leading us up a series of stairs and corridors to the Apron Control Tower, from where our predicament was relayed back to Prestwick.

Breakfast then became number one priority—the instant we discovered that Graeme Abernethy, the Co-Pilot, was flush enough to pay for us all! The only other crew member with any cash was Stevie who, being 'Other Ranks', did not let on, but later confided to me that he had always carried a fiver in his flying-suit—ever since a memorable and miserable SAR when they were stranded overnight in Stornoway, with not enough money among them for a drink, far less the hotel bill!

Still in heavy flying gear, and conscious of curious stares from hundreds of even more outrageously dressed holidaymakers, and natty-suited shuttle commuters, we clomped through the main concourse to the cafeteria, where mixed grill (on the Navy of course!) was the order of the day.

Happily replenished—and no one happier than myself at the near certainty of missing a Monday morning surgery—we settled down again in the Control Tower to await a clearance. The early-morning London shuttles and Mediterranean charter flights seemed to be taking off as usual, in no more than four hundred yards visibility, which prompted me to ask Jeff Ainsworth what his problem had been.

He explained that all Pilots had different instrument ratings, and though he was in fact the Instrument Rating Instructor at Gannet, he was only qualified to fly, like the other helicopter pilots, within strictly defined parameters, especially in areas such as the Scottish Control Zones round Prestwick and Glasgow Airports. Only Pilots with blind-landing instrument ratings, flying commercial aircraft fitted with sophisticated automatic landing equipment, were allowed to approach and land in fog, and although Sea Kings had excellent radar, they had no blind-landing facility and therefore, like light fixed-wing aircraft, could only make a landing approach under what were called Special Visual Flight Rules, keeping below cloud and having good visibility all round.

'So when I told them we had a seriously injured casualty on board and urgently needed to land, they had to clear the Glasgow airspace of all these buggers before they could talk us down!' He chuckled, thumbing at the rows of jet airliners behind him.

'There's one of your pals across there,' interjected one of the Controllers, nodding towards a hangar complex on the far side of the apron. Puzzled, we all turned round, to see a bright red Wessex helicopter of the Royal Flight parked in front of the hangar. It was being loaded with baggage.

'Who's flying in that?' Someone voiced our collective curiosity.

'Charlie's going down to Rothesay—but I don't think it's today. If it had been, we'd have had Special Branch on every roof-top. But the helicopter is cleared for take-off at ten hundred hours... probably taking down his spare suit... and Di's frocks!'

Bang on ten o'clock, the red Wessex taxied out past our forlorn Sea King, took off and disappeared into the fog, much to the chagrin of the Navy boys—having to watch the RAF put one over on them.

'All right for some!' was the disgruntled response. 'That bloody Wessex is fitted with every electronic gadget known to aviation science. It's got so much gear in it I'm surprised it can get off the ground.'

'Could you not have asked him for a tow down the Clyde to Rothesay?' I asked mischievously.

'Hardly. But... maybe we could ask him for an update on the weather down the Clyde... can you do that, Control?'

'No problem! Royal Flight Wessex... Glasgow Control... we've a Sea King grounded here wishing information on weather conditions in the Rothesay area... can you assist?'

'Glasgow Control. This is Royal Flight Wessex...' a very pukka-sounding, stiff upper-lip, 'anyone-for-tennis' voice rang out across the control room. 'I'm flying at fifteen hundred feet above the fog, and can see Arran... looks as if it may clear from the South.'

'My gosh! How frightfully RAF!' was the Navy crew's amused reaction. 'I bet he's got a big moustache! Still, thank him very much for the info. Sounds as if we might get airborne within the hour.' It's not every day the Navy finds itself beholden to the Crabs—and to the Royal Flight at that!

About 1100 hours, the fog lifted enough to let us locate the main hazard and obstacle affecting our take-off—the huge pylons to the north-west of the Airport, stretching their 370,000 volt cables across the Clyde to the Kilpatrick Hills beyond Bowling. We hurried to take advantage of this weather window, but had only flown downriver as far as Dumbarton and Greenock when we again hit thick fog, forcing Lt Holman to re-apply his nose to his rotating radar grindstone and churn out yet more vital directional info for the Pilots.

With no patient to look after, I went up front and was recruited as an extra pair of eyes. It was fascinating to see how accurate Holman's radar predictions were, as we peered ahead and located the large ship, exactly a mile away at ten o'clock, or the navigation buoy, half-mile at two o'clock. One very small, puzzling 'blip' reported dead ahead at quarter-mile proved especially fascinating, as it was not a small boat which materialised out of the fog, but the snout and dorsal fin of a large basking shark, cruising towards us through a mirror sea. Experiencing such radar sensitivity was a further boost to my ever-growing confidence in the flying abilities of Navy aircrew and the safety of their aircraft.

The Cumbraes once again slipped by unseen, and our first glimpse of land was Horse Island, off Ardrossan Harbour. The cloud ceiling over Irvine Bay was only a hundred feet, and as we skimmed across the water past bemused fishing boats, Jeff Ainsworth started to worry about his final approach to Prestwick.

'It looks like we'll be breaking all the rules again, lads! I can't maintain correct approach altitude, and will have to notify Air Traffic Control. It'll probably put the shits up them, thinking it's an emergency.'

His problem was that, at a hundred feet, we would be flying under the Airport radar, and our approach could not be monitored by the Controllers. Although we could see the Airport, they could not see us—with obvious safety implications for other aircraft in the vicinity.

Clearance was duly granted, and we finally clocked in at 1150—after a six hour marathon—in time for an early lunch rather than a late breakfast!

*   *   *

Amazingly, despite everything being stacked against her, Lorraine Dalgleish survived her severe head injuries, and after two months of highly skilled care from the staff of both Southern General and Crosshouse Hospitals, she was well enough to go home. Several months later, though still disabled, she was able to walk independently and, following a spell of intensive rehabilitation and dedicated specialist treatment at the Astley Ainslie Unit, she made a truly remarkable recovery.

Fifteen years on, she now lives in East Lothian with her partner and ten-year-old son Kevin.

It had been a worthwhile job.

10

September 1987

'Send Three-and-Fourpence...!'

As well as that old favourite, Kim's Game, the visual memory test we used to have fun with as boys in the Scouts, there was also, I seem to recall dimly in the past, another proficiency test which involved listening to, then relaying, a verbal message of twenty-five words as nearly word perfect as possible. Baden-Powell, a wily old campaigner who keenly appreciated the importance of communication, was obviously trying to ensure for future generations that 'Send reinforcements, we're going to advance' would never again end up as 'Send three-and-fourpence, we're going to a dance'!

And our mothers must have harboured similar if less ambitious aspirations—hoping against hope that their simple, thrice-repeated instructions to get 'hauf-a-stane o tatties an a loaf' would not resurface as 'hauf-a-stane o loafs an a tattie' by the time our bikes reached the wee shop!

A full quarter century has passed since that momentous boyhood event when the valve-driven steam wireless gave way to the amazing transistor radio —and the 'Trannie' in its turn has been overtaken by a bewildering succession of electronic marvels—stereo radio, quadrophonic sound, colour and cable TV, fibre-optic transatlantic telephone cables, satellite communications, videophones, and talking computers.

B-P, eat your heart out—the Scouts have long since abandoned your old verbal test—for in this great Space Age, who needs to talk by mouth!

The phone rang at 1030 on Sunday night, as we were getting ready for bed. I'd just tholed a particularly rotten, miserable, fish-less week's holiday, and was already dreading the prospect of Monday morning surgery.

'Doc Begg? HMS Gannet here… MA Ferguson. Sorry to disturb you so late, Doc, but I'm new here, and Doc MacKechnie is away on holiday.' That was news to me, for Suddie usually let me know if he was slipping off for a few days and wanted me to cover the Base; but this time he had obviously forgotten.

'What's the problem?' I enquired cagily.

'Well, Sir, we've just received a signal from HMS Cochrane, Rosyth, to go down to Manchester and pick up a couple of sick crewmen off a ship early tomorrow morning. The briefing is at Oh-Eight-Thirty… Can you come in?'

'What! fly down to Manchester… and pick up a couple of crewmen and bring them back to Prestwick?' I repeated slowly and incredulously. 'Surely there must be a Naval Establishment a lot closer to Manchester than Prestwick?'

'That's the signal we've got, Doc. Depending on how ill they are—one's got an I/v drip up for D and V, and the other's got abdominal pain—we'll have to bring them back here to Gannet, then possibly transfer them to Haslar.' RNH Haslar was the main Naval Hospital, five hundred miles away in Portsmouth.

This was incredible! My hackles—as a major donor to a public purse already overstuffed with my personal tax contributions—rapidly began to stiffen.

'For goodness sake! Do you mean to tell me that the Navy is going to fly a helicopter all the way down to Manchester to bring two guys all the way back up to Prestwick, only to send them all the way back down again to Portsmouth! Can't they get the bloody boat to sail up the Manchester Ship Canal and drop them off at Manchester Royal Infirmary, or something—would be a lot cheaper!'

'Sounds a bit off to me too, Doc… but that's the information I've got from the Officer of the Day.' Something told me he had been fed duff gen, but I couldn't quite fathom it out.

'I'm sorry, MA Ferguson, but this is not really a SAR callout, and I can't justify leaving a busy Monday morning surgery to fly down to Manchester on this sort of jaunt. Let me know when you get back, and I'll assess your casualties at Sick Bay, and arrange hospitalisation as necessary.'

Monday morning, as usual after a holiday, was hellish. Mountains of mail—and millions of moans from the Practice Groupies who had been just dying all week to see me back—but hadn't quite managed it! True to form, the Top Ten were all there, anxious to preserve their perfect attendance records. If we had been a Sunday School, they'd have won prizes every time. With a rare combination of foresight and *deja vu*, I reckoned I could have easily made up the appointment list myself the week before I went on holiday, written in their complaints and prescriptions, and given myself the Monday morning off.

Distinctly disgruntled, and having heard nothing from Gannet, I phoned the Ops Room about ten o'clock, to be told that the MA was still flying. But by 1030, he had phoned to say he was back at Sick Bay with his patients, and could I see them as planned.

That was helluva quick, what the hell's going on? I puzzled as I headed for the Base; and duly said so to young Ferguson when I arrived to find four, not two, crewmen sitting in the waiting room.

'Yeah! Sorry Sir. Signal lines got crossed somewhere. It was HMS *Manchester* they were talking about, on exercises in the Firth of Clyde! And we picked up another two casevacs from a sub and the *Minerva* as well.'

41

Fortunately, they were virtually all 'walking wounded'—jaundice, suspected appendicitis, broken foot, and toothache—so I was able to leave him to arrange disposal locally, to the Sick Bay at Faslane, while I re-applied myself to the Monday morning grind.

Eat your heart out, Marconi! Communications don't seem to have advanced all that much since the old days of the dance—Send three-and-fourpence…!

11

2 February 1988

'Do Unto Others...'

'MA Stephenson here, Doc… Could you possibly come out and examine one of our fliers? I've already checked him out myself this morning, and given him some Maxolon and Mist. Kaolin for his D and V—but he's still got some abdominal pain and the CO wants him seen by a doctor.'

I had barely agreed, and settled back into the humdrum of a late morning surgery which was already leading inexorably towards a late lunch, when the phone rang again.

'It's HMS Gannet for you again, Doctor,' apologised Margaret, our receptionist, 'a Commander somebody-or-other… on Line Two.' I pressed Line Two.

'Hello, Doc… Lt Cdr Kirby here, Senior Observer. I believe you're going out to visit Lt Steiner at Dundonald… Just thought I'd fill you in on what's what!'

'What's what?' I enquired curiously.

'Well. I want you to check if this chap's at all fit for flying. He was due on board ship on a three week detachment this morning, and seems to have taken ill all of a sudden. He's apparently been whingeing a bit in the Mess recently about this trip, and I wouldn't like to think he's swinging the lead.'

'I probably won't be finished this surgery till one-thirty, so I'll see him just after two.'

'Fine. If he's fit at all, I want him on that aircraft… even if you have to stick a cork up his arse!'

'You're a cruel crowd of buggers,' I rejoined. 'Sending a poor sod dying with gut-rot to be tossed about the ocean in a gale!' Recollection of my own sad experience with a pair of kid gloves evoked instant sympathy for the poor, unfortunate and unsuspecting Lieutenant.

'Don't worry! It's a twenty-five thousand ton ship with its own Sick Bay and doctor on board—so he'll be well cared for. If he really is ill, obviously he can't go, but that means calling in a replacement at two hours notice.'

'I'll see what I can do.' I promised.

As ever, Sod's Law lumbered me with an over-run surgery, plus two extra visits left by an anonymous partner keen to get away early on his golfing half-day—no doubt self-justified by the twisted logic—if he's going to Dundonald he might as well do these two in Prestwick en route. Naturally, that same logic could never apply to Royal Troon—also en route!

I grabbed a couple of filled rolls, gulped down a mug of lukewarm coffee, and raced the ten miles up the bypass to the officers' married quarters. The ailing Lieutenant was a young German Naval flier on a two year secondment to Gannet. As I suspected, he was suffering from nothing more than a mild, self-limiting, viral stomach upset picked up from one of his *kinder* over the weekend.

He looked so at home and comfy in his dressing-gown and slippers, that I hadn't the heart to tell him what was in store for him—apart from hinting strongly that he'd be fighting fit by tomorrow!

As I drove back to Gannet, heavy grey rain squalls scudding across a stormy grey Firth buffeted the car, and caused me just a tiny wee pang of guilt at the thought of sending a fellow human being out over the heaving deep on such a day. Lt Cdr Kirby had no such qualms, and promised to employ me again for doing such a fine job!

I checked over my two old ladies in their Prestwick nursing home on my way back to the Surgery, and consequently sat down to my first appointment ten minutes late—and under pressure. Midway through my third consultation, the bleep went.

'Yeah, you are needed, Doc… a guy at a lighthouse at Mull of Kintyre bleeding from the abdomen. I'll look out your gear.'

The flying MA was Stevie—again! And the Sea King was flashed-up and ready for take-off as I grabbed my lifejacket and helmet from him and hurried across the tarmac.

'Know any more about what's happened?' I panted as we climbed aboard.

'Just that it's a Lighthouse Keeper on some island called Sanda, with abdominal bleeding.'

'Internal or external?' I pursued.

'Dunno, could be either.' Big help!

After a few minutes' delay while the Bowser off-loaded six hundred pounds of fuel, we were finally airborne at 1600 hours. Unfortunately, as sometimes happens, I was plugged into a subsidiary circuit, not the main intercom, and so missed the two-way exchange of information between the aircraft and RCC Pitreavie. Suddenly I heard the word 'overdose', being tossed around in a conversation between the Pilot and Stevie.

'Did you get that message, Stevie? The guy's had an overdose… confirmed.'

'Yeah. Doc's not on the radio… he'll have missed it.'

'What do you mean—"overdose"?' I butted in. 'I thought he was bleeding… could you confirm if he's had a bleed as well?'

There was silence for a couple of minutes while they checked this out, then back came the affirmative that he was bleeding, but what type of abdominal bleeding was not established—maybe he had fallen as well, someone conjectured.

While, to a doctor, the most obvious, simple, but dull explanation, was an aspirin overdose leading to internal bleeding, the subsequent lurid cabin conversation envisaged a much more vivid scenario.

'Yeah! These Lighthouse Keepers all go loopy eventually. And if they're not throwing themselves off cliffs or the top of their lighthouses, they're trying to do in their Oppos! Wouldn't be surprised if this guy's been at the cocaine, and done something real stupid—like swallowing a bottle of pills and then committing Hara Kiri!'

We flew at 200 feet to avoid the worst effects of the thirty knot head wind, which, even so, caused a fair bit of pitching and yawing as we shuddered round the south end of Arran, before making visual contact with Sanda, a few miles off the tip of the Mull of Kintyre.

'If it continues like this, we might have to winch the Medic and Doc down… depends on how much turbulence we get from these sea cliffs, and where their helipad is located.'

As I had dire visions of having to suck out this casualty, put up an I/v drip, and perhaps dress severe wounds, I was not enamoured by the prospect of having to winch down all the requisite gear as well. Fortunately the tiny helipad, though much too wee for a Sea King, was conveniently sited, and we set down safely.

'There's a Landrover just over to the left, with two men beside it waiting for you,' we were informed as we left the aircraft on the blind side. Stevie was out first—the big chancer—and true to form when he could get away with it, he left me five yards astern, staggering under the weight of two heavy cases of medical kit.

There were indeed two men standing by the Landrover, one scruffily dressed in an old tweed jacket, jeans, wellies and a woollen bunnet, and the other smartly turned out in an orange all-weather suit and white lighthouse keeper's cap.

I panted up just in time to hear Stevie shout over the roar of the engines—'Are you taking us to the casualty?'—gesticulating towards the lighthouse, the lantern of which we could just see a few hundred yards away, sticking above the top of a small hillock, round the shoulder of which twisted the rough track from the helipad. Then his jaw dropped gob-smacked, as the Keeper pointed to himself, and I could lip-read the words—'I am the casualty!'

So much for a case of near-fatal overdose and Hara Kiri, I thought to myself—more like another typical case of 'Send three-and-fourpence'!

Brushing all such uncharitable thoughts aside, I introduced myself, and quickly got his story of having suffered excruciating pain from severe facial neuralgia for several days, and of having in desperation taken twelve paraceta-mol tablets over the previous twenty four hours—which hardly constituted a major overdose. The tablets had obviously eroded his gut and caused some internal bleeding. He had subsequently passed several black motions and real-ised something was far wrong when he felt faint trying to climb the lighthouse stairs to check the lantern. Very sensibly, he had radioed for help.

Having in the past seen some of my own patients collapse suddenly with massive haemorrhages after similar, apparently mild episodes of bleeding, I knew he had done the right thing; but couldn't help smiling at the incredulous looks on the faces of our two Pilots as, one on either side for support, we walked our 'bleeding overdose' under their noses to the starboard door, and helped him on board. Although I wanted him to lie down, he declined, saying he preferred to sit up because lying flat made his headaches worse.

With a strong following wind pushing our ground speed up to 150 knots on the return journey, we were able to deliver him safely to the waiting staff at Crosshouse Hospital and be back at Prestwick by 1700 hours—a one hour SAR—the shortest yet!

Following the debrief, as we stowed the SAR gear back in its locker, I squinted at the Squadron Flight Log Book, lying open on an adjacent table. I couldn't help but notice the flight logged before ours, embarking my earlier patient, Lt Steiner, on the *Armeda*—and, exhausted as I was with the day's efforts, that old maxim flashed through my mind—'Do unto others…'

Served me right!

12

8/12 February 1988

Missing the Boat!

With eight SARs pinpointed on my wall-map for 1987, and one already in the bag for 1988, I was beginning to suspect that Suddie MacKechnie's prediction of 'two or three a year' had been a bit of an underestimate—though, admittedly, very helpful at the time in persuading Helen to let me take on the job in the first place!

In actual fact, Suddie had been telling the truth as far as his experience went, but for some reason or other—perhaps the increasing popularity of outdoor pursuits, coupled with increasing familiarity in the use of helicopters by island doctors—callouts had risen dramatically over the past eighteen months, and, inevitably, so had my share of them.

Having said that, there was no set pattern to SARs. It was either, to use an auld Scots expression—'a hunger or a burst'—the early rush had been followed by a six month spell in the doldrums, during which there was a noticeable dearth of callouts. In fact, two intrusive SAR missions into 'our' territory by East Coast Crabs—to Rum and Jura—had prompted the CO of 819 Squadron to pay a visit to RCC Pitreavie just to remind them that we still existed!

Thereafter, a flurry of callouts, thirteen in the first six weeks of the New Year, had set bleeps a-bleeping with a vengeance, and left me several times sadly disappointed.

On the first occasion, I had been quietly slurping soup with fellow Ayr Rotarians at our Monday lunch meeting when Jean the waitress leaned across the table to inform me there was a phonecall. It was not the Surgery as expected, but Helen—'Gannet have been looking for you—there's a SAR on and they need you—a man with a broken back... Is your bleep not working?'

I looked down at my belt—yes, it was switched on. Hurriedly making my apologies, I did a fast 'Green-light job' through town, and arrived at the Base gates just in time to see a Sea King burning and turning on the apron. The MOD police waved me quickly through and I rushed up to Sick Bay, only to be stopped in my tracks with the jaw-dropping news—'Relax, Doc! They've just left without you a couple of minutes ago!' Trying hard to hide my disappointment, I asked why the hurry.

'There's a guy on Ben Nevis with a severe back injury, and with all that hellish weather out there…' he gesticulated towards the north, where heavy snow-laden clouds were swirling across the watery-blue sky, 'they had to get a move on before it really closed in and the light failed.'

I appreciated the urgency of their departure, and cursed my duff bleep. Ben Nevis—what an experience that would have been!

A few days later, when I dropped in at Gannet to check over some fees due for locum work I had done during Suddie's leave, I met Jack Sibbald the POMA, a tall, lean, pleasant and capable Marine Medic who had recently taken charge of Sick Bay.

'How did it go on the Ben on Monday?' I asked enviously.

'We only acted as back-up.' he shrugged. 'A Crab from Lossiemouth got there ten minutes before us and lifted the climber off. But it was interesting. The weather was a bit dicey for a time up the mountain… one of those whiteouts where you couldn't tell snow from granite. We hit a big downdraught too, which scared the shit out of us in the back—not the Pilots though—all we got from up-front was—"Oops, that was a big one!"'

'Then,' he added, almost as an afterthought, 'we were diverted up to Plockton in Wester Ross to pick up a Navy Rating from the Base there, with a similar back injury, and bring him back to Glasgow—so it wasn't all time wasted.'

My envy greened by the minute. What a scenic trip that would have been—an aerial version of the West Highland railway—flying below snow-capped hills, over black lochs and yellow moors, to the beautiful West Coast and the silver sands of Morar!

I was on call for the practice that night, and had been lying wide-awake, tossing and turning since four o'clock—a condition well known to every GP who has had the misfortune to lift the phone for that classic, dreaded, early-hours 'advice' call—'Wee Darren's burnin up, Doactor, an his temperature's no gaun doun wi the Calpol Ah've gave him!' (Usually a half-strength dose administered only five minutes previously!)

If we had to rise and visit every bairn with a temperature, we would never get to bed, but the GP's standard, visit-parrying response of—'Give it time to work and phone me in an hour if he's not any better'—as shuddering senses register the rattle of rain or sleet on the windows from the dozey depths of a warm bed—invariably leads to a wide-awake mind anticipating the inevitable follow-up phone call.

True to form, the phone rang at a quarter-past-five—but this time Wee Darren must have cooled off!

'PO Sibbald here, Doc. We've got a SAR on… to the West of Ireland.

Fishing boat with two injured. One with a head injury and fractured femur, and the other with broken ribs and a broken leg. You'll be needed.'

With fresh memories of Monday's missed opportunity I dressed in a hurry, gulped down half a glass of milk proffered by a deeply anxious Helen, and sped up the bypass crunching a couple of Stugeron tablets as insurance against possible 'kid-glove syndrome'!

To my surprise, there was no flurry of activity at Gannet when I arrived, and I was able to kit up leisurely before accompanying Jack Sibbald down to the Ops Room, where the aircrew were busy with rules and plotters, planning their route and determining the location of the nearest hospital in Southern Ireland. Apparently, at night, the designated response time for Gannet, from call alert to airborne, was ninety minutes, to allow the maintenance crew time to assemble.

' 'Ave you seen the Chief Tiff?'—a white-capped, agitated PO burst into the room.

'They've been bleeped—same time as everybody else.'

'Well, they've bloody slept in or summat—for they're not 'ere and the bloody 'elicopter's still in the 'angar!'

Consternation all round!

More precious minutes ticked away, till eventually the missing Maintainers materialised, and dragged their reluctant charge down to the apron.

'OK, chaps. Better get loaded up. We've been hanging around here long enough.'

Relieved that the long wait was over and I didn't have to drink the rest of that revolting, black, sugar-less coffee in my mug, I helped the POMA hump our gear across the tarmac and clambered on board.

Strapped in, instrument checks completed, we sat in darkness as the turbines whined and the engines throbbed into life. The distinctive whoosh, whoosh, of the rotor blades merged as they picked up speed—and then:

'Jesus... I don't believe it. We've been cancelled!'

The note of disappointment and annoyance in the Pilot's voice was echoed all down the line.

'Too late in getting off the bloody ground! That's why!'

'The Old Man will be furious about this... especially after going through to Pitreavie and kicking up stink about not getting enough SARs... and then when we get one, we can't respond in time.'

Disheartened and dejected, we trudged back to the Ops Room where the soul-searching and recriminations continued. We discovered that a Gazelle and Lynx from Northern Ireland, simultaneously scrambled with us, were scheduled to reach the trawler by 0730, thus rendering us surplus to requirements.

'Well, that's the second disappointment in four days,' I lamented to Jack as we headed back to Sick Bay in the grey dawn.

'You're not the only one, Doc,' he replied. 'The aircrew enjoy SARs. Gives them some real flying… a change from the dull routine of sonar-dunking patrols. You've at least had some SARs. Just pity that poor guy on Monday!'

'What guy?' I asked.

'The pilot of the Sea King we used on the Ben Nevis run. It was a quick turn-around job with a change of crews. He'd just come in from a routine sortie and had to hand his aircraft over to a fresh crew for the SAR… Been here eighteen months and never had one himself. Sick as a parrot he was—the poor sod!'

Mark 6 ASW Sea King from HMS Gannet *patrols near the huge gannet colony on Ailsa Craig in the Firth of Clyde.*

Sick Bay Staff, HMS Gannet 1989. LMA 'Stevie' Stephenson, 'Boss', POMA John Bennett, MA Don Bradshaw, MA Liam McNamee.

Mountain winching exercise, Isle of Arran.

RNAS Prestwick, home to HMS Gannet *and 819 Squadron from 1971 to 2002. HMS* Gannet *SAR Flight still occupies the airfield site beyond the road—two large hangars. Two SAR Sea Kings can be seen on the apron.*

Sick Bay Staff 1991. MA Jarlath Cooke, MA Jamie McCracken, POMA Ian Lindsay, 'Boss', POMA Rod Newman.

Pool drills, Ayr Baths. Aircrew listen intently to briefing from LA(SE) Woodbridge.

One-man liferafts—just recovering from being tipped upside-down by PO(SE) Lawrence (in water) and clambering back into the dinghy. Note PLB aerial on PLP.

Classic highline transfer from yacht, with the Sea King pilot keeping winchwire and highline well clear of yacht's rigging.

Winchman's view of the same rescue, with Aircrewman safely on board yacht and winchwire slackened off.

Aircrewman going down the wire on to a small motor cruiser.

Aircrewman being lowered with strop to lift off passenger or casualty. Note tight highline controlling direction of descent, and anti-static earthing wire dangling below him.

Cockpit view of Highland glen on Navex.

Heavy operational Mark 6 ASW Sea King used for years—and at increased risk—on mountain SARs prior to the long-awaited arrival of lighter Mark 5 aircraft specially adapted for SAR.

13

12 March 1988

The Aberdeen Spaniards

'Come on! You can finish laying these slabs later!' Helen was impatient—but so was I. For weeks I had been trying hard to finish the damned patio, grabbing a few precious hours here and there between downpours, as depression after depression swept across the country, perversely saving their heaviest deluges for half-days and holidays.

A stationary front had loitered NW to SE across the British Isles for several days, dumping most of its load on Ayr, and in desperation I had been working outside all morning in a heavy drizzle slapping preservative on a newly erected rustic fence. And now, typically, at the very moment when the weather finally looked like picking up, the Parental Taxi was being hailed to collect Fiona from the Young Naturalists' Club at Culzean Country Park. And the dogs needed a walk. And Colin, a Team Leader with the Young Naturalists, was doing some conservation work and would need to be collected later in the afternoon!

'I'm coming, love!'—famous last words—'I'll do the rest when I get back.'

'Oh, no, you won't. You are going to hear Fiona playing in her orchestra at the Music Festival at two o'clock. Don't tell me you had forgotten that!'

'No, dear, of course not,' I lied through clenched teeth.

Welly-clad and anoraked for muddy Culzean woodland paths, we took the old high road to Maybole—a road which often rewarded us with bonny scenic views of rolling South Ayrshire countryside bisected by the wooded, winding course of the River Doon, whose source rose far off to the south east among the distant whale-backs of the wild Galloway Hills.

Today, however, away to the West, Arran was obscured by low menacing grey cloud, against which only the faintest outline of Holy Isle could be seen, so we were pleasantly surprised, on cresting the Newark brae and looking east, to find the far summit of Shalloch on Minnoch, at 2,600 feet, clear of cloud and freshly dusted with new snow, contrasting vividly with the rich, brown, plough-patterned patchwork of the roadside farmland.

I commented to Helen on this unusual weather pattern, and hoped that the louring skies over Arran were receding and not advancing to drop even more rain. Fortunately the wind was from the east, and it stayed dry for our walk along Happy Valley to the Swan Pond, where the two Cairn Terriers obviously relished their exercise, with old Biddy, as skeich as ever at fourteen, louping sheuchs in pursuit of young Islay, who at three and with all the boundless mad energy of youth, was dashing through the undergrowth in hot pursuit of imaginary rabbits.

The Park Centre was crammed with parental taxis, and seething with a couple of hundred excited youngsters, well-greased from their 'sausage-sizzle', and well-caked with mud after their exploration of the smugglers' caves beneath Culzean Castle. Fiona chattered on about her adventures all the way home till, five miles out, near Culroy Smiddy, she was interrupted by the dreaded Bleep.

'Oh, Shi—ugar!' exclaimed Helen in exasperation. 'Don't tell me you've got that bloody thing with you. Don't we ever get any peace? What are you going to do—we're a long way from home?'

I'd often carried the bleep on our visits to Culzean, which was about eleven miles from Ayr, calculating that the probability of a callout was remote—but this time, dammit, it had happened. The only saving grace was that it had not gone off en route to the Park, leaving Helen to go back down in her own car to pick up Fiona. That would have spelt Big-T Trouble.

'I'll use the radio and ask Ayr Ambulance Control to ring Gannet and see what's what.' I had already foreseen this problem arising at sometime or another—of being far out in the country, perhaps at a house visit, a road accident, or even fishing—and had made a prior arrangement with the Controllers to cover the eventuality.

As we raced expectantly towards Ayr, the radio crackled—'Medic Eleven... Ayr-Am Control... Gannet have a report of a fishing boat, thirty miles north of Malin Head... seaman with a bad eye injury... can you attend?'

I dropped Helen and Fiona at the top of our drive, apologised regretfully (and honestly!) to the wee soul for not being able to come and hear her fiddling at the Festival, and headed for Gannet.

The duty SAR crew were again from 824 Squadron, recently transferred up from Culdrose to join 819 at Prestwick—all dressed up and raring to go on what was probably their first SAR—and anxious to make amends for that abortive effort of a few weeks back, when they had failed to get off the ground. Efficiency triumphed this time, and we were airborne within thirty minutes of callout.

As we approached Arran, on a heading of 280 degrees, it became obvious that the low stratus cloud might cause problems. Skirting the northern shoulder of Holy Isle, we dipped over Lamlash Bay and followed a wooded glen which led up into the misty hills. Skimming heather and granite-clad slopes, we only just managed to squeeze over the ridge through a tiny hole in the cloud blanket, emerging thankfully on the far side to see the glinting, spindly fingers of the Machrie Water delta spread out beneath us.

The crook of Carradale Point across the Kilbrannan Sound was our next landmark, and the high ground of the Kintyre peninsula beyond was similarly shrouded in grey mist. There was now a choice of flying south through the Machrihanish Gap, or trying further to the north where the ground fell away a little. Gurney Hickey, our Pilot, chose the latter option, and again found enough space between mist and mountain to see us safely through.

'There's Gee-gah down to our right now!' someone exclaimed, and as the only Scot on board, I cringed at their mispronunciation of magical Gigha, 'God's Isle', one of the scenic gems of the West Coast.

Since our route took us across the Sound of Jura to overfly Port Ellen and the southern end of Islay, I eagerly anticipated the view, only to be disappointed when the weather clamped in again. We did get a glimpse of the Mull of Oa with its impressive seacliffs and memorial tower, and I recounted to the lads the tragic story of the troopship *Tuscania*, torpedoed off the Oa in February 1918, only a few months before the end of the Great War, with the pointless loss of hundreds of young American lives.

Thirty miles west of the Rhinns of Islay, we made visual contact with the *Grampian Admiral*, a large blue-hulled trawler with a white superstructure, registered, as the name would suggest, in Aberdeen.

On instructions radioed ahead, she was steaming directly into the easterly wind at ten knots, which allowed us to come up astern into the hover, taking advantage of the uplift created by a combined seaspeed and windspeed of around twenty knots. With an offshore wind, the sea was fairly gentle, and posed no real problems for the flight crew or POACMN Sykes, who made himself ready and was swiftly lowered with a radio to assess the situation on board. As I watched intently through the starboard window, I was intrigued by the incredible number of seamen who spilled on to the trawler's decks to spectate. At one point I counted at least fourteen, and that presumably did not include the Skipper, Helmsman, Engineer or casualty.

As we circled overhead, the PO radioed up that he needed a stretcher, and the aircraft was taken in again, shuddering, dipping and yawing to keep station with the trawler's stern, as the Stokes Litter was highlined down to the deck where it was unhooked and carried for'ard to the crew's quarters.

We stood off till the loaded stretcher reappeared, with the injured seaman kitted out in a bright red immersion suit and lifejacket. The lift-off was textbook stuff. Once back on board, Sykes plugged himself into the intercom to update myself and 'Daisy' Adams, the LMA, as we knelt to examine a badly swollen and bleeding left eye.

'Nasty one!' he said. 'Seems a winch cable snapped and hit him across the face. Could have been a lot worse though... he might have lost his head instead of his eye.'

There wasn't much for Adams or myself to do, apart from applying a field dressing and making him more comfortable. He was fully conscious and lay with his hands clasped, quite composed. He looked foreign for an Aberdonian.

'His papers are in his kitbag.' Sykes continued. 'He's Spanish. They're all Spaniards on board—every damn one except the Skipper—and he's from Hull! That's the bloody Common Market for you. After they've fished their own waters to extinction, the French, Danes and Spaniards all want a free go at ours. But the Fisheries Agreement has only allowed a limited number from each country into our territorial waters, so to get round that, the Spaniards are buying up British registered boats with British Skippers, manning them with Spanish crews, and going their own sweet effin way!'

As if on cue, Channel Sixteen crackled again.

'Rescue One Seven Seven... This is Grampian Admiral Skipper... Can you hear me, old man.'

'Grampian Admiral. This is Rescue One Seven Seven... Loud and clear.'

'Can 'e tell me wot 'ospital my crewman's goin' into, an 'ow bad 'e is, old man... 'as the doctor seen 'im?'

The Captain relayed my assessment that, apart from making him comfortable, there was little else we could say until his eye was examined properly by an eye specialist—and added that he would be going to Limnavadie Hospital in Northern Ireland.

'Lim .. na .. va .. die... Thank 'e very much, old man!'

We banked and set course for Londonderry to the chuckles of the crew over the intercom—Gurney Hickey was getting some stick! 'Now we know who's the Grandad of the Squadron... Time you hung up your wings... Old Man!'

I shuffled quickly through the Spaniard's papers for some details for the casualty note I was writing for the ambulance men—a shaky scribble in chinagraph crayon barely legible due to the vibration—'Rodrigues Sines, Spanish Seaman. Off Grampian Admiral. Severe injury right eye. Hit by snapped winch cable. Conscious. Has taken two Spanish painkillers (mild).'

Then I had a moment to sit back and reflect on our own situation. Here we were, half an hour's flying time from Londonderry, and less than an hour's journey back to Crosshouse. The patient wasn't desperately ill, and another half-hour would make no difference. Why couldn't we just fly him back to Scotland?

Jeez... The SAS had just shot three IRA terrorists in Gibraltar last Wednesday, and the show funeral was in Belfast the day after tomorrow! And the last time we had flown into Ballykelly, we had been joking about SAM missiles, but after the seizure of *MV Eksund* with one hundred and fifty tons of arms on board only a few months back, it was now one hundred per cent certain that the bastards actually had the bloody things—for use against helicopters—at ranges up to two miles!

Hell's teeth, I didn't mind flying into Northern Ireland if someone was critically ill, but this guy—and the Norwegian sailor with the renal colic—could easily have been flown safely to Scotland. A calculated risk was fair enough, but not an unnecessary one.

I voiced my thoughts as we flew in low over the Antrim coastline. 'Who decides which hospital a casualty goes to?'

'We just go where we're sent, Doc. As far as I know, it's decided between Pitreavie and the Ops Room… usually the nearest hospital.'

'That's fair enough if they're critical, but somebody like this guy could just as easily have gone to Crosshouse and been transferred by road a few miles to the Eye Unit at Heathfield Hospital in Ayr. I'll have to make some enquiries about this.'

We were now moving south east, back along the Antrim coast towards the entrance of Lough Foyle.

'Suppose we'd better go operational now.' said Hickey laconically. 'I'll take her down below a hundred feet.'

'This railway line goes to Londonderry, via Ballykelly,' chipped in Dave Tribe, the Co-Pilot. 'If we follow it… should take us right there.'

Leaving Daisy Adams with the Spaniard, I went for'ard for a look, as we scattered sheep and bullocks left and right while skimming over a vast, flat expanse of waterlogged farmland, criss-crossed with brown, brimfull drainage channels. The railway skirted the base of a curved escarpment well over a mile from the sea, which was, in fact, the old raised beach shoreline dating from the last Ice Age—when Lough Foyle must have been much larger—and the country a damn sight more peaceful!

Moments later, the Sea King landed on at Ballykelly. While it was being refuelled, we quickly transferred our fisherman to the waiting ambulance, gently divested him of his lifejacket and survival suit, and humped the stretcher back to the aircraft.

Then we were off, flying low back along the railway, effortlessly overtaking a passenger train, and swerving occasionally to avoid the unnecessary noise disturbance of directly overflying farmhouses and bungalows. This was not a very clever idea, I thought to myself, going in and out by the same route—and I breathed a deep sigh of relief when we eventually veered off at a tangent towards the coast.

'Are these geese?' Dave Tribe nodded down towards a flock of sixty-seven large white birds grazing a field of waterlogged winter barley.

'No. They're whooper swans.' I enlightened him. 'I saw them on the way in… they're wintering here from Iceland.'

'These SARs are marvellous for birdwatching!' I added as we left the raised beaches behind and flew parallel to grey basalt cliffs, their ledges already packed with courting, house-hunting fulmars and kittiwakes. I was too busy watching birds to notice the three men diving into a cave as we roared overhead towards Portrush—but Gurney Hickey saw them. God only knows what mischief or evil they were up to!

Keeping clear of Rathlin Island, regarded as unfriendly territory, we headed for the Mull of Kintyre and the safety of home.

A week later, I broached the subject of flying into Northern Ireland at a meeting with Suddie and Captain Davis from FONAC in Sick Bay, and was relieved to learn that, in future, I personally would have the clinical responsibility to decide on medical grounds where a casualty should be sent.

'Have a word with the CO, Jimmy.' Captain Davis patted my shoulder reassuringly as we left. '...But I wouldn't worry a lot about Northern Ireland. They don't seem to bother with the Navy too much.'

All right for you to say, I thought, but they did manage to get Admiral of the Fleet, Lord Mountbatten!

14

7 December 1988

The Fankle

'That's the third time in two days!' I apologised to a startled, bemused Trainee as I fumbled under the desk to switch off the bleep which had just burst into warbling song from the depths of my waistband. 'Sometimes goes off like this when the battery is running low… but I'd better phone Gannet anyway.'

At least it would be a momentary diversion from the boring tutorial I'd been inflicting on Pauleen about the functions of Social Work Departments, I thought to myself, as the phone rang at the other end. It had been a quiet summer, and nine months since my last callout—although Scott and Big Paul had collected two SARs in July while I was on holiday—both in marvellous weather; Scott having to medevac a meningitis case from Benbecula; and Paul helping to manhandle a Neil-Robertson stretcher down ladders from the top of Skerryvore Lighthouse, where the keeper had fallen and broken his ankle. Skerryvore! On a flat calm! How I had envied the Big Yin that job.

'Could you come in, Sir?' a quiet request from Daisy Adams, the duty LMA.

'What's the score—any details?'

'Just that it's a ship call, Sir… somewhere off Barra Head. Crewman with chest pain.'

Typical! It was my half-day; the car was due to have a new tow-bar fitted; Helen had me earmarked for Christmas shopping—and would probably want to earmark me further, physically or verbally, when she got the message from the Surgery that I was airborne!

Daisy was all kitted up and ready when I arrived, and together we lugged the SAR gear out to the waiting Sea King. It was very mild for December, with a moderate south-westerly breeze, and the cloud ceiling around a thousand feet—just high enough to allow us to sneak over the southern Arran hills and the Kintyre peninsula above Carradale without having to depart from our 283 degree heading.

The long grey smudged outline of Islay now filled our horizon, with the northern high ground of Ben Bheigeir and Glas Bheinn enveloped in cloud and directly ahead. The steep promontory of McArthur's Head, with its white-walled lighthouse, slid below and to starboard as Lt Jock Alexander, the cab Captain, steered us up and over a col momentarily free of cloud, and down the other side towards the gleaming broad expanse of Loch Indaal. To my delight the heading took us straight over Bruachladdich and our favourite wee holiday hotel, but nobody came out to wave!

'How far now?' I queried as we overflew Loch Gorm and the sands of Saligo Bay and headed west—next landfall America!

'About ninety miles west of Islay... forty-five minutes flying time,' interjected Jerry Scott, the Observer—and for the benefit of the Pilot, added, 'Wind speed increasing, twenty-three knots, two thirty degrees.'

Below us, the Atlantic looked deceptively still, and only the tell-tale streaks of foam trailing the breaking waves gave some indication of the real weather conditions. Visibility quickly dropped to one-and-a-half miles as we flew through rain squalls, and two radar blips to starboard eventually materialised as a pair of deep-sea trawlers pitching and rolling in a heavy swell as they headed east towards the mainland and shelter.

'Jesus, look at these buggers roll! I hope it doesn't get much worse further out or we might have problems.' It did!

'Fishing boat should now be visual, three miles on the nose... wind speed thirty-two knots, coming up on gale force eight,' intoned Jerry.

'Yeah! Sea state six or seven... pig of a swell... I've got her. Bloody Hell! She's rolling all over the frigging place... just look at that.'

The Peterhead registered *Voracious* was a big eighty-four foot trawler, its stern wheelhouse bristling with whip aerials, and precious little space between the fore and aft masts into which to drop a stretcher. She was steaming downwind at a steady ten knots to minimise rolling, but she still pitched violently as she rode the twenty-foot following seas.

'I think you two would be safer up here... it's too dangerous!' instructed the Captain. 'We'll put the Aircrewman down first, then the stretcher, and get this guy on board for treatment.'

Daisy and I made suitably relieved noises as LACMN Bob Yeomans deftly prepared the Stokes Litter, calmly strapped himself into the harness, and disappeared down the wire.

Skilfully directed by Jerry Scott manning the winch, Jock Alexander equally skilfully kept us on station, and Yeomans was safely deposited on the heaving deck at the first attempt. He promptly radioed up that the casualty would be able to walk out to the stretcher, and that there would be no need for Daisy or myself to follow him down—thank goodness!

The sand-bagged high-line lead rope, lowered first to guide down the stretcher, momentarily snagged on the mast but was quickly freed, and the stretcher was pushed out, lowered, and safely hauled down on to the deck. Then real trouble!

'Back three yards! Back three yards!'—a hint of alarm in Jerry's voice over the intercom—'The wire's caught in the crosstrees of the fore-mast... I've run off a lot of slack... no problem... but go easy! Hold it!

'Now right two yards and up five feet... No! Back four yards... back one yard. Right again two yards... one yard... now up six feet... Steady! That's it free... Relax!'

The professionalism of the crew was superb. Helicopters are difficult enough to fly at the best of times, but to keep station with this bucking, rolling beast of a boat, fifty feet below us and pitching downwind at ten knots in heavy seas, meant our Pilot, facing into the teeth of a near-gale, had to fly backwards and blind at a matching speed, relying solely on instructions from his Winchman to maintain his correct height and a safe lateral distance from the ship to avoid a further fankle between the mast and winch-wire. Three-dimensional flying at its best!

I was impressed—and relieved. All the more so when Jock Alexander exclaimed—'I'm bloody glad that's over! My frigging neck is killing me, craning out of that window. Last time I did this, my head got jammed when the bloody helmet visor stuck fast in the window frame!'

After what seemed like an eternity, a white-faced figure in a bright red survival suit was led out of the wheelhouse, strapped into the stretcher, and safely winched aboard.

It was now our turn. We had already received a communication from the Skipper that our patient had been suffering severe chest pain for several hours, unrelieved—not surprisingly—by the two Trinitrin tablets he had been given to suck. He wasn't shocked, but indicated with a nod of his head that the pain was still there.

Enveloped in his survival suit, unzipped now to reveal layer upon layer of heavy fisherman's pullovers, there was just nowhere to inject Morphine. Ignoring Daisy's suggestion of simply sticking the needle through what was a perfectly serviceable and expensive piece of Government Property, I persevered, and eventually managed to score a bullseye between my fingers, into a two-inch square of exposed hip.

Monitoring his blood pressure was impossible, but I was fortunately able to lock onto his wrist pulse with a forefinger, and kept it there for the hour-long trip back to Crosshouse Hospital, and his safe transfer to the Coronary Care Unit.

'That guy did have a coronary, after all, but he's doing well,' I informed the lads next morning when I dropped in for a coffee.

'Yeah! It was a good trip. You don't feel so bad when it's something worthwhile like that. Not like some of the bloody rubbish we get... like those two drunken buggers off Campbeltown last month, who pissed in the fuel tank of their boat and had drifted halfway to Ireland by the time we picked them up.'

'Did you hear Bob Yeoman's up for an Admiral's Commendation for yesterday, Doc?'

I wasn't surprised. In fact, the whole crew got one.

15

21 December 1988

Flight PA103

I arrived home to find that the BT telephone engineer had responded swiftly to Helen's call for help, but had been unable to find any fault at our end.

'It's an earthing problem. Could be at the Exchange, or up a pole some-where.' Standing on the doorstep, we both shuddered as heavy rain drummed on the roof of his van. Then, dropping a heavy hint as to his innermost thoughts on the matter, he continued—'A bit risky up a pole in this weather... would need to call out a couple of linesmen.'

It was so near Christmas, and the night was so foul, that I felt sorry for him. 'Och, it's hardly worth it! I was on call last night, so I suppose it could wait until the morning.'

'Oh! You're not on call then?' He sounded a bit peeved. 'The woman said you were on call, and that's why I am here.'

'Well, not for the Practice...' I replied defensively, in case he thought Helen had pulled a fast one, 'But I am permanently on twenty-four hour callout for HMS Gannet—for Search and Rescue operations.'

This produced a compromise—he would at least check the exchange. And results—when he popped back round at teatime to tell us the phone was fixed, he complimented Helen on the smell of her cooking, and expressed a hope he'd now get home for his own dinner. I thanked him warmly for his trouble and, tempting fate as always, added apologetically, 'It's good to know that it's working... even though I'm seldom called out.'

Ninety minutes later, at 7.35pm, the bleep went! I telephoned Gannet. The duty MA—a young Glasgow lad called Bradshaw—answered breathlessly, and I could detect an unusual note of panic in his voice.

'Could you come in, Sir? There's word that a Jumbo jet has crashed! Don't know where yet.'

Numb disbelief had to be my initial reaction—must be a hoax-call from some weirdo pervert! But what if it was for real? Where? A hundred miles out in the Atlantic? The Irish Sea? The approaches to Prestwick or Glasgow Air-ports? The Galloway Hills?

All these scenarios seared through my brain as I raced up the bypass, my eyes anxiously scanning the night sky for the tell-tale glow of flames. There was nothing to be seen—and the Airport area itself was also clear—thank goodness.

MA Bradshaw was ready waiting with the SAR gear.

'Any more news, Don?'

'Yes. It's crashed near to a place called Lockerbie, Sir. Er... where is Lockerbie? On the west coast somewhere?'

Mildly surprised at this geographical gaffe, I enlightened him. 'Heavens, no! It's a wee town near Dumfries, on the A74 Glasgow-London road. There's a lot of hilly, wooded countryside down there. Could be anywhere in that lot. Get the spare SAR Box as well, and as much I/v fluids and dressings as you can find.'

As I limbo-danced into my flying suit, pulling the tight rubber neck-seal over my head, a young airman, returning to collect his briefcase from the locker room, stopped and smiled.

'Hi! Are you the dawktor?' The soft American drawl surprised me, till I realised he must be one of the exchange aircrew on regular two year attachments to Gannet from allied foreign navies. I shook his proffered hand.

'I'm Scott Bruce. Left-hand Pilot tonight... No, not the Captain.'

Even when we got on board, neither he, nor Lt John Newell the Captain, nor the Observer Lt Bill Lines, knew much more about the crash, apart from the fact it was not a hoax, and the locus was somewhere near Lockerbie.

By a tragic coincidence, our course overflew my birthplace, the small Ayrshire mining village of New Cumnock, where, in September 1950, the greatest rescue in British mining history had averted one of its greatest disasters. While extracting shallow coal from an inclined seam, a heading had been driven up too near the surface and had broken through into a peat basin underlying a farmer's waterlogged field. Within minutes the field had disappeared as a huge crater opened up and thousands of tons of liquid peat rushed at frightening speed down the incline, blocking off the pit bottom and trapping one hundred and twenty-nine miners. The world's attention was focussed on Knockshinnoch Colliery for three days as rescuers tunnelled and fought their way through gas-filled disused workings, and eventually brought out one hundred and sixteen men alive. Thirteen men died.

I was only seven at the time, but still retain a vivid recollection of the rescue teams, the arc-lights, the press photographs, the expectant crowds at the pithead, the school friends who had lost their fathers, and the hushed numbness and grief which had settled on the village for a long, long time afterwards.

Leaving New Cumnock behind, the small Nithsdale villages of Kirkconnel, Sanquhar, and Thornhill slid beneath us as the rain cleared to reveal the distant lights of Dumfries to the south east. Lockerbie would be somewhere beyond and to the north. We flew on.

'Visual on Lockerbie!' Lt Newell announced calmly. Then as we drew nearer, he let out a cry of horror and disbelief. 'Christ! It's crashed onto the town! I can see flames!'

Standing just behind him, we could see, not a raging inferno as anticipated, but multiple, small, scattered fires blending with the orange glow of street lights; the flashing blue lights of the emergency services; and a confusion of car headlights as tailbacks tentacled out of the town in all directions. The red navigation lights of another helicopter, probably a Crab, drifted through the black sky to the south.

Confusion reigned. The radio channels were choked with fragmented snatches of conversation—Liverpool Coastguard—Edinburgh Rescue—Kirkcudbright Coastguard—and others less readily identifiable.

We circled for over quarter of an hour, getting bloody nowhere, before John Newell, in frustration, put us down in a ploughed field; then Bill Lines jumped out and managed to commandeer a passing police car to drive him to the Emergency Control Centre being set up in a school on the far side of the town. The next twenty minutes were spent in agonising tension, trying to glean some grains of sense from the confused chaff of radio communication, while our Aircrewman, Jim Scott, kept peering worriedly under the fuselage as the Sea King's wheels sank further and further into the glaur of the ploughed field. Eternities later, Lines returned and plugged into the intercom.

'The town's a disaster area… The plane has crashed on to a street of houses, and they reckon there's hundreds of casualties… Seems to have come in from the east. They want us to track east and look for wreckage, bodies, survivors, whatever we can find.'

I could see the frustration in young Don's face mirror the feeling of impotence and anger welling up inside me at the delay in getting us into action. Bloody Hell! Here we were with a plane load of medical gear; a Medic and a Doctor; hundreds of reported casualties; a town on fire; and we were being asked to go farting about the countryside in pitch darkness looking for bits of wreckage! I voiced our combined feelings to John Newell—could we not be off-loaded?

'Sorry, Doc! This is what we have been tasked to do. The town is crawling with ambulances, and I need you both here. We'd be no friggin' use on our own if we came across injured casualties.' Despite our gut reaction, there was a lot of sense in what he said. A sound Captain's decision.

As we flew over the crash scene, where two burst gas mains still flared, a terrible smell of burning kerosene and charred wreckage filled the aircraft through the open cargo door. Below us, fire engines, ambulances and police vehicles flashed their little blue lights like dinky toys in a toy town. Apart from the all-pervading smell, it was too unreal, too unbelievable, and could not have happened. Five hundred feet above Lockerbie, we were strangely detached from the grim reality and from the subsequently revealed horrors of the dawn—

of bodies and limbs on rooftops, in gardens, strewn on the golf course; of roofless houses, and scorched cars on the A74; of the thirty-foot deep crater and the homes and people vapourised in a fireball of one hundred tonnes of exploding aircraft fuel.

We experienced nothing of the scale of the tragedy on the ground, but learned a lot about the scale of the catastrophic break-up of the Boeing 747 as we located wreckage spread over a wide area up to five miles east of Lockerbie. It soon became obvious that few fragments were bigger than eight feet long, and the scatter—even to our inexperienced eyes—indicated a total disintegration at high altitude. Sudden decompression at 30,000 feet, or whatever, meant certain death—there could be no survivors. Our searchlights picked out a rudder section bearing the Pan-Am emblem.

Whether it was the horrible knowledge that so many of his countrymen were on that plane, or whether it was just a characteristic of his transatlantic temperament, I don't know, but our young American co-pilot reacted more volubly than the others.

'There's three seats down there! at ten o'clock! Shit! We've overflown them. Turn back! Turn back! We gotta go down and check them. Goddam! There were guys fell outa planes at twenty thousand feet in the last war and survived! There could be somebody down there for Chrissake!'

There was little we could say that would persuade him of the futility of such action, but all exchanges were abruptly terminated when a white object spun rapidly upwards through the searchlights and hit the rotors above the windscreen in a blur of wings.

'Bird strike!' shouted Newell. 'Anyone feel anything wrong… vibrations?'

For a few seconds it was white-knuckle time as I tightened my grip on the back of Scott Bruce's seat. There was an expectant hush.

'No!' A sigh of relief all round.

'We'd better return to Lockerbie now and check for any damage. Looked like a duck or a wood pigeon.'

By this time, a semblance of order was creeping into the aerial chaos, and we were directed down on to a grass playing field beside the Primary School, where we were joined shortly afterwards by a couple of RAF Wessex Crabs. Parked by the school gates were a number of ambulances and police vehicles, including a large Police Incident Van.

John Newell clambered up the side of the aircraft with a torch to check rotors and turbine air intakes for damage, and reported all clear. Then Bill Lines disappeared to the Incident Control HQ for an update briefing on the crash, and the rest of us were left twiddling our thumbs.

'To Hell with this, Don!' I was still a bit twitched about our non-involvement on the ground. 'I'm going over to find out from these ambulance lads what is happening.'

In the group fortunately were several local BASICS Immediate Care Doctors, some of whom I knew, and I was amazed to learn that only five local people had been badly enough injured to require hospitalization. The sense of relief that this engendered, that our skills after all had not been wasted, was shattered by the subsequent news that around twenty townsfolk were missing, feared dead, in the burnt-out ruins of their homes. It was also rumoured that the plane had been full of US Servicemen going home on Christmas leave, raising speculation that a bomb had been planted on board.

The implications for world peace of such an outrage, just at a crucial time when Yasser Arafat's PLO had renounced terrorist violence and was prepared to recognise Israel, were only too horribly obvious, and hit me like a kick in the guts. I only hoped that some other precipitating cause would be found to explain the structural failure of the 747.

Bill Lines returned from his briefing with the news that another Sea King from Gannet was flying down with Malcolm Rifkind, the Secretary of State for Scotland, and various other politicians, to view the scene and give a press conference. As if on cue, the recognisable throb of a Sea King materialised from the darkness in a blaze of landing lights, and set down on the playing field, synchronising perfectly with the arrival of a couple of large police cars.

Escorted by the aircrew, a group of trench-coated gentlemen, heads bowed against the driving rain, emerged into the light and split into two groups—the Government Ministers whisked away by police car to the main control building —and Donald Dewar, the Shadow Secretary of State, and his colleague, left to fend for themselves and make their own enquiries at the secondary Incident Van!

'We've to do another sweep east of the town.' Lines informed us. 'They've found the aircraft's nose and flight deck and scores of bodies in a field just south east of the town, but want us to go as far east as Langholm.'

East we went for twelve miles, as far as Langholm, and located pieces of wreckage more than eight miles from Lockerbie. Searching became increasingly difficult due to the hilly terrain, the black night and a wind gusting to twenty-five knots—with down-draughts, rain squalls and patchy low cloud to add to our problems.

For the searchlights to give maximum illumination, it was essential to fly very low, but the prevailing conditions necessitated keeping at a safe, rather than an effective altitude, and for much of the time our eyes strained to focus on an amorphous, grey landscape where vague white lumps of 'wreckage' would suddenly scatter as sheep.

We landed beside one group of three chairs, seatbelts unfastened, a grim clue as to the suddenness of the fate which had befallen their occupants. On the same hillside lay an intact parcel of computer software for an address in Massachusetts, a bag full of business papers, a bar of soap, some duty-free perfume and a hostess trolley still containing the remains of half-eaten meals.

With these finds, the hitherto remote, impersonal nature of our task suddenly changed, and the realities began to sink in. These objects had belonged to people; people who only a few hours previously had been happily flying home for Christmas; people who were now dead—scattered like their possessions over dozens of square miles of Scottish countryside. Our task seemed at once more and more futile in this worsening weather. It was time to go home.

At the makeshift canteen in Lockerbie Academy, we had our first experience of the toll exacted on those in the front-line. Kindly Red Cross ladies from nearby Annan were busy supplying tea, sandwiches and sausage rolls to haggard, white-faced policemen; to a team of part-time firemen from Dumfries, smoke-blackened, bleary-eyed, numb and exhausted—the real heroes of the night; to lads and lasses from Mountain Rescue Teams and the Services—who had all witnessed terrible scenes which would haunt their dreams for years to come; and to an old man with shaking hands and a blood-crusted scalp—and nowhere to go.

Outside, on the road leading back to our Sea King, the unleashed potential for even greater devastation was forcefully demonstrated by the presence of a huge 747 engine buried vertically, like a bomb, deep in the pavement, with just its cowling visible above ground, only five yards from a terraced row of houses—and not a single window broken! Unbelievable luck—for some.

It was about a quarter to four, and the school playing fields now held four Wessex, three Sea King, and two Puma helicopters, all dwarfed by two huge Chinooks which had just flown in with fifty RAF personnel—and body bags for the morning's grim ordeal.

We were now surplus to requirements, and homeward bound. In a few hours' time, the night's veil would be lifted, and the horrors of Lockerbie and Flight PA 103 revealed to a shocked and disbelieving world.

16

9 February 1989

SAR Thirteen

'A most useful meeting, gentlemen. Thank you for coming. I will be in touch with you later, Mr Dawson… and I'll see you around, Doc.' Famous last words!

Lt Cdr Roy Lewis had been tasked to organise the new SAR set-up. With its burgeoning workload and its increasingly important role in Search and Rescue operations around the west of Scotland and Ireland now widely recognised, Gannet had just been designated as a fully fledged front line SAR Unit similar to RAF Lossiemouth and RNAS Culdrose. This had necessitated a complete change of philosophy from the old-style, gentlemanly amateurish, TYT (Take Your Time) SARs, with their leisurely response time limit of forty-five minutes by day, and ninety minutes by night, to a highly professional approach, with a rapid response target set—of having to be airborne within fifteen minutes, dawn to dusk, and thirty minutes overnight.

Consequently Roy had approached me for advice on provision of facilities for medical training of aircrew, either at the local Casualty Departments, or with the Ambulance Service. The end result had been this very constructive session in which Jeff Dawson, the Area Ambulance Training Officer, and myself, together with the Lt Cdr and POMA John Bennett, had discussed various options: initial medical training to be carried out by the Sick Bay Medic Instructors; with a follow-up arrangement for aircrew to ride shotgun as observers on the Saturday night front-line ambulances, to get themselves battle-hardened.

The official thinking behind this training scheme was that a SAR crew on permanent standby could easily be airborne within seven minutes on a search for missing climbers or boats, and might well leave without a medic or myself on board. In which case, the Observer or Aircrewman would have to be capable of dealing with any injuries encountered on arrival at the scene. I was personally unhappy with this idea, and had argued strongly that an extra two or three minutes spent at this end, waiting for a Medic to come down from Sick Bay, would very likely mean a life saved at the other end; and that the MAs should be incorporated as regular SAR crew members. Where there was a callout to a severely injured or ill patient, the take-off would have to be delayed long enough anyway, to allow the MA or myself to participate.

It was going to be a completely new ball-game for Gannet. Up until now, the SAR commitment had been of a second-line, casual nature, using any old Sea King which might be available; with the SAR gear permanently stowed on a large trolley and wheeled out to the aircraft on receipt of a callout. My goon suit and those of the Medics were kept up in Sick Bay, and we had to change there and run the two hundred yards down to the Ops Room, where our medical kit was kept in a cupboard—ready to be lugged across the tarmac by ourselves, if we were unlucky enough to miss the trolley!

The present level of Service medical equipment carried on board the SAR Sea King was of a pathetically poor, second-rate standard, and totally inadequate for dealing with major trauma—compared with the civilian gear we were accustomed to use at road accidents as BASICs doctors, and what was now being carried by front-line ambulances. It comprised a big, white, unwieldy, heavy plastic, basic Ship's Doctor's Box, which was a bugger to carry with one handle, dangerous to lower on a winch, and hopeless to use in a confined space. In addition, the drugs and dressings it contained were often inappropriate or antiquated—or just not there! What on earth would I use Sal Volatile (smelling salts) or Calcium Carbonate for nowadays? And several of my first casualties had been severe head injuries—when there was not even a cervical collar on board, or spinal immobilisation splints. There was certainly a Pneupac Ventilator, and a Laerdal Suction machine, but nothing else of any practical use.

Weight, or excess weight, always seemed to be a limiting factor, and the illogical reason—or excuse—put forward for not being able to carry more gear. The back-seat crews had a rigid military mindset about this. Every extra pound carried, so I was told, meant a pound less fuel, and reduced flying endurance. Initially the cab only carried *a single oxygen cylinder*, and early on I had a terrible argument trying to persuade an Observer and Aircrewman to allow us to carry a second oxygen cylinder—because it weighed something like twenty pounds! They capitulated eventually, when I pointed out that, while their aircraft might well have plenty of flying endurance, the endurance time of an oxygen cylinder was only forty minutes, and that of an anoxic patient's brain— *only three minutes* if it ran out! If the return trip was going to take an hour, their casualty would most likely be dead for the last twenty minutes of the flight. We now carried three cylinders—and even that was not enough.

Over the last two years I had campaigned and agitated for better equipment, but had managed to secure very little in the way of practical improvements—mainly I felt, because I had no official status or authority at Gannet, being simply Suddie MacKechnie's locum for SAR callouts. Suddie, who had had more retiral dates than Frank Sinatra, was finally due to hang up his stethoscope at the end of March, and I hoped then that Naval purse strings might be loosened sufficiently by powerful arguments from the new CMP to allow the purchase of spinal supports, up-to-date splints, and other vital equipment. But that was still two months away.

The decision to upgrade Gannet to full SAR status had come about as the result of a recent policy decision to restrict the Wessex Crabs from RAF Leuchars in Fife to daylight and weekday flying only, as a face-saving compromise following vigorous opposition to an MOD plan to scrap the Leuchars SAR cab altogether in the interests of economy. The workload of what had always been one of the busiest SAR stations in the country was to have been shared by RAF Sea Kings from Lossiemouth, and Boulmer in Northumberland, together with the Navy Sea Kings from HMS Gannet. However, a public furore from Mountain Rescue Teams, local authorities, fishermen's organisations and MPs, coupled with some skilful PR work involving lots of yellow Crabs on TV, had forced the MOD to think again—and allowed us all a sigh of relief.

Even so, as from 1st August 1989, Gannet would have a much higher SAR profile, and Navy pride dictated that their crews would have to be every bit as professional as those of the RAF. Inter-Service rivalries were always intense, and what else could Roy Lewis do but arrange these courses—in the face of RAF propaganda that their chappies could resuscitate, intubate, amputate, fornicate and even perform open-heart surgery in the back of their Crabs!

Next day, I was taking advantage of a slack hour before evening surgery to get on with some paperwork at home, when the bleep went.

'John Bennett here, Doc. It's to Oban… a man with internal bleeding. I'm sending young McNamee—it's his first SAR—and I'd like you to go along. Can cause problems, these internal bleeds.'

'OK. I'll come in, but I'll have to call the Surgery first and arrange for someone else to do my evening appointments.'

'How long will you be, so that I can inform Ops Room?'

'Fifteen minutes.' I glanced at my watch—1445 hours. Twelve minutes later I was at Gannet, to find the Sea King already burning and turning on the apron—obviously a quick turn-round job, which put added pressure on me. Diving into my goon suit, I grabbed helmet and lifejacket and rushed dishevelled on to the tarmac, only to be pulled-up and firmly told to get my helmet fastened on properly before going anywhere near the aircraft, by the ground crew—and the rest of me buttoned and zipped-up properly before we got airborne, by LACMN Crosby. We were almost at our destination before I remembered to tie my bootlaces!

Our destination, in the finest tradition of SAR signal communication cock-ups, was not Oban, but the island of Coll. Leaving behind clear skies over Ayrshire, we found, as so often in the past, a marked change in the weather beyond the Arran hills and Kintyre. Visibility had closed to three or four miles going up Loch Fyne, and a cloud ceiling of 1000 feet meant we had to fly visual through the Crinan Gap rather than beeline it on a high altitude bearing straight for Coll.

Corrievreckan was, once again, sadly unimpressive as we overflew it on a slack tide and, as we traversed the Ross of Mull just to the east of Iona, low cloud forced us down to 500 feet for the rest of the trip. The torrential rain of recent weeks had left a waterlogged Coll landscape, and there was some concern that even the grass landing strip might be too soft for the Sea King.

Roy Lewis—he of the famous last words—was right-hand Pilot, and managed to set the cab down gingerly on a surprisingly firm piece of ground.

'I might have to put up a drip and stabilise this guy before we bring him back on board,' I warned him as we left the aircraft.

'I can give you fifteen minutes, no more… because we want to get to Oban hospital before it gets too dark!'

Ducking the rotors, we hurried over to a small knot of people by a gate. Dr de Mornay, the island GP, was there, and handed me a referral letter.

'What's his condition?' I asked. 'Does he need a drip?'

'No. He is quite stable. BP and pulse are normal. He had a small haematemesis and melaena this morning, but nothing since… See for yourself.'

She gestured towards the Coll 'front-line ambulance'—an old farm pick-up truck with a glass-fibre hood, and the end of a grubby mattress and a pair of feet jutting over the tailboard!

I peered in, to find a somewhat embarrassed middle-aged man, whose ruddy complexion and cheery grin clearly indicated he was not *in extremis*. He had one of those vaguely familiar West Highland faces you can see on any MacBraynes ferry, and his hands were clasped behind his head in a display of nonchalance.

'How are you feeling?' I enquired.

'Fine! Just fine! Nothing much wrong with me!'

'Well—away hame then!' I rejoined, to laughter from the surrounding group, '—and we'll do the same!'

Back on board the helicopter, 'Bing' Crosby fitted him with earmuffs and plugged him into the intercom. He lay there, relaxed and content. During the hubbub of navigational cross-talk which always occupies take-off, young McNamee looked across at me, produced his chinagraph pencil, and scribbled 'Name' on his kneepad.

I opened the referral letter, glanced through the case details, caught the name—'John McIntyre, Inveraray'—and handed the note to him. Then memory cues began slowly to slip into place—that grin—that vaguely familiar face—the name McIntyre—who, where, when? Suddenly it clicked! There was a lull on the intercom.

'Doc here! Permission to speak to the patient?'

'Go ahead, Doc!'

'Is your name John McIntyre?' A nod of the head.

'Have you ever been on Islay?' Two nods of the head.

'Did you ever stay at the Bridgend Hotel?' More nods of the head and a wide grin.

' "Teak" McIntyre? Remember me? Doctor Begg... on our holidays?' Vigorous nodding and an expression of delight. I leaned over and we shook hands warmly.

It was the 'Inveraray' address which had given me the clue that he was not a Coll man. Teak was an agricultural traveller to the islands, whom we had met on several occasions while on holiday on Islay. He was a real character, whose visits to Bridgend were always eagerly anticipated by the staff; and something which had always stuck with me was his home address, Furnace, near Inveraray. It had been at least eight years since our last encounter, and I was delighted to meet him again. Although Islay was no longer on his patch, his black briefcase, dumped on board with his weekend bag, indicated he was still stomping an island beat.

We settled down for the short, twenty minute flight to Oban, and very soon were past Ardnamurchan Point and into the Sound of Mull. The aircraft began to pitch and yaw. 'Sorry if you might find the going a bit rough,' apologised Roy Lewis. 'We are in the lee of the island and the downdraughts are making it a bumpy ride.'

'As long as it's the weather, and not the bloody Pilot!' someone quipped from the back.

We flew on past Tobermory and out of the rough stuff. Then, surprisingly, there came what sounded like a request for 'Doc' to go up front. I scrambled for'ard, to find it was a mistake. It was LACMN Crosby the Captain had wanted, and when he joined us, Lewis scribbled something I couldn't quite decipher on his kneepad. Crosby silently returned aft, and I followed, to find him unplugging Teak's intercom.

'Intercom unplugged, Sir!'

'Didn't want to alarm our passenger, chaps,' announced the Captain calmly, 'but there's a smell of burning in the cockpit. Lead Crosby, could you walk slowly for'ard sniffing carefully as you come, and try to locate the source.'

Liam McNamee and I just looked at each other. Crosby duly obliged, and ended up in the cockpit, confirming a strong smell like electrical arcing, possibly from behind the instrument panel. At least there was no smoke.

'Probably a short circuit somewhere... would explain that crackling on the intercom when we're operating switches, and that break in the intercom a few minutes ago. We'd better shut down completely when we get to Oban.' The Captain was for taking no unnecessary risks.

The next five minutes seemed like twenty-five as our noses strained like smoke sensors to detect the faintest whiff of anything, and our ears tuned anxiously to the pitch of the rotorblades; while Teak lay there with a big contented smile on his face and his eyes closed in blissful ignorance.

Swinging round to the north of Oban, we topped a rocky, wooded hillside and dropped into the shinty park landing site without further incident. Teak was hastily evacuated to the waiting ambulance, where I bade him farewell. Lt Goldsmith, our Observer, went off likewise in a Coastguard van to inform Gannet by telephone that we had a shutdown, while the Pilot and Co-Pilot checked all systems.

No malfunctions were found, but there was a suspicion that perhaps a windscreen wiper motor was overheating. In any event, Gannet Maintainers gave us clearance to return to Prestwick after a half-hour delay, and we finally arrived back at 1800 hours, just in time for me to go on call overnight for the Practice.

So much for SAR Thirteen!

17

24 February 1989

Busy Spell

'Sorry about that, Craig!' I apologised profusely to my partner next morning. 'How did you get on?'

I had left him reluctantly holding the bleep for a couple of hours while Helen and I went to listen to James Galway and his golden flute in concert with the Scottish Chamber Orchestra, at Ayr Town Hall. Enthralled by the performance, we had gone back to collect it after the concert, only to discover from a very anxious-looking Carol that he had been bleeped for his first-ever SAR less than half-an-hour after we had left, and was away to—of all places—Barra!

'Oh, fine,' he replied. 'It wasn't as bad as I thought—after the mad rush I had to get there. Carol had just popped out to Safeways for a few minutes, and there was a helluva panic on… with me bleeped for Gannet, on call for the Practice, minding the kids, and no one at home to man the phone. Took me twenty-five minutes to get out, then a guy waiting at the gate grabbed me and got me kitted out while the helicopter was revving up on the tarmac.'

'What was the callout for?' I asked.

'It was a nasty one. A wall had collapsed on this poor bloke's leg and mashed it up so badly that they thought it might need amputated. The Barra doctor had already pumped about seven units of plasma into him, and goodness knows how much morphine, so he was in good condition for the journey—quite oblivious! In fact, the young Medic cracked, "You'll not need to worry about your patient, Doc. He'll be flying five hundred yards ahead of the aircraft all the way back to Glasgow!"

'I enjoyed the trip back down from Glasgow to Prestwick about midnight. It was magic looking down on the lit-up towns, with a big silver moon shining through the clouds.'

Craig—not the most poetic of men—was waxing lyrical! He sounded so enthusiastic, with his first SAR under his belt and his fear of the unknown overcome, that I felt quite relieved, and would worry less in future about leaving him with the bleep—though I was glad it had been to a solid island and not a heaving trawler!

It had been a busy fortnight, I mused, as I started the two o'clock surgery—I'd been to Coll, Craig to Barra, and big Paul had recently escorted a dehydrated baby from Arran to Glasgow. Edith interrupted my thoughts with a buzz from the front desk—'It's Sick Bay for you, Doctor.' I groaned.

'Stevie here, Doc. We've got a call to medevac a six year-old child from Machrihanish, and,' he added ominously, 'they've asked us to bring resuscitation equipment. Can you come in?'

Fortunately, as usual on most winter Friday afternoons, there was a surplus of consulting doctors, and the twin burdens of my conscience and my remaining patients were spread lightly among four of them.

Bloody Hell! What's this I'm going to? I turned over in my mind all the horrific possibilities I could think of as I tore up the bypass—head injury, crushed chest, pneumonia, meningitis, drowning... Typically, even on board the Sea King, there was no more accurate information forthcoming from Edinburgh Rescue than contained in the original message from Stevie.

Liam McNamee was the duty MA, and the aircraft Captain was Roger Stringer, who had last flown with me on the day of the barbecue and kid gloves—as he kindly reminded me. The short trip across to Machrihanish took twenty minutes; spent checking the Laerdal suction apparatus, the Pneupac oxygen ventilator, endotracheal tubes—which I had never used on a kid—instead of enjoying a beautiful afternoon of still seas, blue skies and a sunkissed Arran landscape of tawny winter hills, bottle-green forests and whitewashed cottages.

Touchdown at Machrihanish Airbase was an anticlimax. There was no waiting ambulance. Twenty minutes passed before it finally arrived, bearing not the desperately ill six-year-old we'd been led to expect, but a six-month-old bouncing baby boy in the arms of his anxious mum. Hovering solicitously in the background was a bearded chap who turned out not to be the baby's father, as we thought, but the local health visitor.

I examined the infant. He was contented, bright-eyed and alert, no vomiting, and no signs of increased intracranial pressure. Apparently he had been violently sick earlier in the day, and had gone very limp and cyanosed. His doctor had suspected meningitis and decided on hospital. Again, a difficult decision for a GP to take, a hundred and fifty miles by road from the nearest paediatric hospital—and knowing there were no medals to be gained from a tragic delay.

The health visitor insisted that he should come with us because he had 'resuscitation equipment'—a hand-operated suction pump—despite the presence of myself, the MA, and all our own gear! Bob Yeomans, the Aircrewman, was non-plussed. He'd been told only one would be travelling. However, an extra set of earmuffs and a lifejacket were produced and, after telling the chap he'd have to hoof it, or get the bus back to Campbeltown from Paisley, we boarded the aircraft.

True to form, ears plugged against the aircraft noise, muffled in warm blankets against the cold, and snuggled up against his mum, our wee patient slept all the way to Glasgow Airport.

The waiting ambulancemen were bemused. 'We were expecting a six-year-old boy!' said one, as Bob Yeomans, showing a degree of paternal tenderness, skill and dexterity none of us would have dreamed he possessed, cradled the baby in his arms and carried the tiny bundle across the tarmac to the ambulance. 'So were we,' I replied. 'You obviously get the same bum info as we do from time to time!'

*　　*　　*

A fortnight later and I was airborne again. Surgery interruptions had become so much the norm in the last few weeks that yet another late morning call from Sick Bay, announcing yet another SAR, this time to Arran, scarcely raised a staff eyebrow when I left in a puff o' stour. Whether it raised the hackles of my few remaining patients, I did not wait long enough to find out, but it momentarily crossed my mind that some of them must be thinking (and not without a grain of truth in it) that I'd do anything to avoid seeing them!

Speed and smooth efficiency were the order of the day. I was met at the Ops Room door by the OOD, briefed that the patient had early pregnancy complications, got kitted out, and was onboard the Sea King within fifteen minutes of leaving the Surgery—much to Roy Lewis's surprise.

Flying low to cheat a strong thirty knot headwind, we reached the Whiting Bay rendezvous ten minutes before the ambulance arrived from Arran War Memorial Hospital. As we prepared the stretcher, Bob Pheasant the Aircrewman looked up with a grin. 'First time we've been out together, Doc—since that girl, on the yacht, with the fractured skull—remember, the time when you were... er... not very well?'

Seems Pheasants, like elephants, never forget!

Fortunately, and typically, the girl's condition was stable, and nowhere near as grim as that portrayed in the original signal from Pitreavie. With the wind behind us, it was only a short ten-minute hop back to the Maternity Hospital landing site at Irvine, and I relayed this reassuring piece of information to her on a piece of paper.

She smiled, gestured for the pen, and wrote—reassuringly—'Brother... trained Chopper Pilot... Air Corps.'

Thumbs up and camaraderie all round!

Ten minutes later, as promised, we were on the ground, twiddling the same thumbs again, as we waited—this time for the Irvine hospital ambulance. Such speed, such efficiency.

18

10 June 1989

High Drama

'Is she tied on?' asked a wide-eyed young Susan, as Helen, 'The Girl on the Wing', waved bravely to the Prestwick Air Show crowds from the top of her Steadman Biplane while it skimmed past only twenty feet above the runway.

'No. She holds on with one hand, and grips with her long curved toenails—just like a bird!' we teased her. 'Oh, look! Isn't that clever?' The girl had just posed with one leg raised, then lowered it smartly as the small plane roared into a vertical climb and looped the loop.

'I think she must be tied on, Susan!' Her dad nudged her and winked as both plane and girl hung momentarily motionless and upside down, silhouetted against the lead-grey sky. It was threatening rain, not the best of weather for an Air Show, but the Red Arrows had already managed to slot their impeccable performance of precision flying into a 'window' of high cloud and blinks of sunshine; and cousin Jim would have been quite happy with that experience alone to savour as the highlight of his family day out.

Now officially the Civilian Medical Practitioner at Gannet since Suddie MacKechnie's retiral on 31st March, we were able to have our picnic lunch, of all places, in the comfort of my very own Sick Bay, safely out of the wind and weather, but with the kids strictly warned to leave no crumbs lying around for the Monday morning Sick Parade.

Then it was back to the display area to watch the incredible manoeuvres of a Sea Harrier dipping and bowing to its audience. The static display contained an impressive array of aircraft old and new—a Victor V-bomber, now converted to a refuelling tanker, vintage Hawker Hunter and Corsair jet fighters, an AWAC Boeing 707, and modern, multi-million pound Tornadoes. Close by, our attention was drawn to a comprehensive demonstration by the local Emergency Services of rescue equipment used for fire-fighting, underwater searches, mine rescue, entrapment and transporting casualties; and an Irvine GP colleague, Dave Carson, had mounted a fine photographic display of the work done by BASICs doctors attending road accidents and major disaster exercises.

As we tagged on to the tail of a long queue slowly disappearing up the backside of a huge USAF Starlifter, the splutter and roar of a piston engine drew our eyes to a veteran single-seater Fleet Air Arm Sea Fury of the Royal Navy's Historic Flight—the only one of its kind in existence—which was warming up just a few yards away. The children gazed with great interest as its folded wings lowered and clicked into place, and the plane taxied off out of our view.

'I'm fed up with queues!' I signalled to Jim, as our progress up the Starlifter ground to a halt for the third time. 'Aye, let's get underneath one of these loudspeakers with a good view of the runway, and the kids can watch the flying display,' he replied—with more than a hint of self-interest.

As we jumped down from the big plane, I glanced with some curiosity over to my left towards a long line of fire engines, ambulances—and Dave Carson's BMW—assembling at the edge of the main runway. Don't tell me we're going to get a display from this bunch as well, I thought to myself, as we moved to a vantage point near the Tannoy; and simultaneously, my attention was diverted by the roar of the Sea Fury's engine as it flew overhead.

'Funny! It's only got its left wheel down.' I remarked to Jim. 'I suppose he'll free the other one fairly smartly before his display... Or maybe he's doing tricks like that lassie on the biplane!'

Then yet another distraction—as the Show Commentator matter-of-factly announced that a British Airways Jumbo was about to make an emergency landing because of smoke in the cargo hold! This must be the lead-in to the Emergency Services display, was my initial reaction—followed by the swift realisation that it would be bloody expensive to fly in a Jumbo-jet just for an exercise—a damn-sight more than for that Lynx helicopter with its half-dozen abseiling Marines we'd watched perform earlier.

'Jim, I think this is for real! I'd better go across and see what's happening. Tell Helen and Sheila I won't be long—I hope.'

I'd no sooner joined Dave in his BMW than the massive bulk of the 747 flew in low over the sea to a perfect landing, rolled to a halt abreast of us, and immediately taxied off on to a subsidiary runway. Led by a yellow Airport van, we sped across the tarmac and took up our positions to windward of the giant plane.

Three huge Airport fire tenders converged on the aircraft as stairs were quickly manouevred into place and the passengers hurriedly evacuated. Only then were the cargo doors opened, to reveal—nothing! It had been, as we discovered later, a false alarm due to a fault in the plane's smoke sensors. 'We're not finished yet!' The Incident Fire Officer poked his head through the car window. 'One of the Show aircraft is flying about with undercarriage problems, and he is going to try an emergency landing here, along the grass beside the runway. He's burning off fuel at the moment while we shift this Jumbo out of harm's way.'

The atmosphere was charged, tense and hushed, as we watched and waited, and feared, for the poor chap in the Sea Fury; wondering what must be going through his mind as he flew his lonely laps in front of 60,000 onlookers. Most of the spectators, in fact, were more clued up as to what was happening than we were—listening to every word of the drama on their UHF radios.

At last, he made his final approach—a tiny insignificant speck in the sky in comparison with the earlier, lumbering, giant 747. As he flew in low over the grass, we soon realised, by his height and speed, that he was simply going to overfly and not attempt a crash landing.

This was confirmed a few moments later by the Airport Manager, who informed us all that the Pilot now intended to bale out over the Firth of Clyde, and that we could stand down. A Sea King, which had been parked close at hand on standby for both incidents, took off and headed back over the airfield to HMS *Gannet*.

'I might be needed by Gannet for a SAR!' I called to the Manager. 'Any chance of getting me back across there quickly?'

'You should have fifteen minutes, Doctor… they've gone to refuel.'

Our procession of vehicles was escorted swiftly back across the runway, and Dave dropped me off by the Ops Building. I rushed in and encountered Lt Cdr Ian McKellar, OIC Ops.

'Will I be needed for this one?'

'Oh, yes, Doc! Get changed quickly. We're kitting out a Diver at present, but you should be able to get up there before him if you're lucky. If not, too bad. They may have to leave without you.'

There's nothing like hurrying three hundred yards up a hill in heavy flying gear to make you realise you're twice as old as most of the aircrew—and half as fit! I was knackered by the time I reached the Sick Bay car park where, to my surprise, I found Helen, with Colin and Fiona, standing key-less by the car. Jim and Sheila were packed and ready for home. My car key was—naturally —zipped-up and completely inaccessible inside my goon suit. I could only gasp my apologies, hope that retribution would be minimal, and wave cheerio to an awestruck William and Susan (their Uncle Jimmy really did fly in a helicopter!).

Barging into Sick Bay, I discovered that no Medic had been alerted for the SAR, and consequently there was no SAR gear on board. Grabbing the spare Pneupac and SAR Box, I was decidedly more buggered than knackered by the time I had clambered aboard the Sea King which, for the duration of the Air Show, had been stationed a further hundred yards uphill beyond Sick Bay, on the playing fields opposite the Wardroom. Roy Lewis looked surprised to see me. Jock Alexander, a qualified Diver as well as a Pilot, followed me on board, and within seconds we were airborne and heading south over the Air Show crowds.

I had no idea where we were going, and was surprised when we overflew, first Prestwick, then Ayr, then the fishing village of Dunure—till it dawned on me that the Sea Fury must have been directed as far away as possible from built-up areas to minimise the risk of casualties once the Pilot had baled out.

Five miles further on—five-star resplendent following a recent seven million pound refurbishment—and standing isolated in red-roofed gleaming glory on a tree-clad hilltop overlooking its famous golf courses, Turnberry Hotel was obviously expendable. An honorable Kamikaze attack by a pilotless World War Two, Far East fighter would probably be received with full and sympathetic understanding by its new Japanese owners! So we took up station just offshore, at the southern end of the Ailsa Championship Course, to await developments.

'I want every man on board looking for this aircraft!' ordered Roy Lewis. 'Get yourselves to a window—and when you see it, for God's sake don't lose it!'

Jock Alexander went for'ard as an extra pair of eyes, his diving services not being required. The Observer and Aircrewman placed themselves in readiness at the open cargo door, and I clambered into the Observer's window seat.

'Got him!' someone called up front. 'Flying very high at two o'clock. Shit! He's flying into the sun... I've lost him.'

'Alright! I see him now... heading south east at twelve o'clock. Can you all see him? Don't lose him again. Watch as he goes through that patch of thin cloud.'

I was on the wrong side of the aircraft for all this high drama, frustrated at being able to see nothing. Then the plane changed direction, the helicopter banked to follow it, and, through the starboard door, I finally saw a small speck 6000ft up, flying through wispy cloud towards Arran, and difficult to track because of the sun's glare.

We tacked again and I lost it. Then a cry went up—'He's baled out! I can see a parachute... at that height and windspeed he should be able to drift in overland.'

'There goes his plane into the sea... what a bloody shame!'

'It looks like the poor bugger's not going to get a dry landing after all. I'd better go in closer... get ready to pick him up in the two-man strop as soon as he hits the sea!'

As we maneouvred, I could see the Pilot swinging slowly like a pendulum, as his chute gently carried him to a watery landing half a mile off-shore. Fortunately the calm sea, with two foot waves, would pose no problems.

'He's down! Right. Go! Watch your height!'—this last instruction in a note of alarm, as the helicopter banked steeply into a tight turn, its angled rotor blades perilously close to the water. We were almost instantly over the Pilot, his discarded parachute skimming over the waves away from our downdraught. Marcus Wilson, the Observer, was quickly lowered, and within a minute of ditching, had the bedraggled figure of Lt Cdr John Beattie safely on board, unscathed apart from some spherical bruising caused by the crutch of his parachute harness.

Smartly wrapping him in a survival blanket, we beelined for Gannet, since there was obviously no need for a hospital check-up; leaving the back-up Sea King to fix accurately the Sea Fury's point of entry for future diving/salvage attempts.

Following his medical all-clear in Sick Bay, and before we sat down together to fill in the intimidating and lengthy F/Med 154 Report which must be completed for all air accidents, a tatty but dry old pair of overalls were eventually found for him by Stevie, after an extensive search—probably the only spare clothes available from Gannet which did not require to be signed out of Purser's Stores in triplicate!

As Lt Cdr Beattie struggled gratefully into the proffered rags, Cdr Ian Thorpe, Captain of Gannet, poked his head round the door—'Alright, John?... Would you like a large one... purely medicinal of course, Jimmy!' He grinned and winked as he brandished a large bottle of Scotch.

'Sorry! I can't authorise the use of alcohol on medical grounds, Ian!' I replied, tongue in cheek—a typical bloody medical killjoy getting his health message punchline across. 'Worst thing you can do for someone with hypothermia. Those St Bernard dogs have a lot to answer for!'

'You and I must be in different Navies!' he cracked back.

'But,' I continued magnanimously, 'since he was less than a minute in the water, I think we could safely allow him a social dram!'

Honour satisfied, we moved to the door, to be confronted by Phil Ball, the Station Photographer.

'Could we have a photograph of Lt Lewis and Lt Cdr Beattie together—perhaps with the Doc pouring the Lt Cdr a large whisky?'

Needless to say, this was the picture which appeared next day in the national press. Shades of St Bernard. And so much for getting the message across on the correct and proper medical treatment of hypothermia!

19

14 September 1989

Fillet de Frenchman

'I saw your letter last week in *The Herald*, Chris,' I remarked to the CO of 819 Squadron as we towelled down after a liferaft and dinghy Wet Drill at Ayr Baths. 'Didn't do much good though. Did you see page seven?'

He laughed. 'Yes, just typical! I don't know what the Navy has got to do to get some media recognition for our SARs. The same thing happened again last weekend, when we lifted that injured climber off the Cobbler, and the RAF got all the credit. D'you know, it's not all that long ago since the Fleet Air Arm actually had more aircraft than the RAF!'

This Press blind-spot about Royal Naval 'non-involvement' in SAR work had always been a sore point at Gannet. Invariably, any rescue was reported as having been undertaken by *'a Royal Air Force helicopter'*, or—even worse—*'an RAF Sea King from HMS Gannet'*!

The final straw had come only last week. After 819 had saved the life of a windsurfer being swept out to sea by high winds and strong Solway tides near Dalbeattie—next stop Isle of Man—the credit had, naturally, gone to the RAF. And, to rub salt in the wound, on the very day that Chris Denny's letter of complaint was being published in the Glasgow *Herald*, the preceding page carried a follow-up piece on the incident, in which the windsurfer—still rescued by *'an RAF helicopter'*—was claiming he had not been in any danger, and blaming the Rescue Services for the loss of his sailboard!

This prompted further caustic comments from Chris on the unbelievable ingratitude of some of those rescued. 'When I was in Cornwall, we once rescued a woman and her two kids trapped by the tide on rocks near Culdrose, and her husband had the cheek to bill the Navy for a ten pound repair to her skirt. Needless to say, the Old Man sent him a bill for four thousand quid for the rescue, and that was the last we heard of that one!'

'To come back to the Cobbler rescue,' I asked, 'I gather the SAR crew went off without the MA, although the guy was badly injured?'

My Sick Bay staff had been pretty miffed about this incident, worried that the new fifteen-minute response time for SARs was going to leave them out in the cold, with valuable medical expertise being sacrificed by gung-ho aircrew striving to beat their record take-off time of six minutes thirty-six seconds or whatever, without a thought as to what might be waiting for them at the other end. SAR back-seat crews had been receiving extra first-aid training from the MAs for several months, to help them cope with emergencies, and maybe put them roughly on a par with the RAF Aircrewmen, who spent their entire Service career on SAR helos.

It was hoped that this training might just put an end to some of the snide remarks coming from their RAF rivals—whose back-seat crews had first aid skills of such a tremendously high standard (if the Crabs were to be believed), that they could do anything from vasectomies to heart transplants in the back of their helos! If truth were to be told however, highly trained though they were, RAF Winchmen did not have the professional diagnostic training of the Navy's Medical Assistants—who might well be in sole medical charge of a frigate's crew at sea—and, just like the Navy, the RAF would take a doctor along if one was required.

So, as far as the service provided by Gannet was concerned, Chris Denny assured me, the option of carrying an MA was an extra bonus provision. Far from being considered redundant, the back-seat crews—despite their extra training—were more than relieved to have on board the medical expertise of an MA to augment their basic skills. I was delighted to hear this, and further pushed my argument that the MAs should now be included as an integral part of the SAR crew.

'That Cobbler trip was a calculated risk,' he continued. 'We were worried about carrying extra weight into the hills, and because the aircraft was fully loaded with fuel and too heavy for such a short transit, the Captain had to jettison about seventeen hundred pounds over the sea before he could risk approaching the mountain. Even at that, he was developing well over ninety percent torque in the hover... and you know what that means!' I didn't.

'Well, at one hundred percent torque the helicopter goes straight down. So that's why the weight factor is so critical, and why we decided in this instance to risk transporting the casualty without an MA.

'It's an unsatisfactory set-up,' he went on. 'We've been landed with this extra SAR commitment, and frankly we don't have suitable aircraft yet. FONAC have been reluctant so far to allow us a designated SAR aircraft, and have told us to make do with the operational Mark Five Sea Kings, which are too damn heavy for this sort of thing.

'There's over a tonne of sonar equipment in a Mark Five, and that equates with a helluva lot of extra fuel or passenger-carrying capacity. We've been back on at them to allow us to strip down a Sea King, and I hope they'll listen to us this time.'

The boys in Sick Bay were a lot happier next morning when I related the

1987. All geared up and nowhere to go! The author in goonsuit, PLP and bone-dome, with Mark 6 ASW Sea King in background.

First Pilot's view of standard right-hand approach to fishing vessel for a stern transfer in slight seas. Note the potential hazards from masts, derrick and aerials in rougher weather.

Guiding highline being hauled in and stowed properly in a bucket—NOT tied to the vessel!

*Medics in transit to a 'job', sitting in cramped rear compartment of ASW Sea King, just behind the
Aircrewman and Observer's seats.*

Even more cramped—when monitoring and treating a stretchered casualty.

A SAR Medic's dream of the future! Looking for'ard in the spacious cabin.

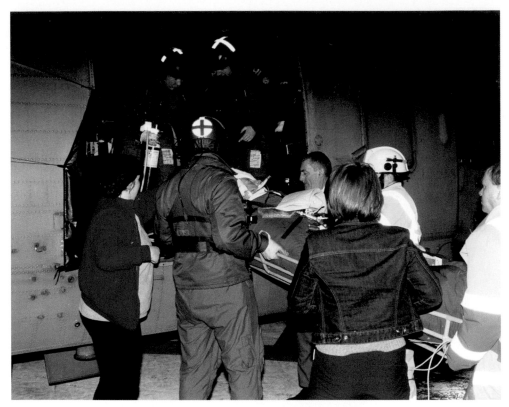

Night time medevac. Loading a heavy patient on a 'lightweight' stretcher—the more help the better!

All Scottish crew—1992. POMA Don Clark, LMA Jamie McCracken, MAQ Magz Brodie, 'Boss', MAQ Fiona McWilliam.

SAR Sea King in aft deck transfer from nuclear submarine.

This is the view a person gets from a two-man strop lift aboard a SAR Sea King with the Aircrewman. It looks a very thin wire!

whys and wherefores of last week's episode; that everybody really loved them, and that they wouldn't have to go and eat worms after all!

Morning Sick Parade went smoothly, with the usual procession of halt, lame, and weary—bruised ribs, backstrains and torn ligaments—with the odd viral infection thrown in for luck. 'Viruses'—in contrast to general practice—seldom come top of the Navy morbidity league. Unarmed combat on the sports field is more than able, on its own, to keep a Ship's Company at permanent half-strength. Who needs germ warfare when you've got hockey-sticks and goal-posts? Put these to the torch, and the Royal Navy's manpower shortages could be solved at the stroke of a match!

I was just assessing a young rating's 'Fitness to Box'—becoming in the process an accessory to yet another potential *'Sick on Shore—seven days'*, when the POMA stuck his head round the door:

'Looks as if there's a SAR on, Sir! it may require a doctor… we're just confirming details.' There was an expectant thirty second pause, then he re-turned. 'It's on, Sir. I want young Jamie McCracken to go with you. It will be his first SAR. The only information we've got so far is that it's a hundred and ninety miles out, and the casualty is a fisherman with a hand injury who has lost a lot of blood.'

I quickly stripped and changed into my flying overalls in the consulting room, mentally going over all the gear and procedures I might have to use, while at the same time entertaining the uncharitable thought that Elastoplast would probably suffice—if it turned out like some of the other recent jobs I'd been on.

Jamie was already in his goon suit when I drove him down to the SAR Cabin, and he shot off to grab a couple of lifejackets while I struggled into my own gear.

'Hi, Doc!' I turned to see Scott Bruce at an adjacent locker. It was our first SAR together since Lockerbie, and probably our last, as he was due to return to the States soon, at the end of his two year secondment to Gannet.

'Yeah. I'm flying left-hand seat again. It'll be a long trip—a hundred and ninety miles. The guy's on a French trawler… seems he's lost a lot of blood and is unconscious.'

Young McCracken arrived at the door with the lifejackets, and we both trotted out quickly to the aircraft. Seatbelts fastened, we had just settled our-selves into the forard seats when the Aircrewman, Bing Crosby, clambered up the flight door steps, and beckoned with his thumb at Jamie above the engine roar—'Get out! You're not going!' Jamie's mouth opened with surprise and disappointment as he looked at me, but he unclipped his seatbelt and obeyed without question. I was heartfelt sorry for him, missing his first SAR like that, but immediately guessed what the problem was—weight—again! Scott Bruce confirmed this over the intercom, when he announced that we would have to refuel at Machrihanish on the way out, to give us sufficient endurance for the whole trip.

It was a beautiful blue morning as we overflew a sun-kissed Arran, skirted Davaar Island and entered Campbeltown Loch. Below us lay moored the sleek new destroyer HMS *Campbeltown*. Recently commissioned, she was on a courtesy visit to Campbeltown where she was to be presented with the original silver plate bought by the townsfolk for her predecessor, the famous old HMS *Campbeltown* which, packed with explosives, had rammed the massive dock gates of St Nazaire in 1941, and had blown sky-high any hopes the German pocket battleship *Tirpitz* ever had of using the port's strategically vital dry dock facilities. The inscribed plate had lain proudly unclaimed in a vault for forty-eight years till this week's visit.

Lt Chris Reece, our Captain, dipped the aircraft in a courtesy roll as we passed over on our descent approach to RAF Machrihanish, where a Bowser was already on tap to replenish our tanks. A few minutes later and we were again airborne, heading west past Islay's southernmost tip, the Mull of Oa.

Most of the SAR gear was stowed for'ard in the sonar well, and I rummaged through it for what I thought I might need; and read up two pages of instructions on how to apply MAST trousers—Military Anti-Shock Trousers—a new and unsolicited piece of equipment which we had hitherto felt was superfluous. But it crossed my mind that this time they might come in very handy. If the guy had lost so much blood that I couldn't get a drip up, I could always squeeze a couple of pints out of his legs and into his vital circulation using the MAST trousers. With this in mind, I stuffed a dripset, I/V fluids, syringes and a sphygmo into the MAST bag which had a good carrying handle, as I felt the big white Ship's Doctor box was too hard, heavy, cumbersome and dangerous to consider lowering it safely on to the trawler.

A full hour passed quickly during this preparation, and by the time I was finished, we had rounded Malin Head, contacted the local Coastguard, and were heading southwards some thirty miles off the Donegal coast.

'Anyone here speak French?' inquired Chris Reece.

'I'm not too bad at it,' volunteered Jerry Scott, the Observer.

'And I'm just back from a holiday in France,' I chipped in, 'but I don't think that counts for much.' My heroic midsummer attempts at rekindling the 'Auld Alliance' through friendly chats with French villagers in the Dordogne, proud though I had been of my efforts, were beginning to fade into distant memory. What was the French for 'blood' again? Or hand… or blood pressure, or drip, or…? Thirty-year-old school vocabulary didn't cover many medical terms except '*mal à la tete*', and '*mal de mer*'—though the latter was more than a distinct possibility once I was lowered on to that trawler!

'Right, Jerry,' Reece continued with his pre-planning. 'When we get there, you go down first, then Doc will follow, OK?' It was agreed. No option!

'What was his last reported position?'

'Fifty-four degrees thirty-two north, nine degrees fourteen west,' responded Jerry Scott promptly. 'I think I've got him coming up on radar now. Steer two-one-zero.'

The Sea King nosed round, and far ahead we could see several scattered specks on the vast grey expanse of ocean.

'Jeez, there's five of them!' exclaimed Scott Bruce. 'Which one is ours?'

'Call him up on radio, Jerry. Use that fluent French of yours,' instructed Chris. 'Ask him to turn bow on to us as soon as he spots us... I'll switch on the landing lights.'

Jerry was hesitant, but agreed. 'Eh, what's the French for "bow"?' he asked plaintively.

'Dunno. Try le front de bateau!' quipped Chris Reece.

'Allo, allo... Fishing boat *Aries*. This is Rescue One Seven Seven... Eh, parlez-vous Anglais?'

'Non, monsieur... Je ne parle pas Anglais.'

'Shit! He doesn't speak English. Eh bien! Je parle un peu Francais. Est-ce que vous pouvez me voir?'

'Non!'

'Cherchez nos lumieres... quand vous me voyez, je voudrais que vous tournez le... er... front de bateau vers nous.'

'Oui. Je comprends, monsieur. Je tournerai l'avant vers vous.'

Ten seconds later, as if by magic, a white bow wave glinted in the sun five miles away, as one of the trawlers turned smartly in our direction.

'There she is! Well done Jerry!' Cheers all round.

We closed in rapidly. The *Aries* was a large stern trawler, but access to that area was barred by horizontal masthead wires, antennae, and derricks. It would have to be the bow. A twenty knot south-westerly wind raised a moderate swell from that quarter, but an older, larger cross-swell from the north-west was producing an uncomfortable rolling motion as the *Aries* dutifully steered six-zero downwind.

Jerry Scott was lowered first, then myself—without incident. The MAST bag followed, attached by a grab-hook to the winchwire, and was hauled on board with the aid of a sand-bagged highline. To the accompaniment of a few 'bonjours', and curious Gallic stares, we were ushered below, and along a narrow passage to a cabin conveniently close to the foredeck.

Lying across his bunk, ashen-faced but fully conscious, his left hand clenched on a wad of blood-soaked gamgee, was a man about forty—the ship's Captain. The bleeding fortunately had stopped, but his pulse was rapid, and his BP a bit low. He would need a drip to be on the safe side for the long trip home.

Brandishing my scissors with an apologetic 'Pardonnez-moi, monsieur!' I slit up the sleeve of his smock to expose, to my immense relief, a large and inviting vein. Cannulation was no problem, and the infusion was set up quickly. From his assembled crewmates, we were able to establish that he'd stuck a filleting knife into the palm of his hand, severed an artery, and lost between one and two litres of blood, following which he had passed out for ten minutes.

With the bleeding now stopped, I judged his condition was stable enough for him to be taken safely back to Crosshouse Hospital, rather than to Northern Ireland—which greatly relieved Scott Bruce, who had already warned Pitreavie that he wanted a military escort if we were going into Ballykelly. Obviously he was keen to get back to the USA in one piece!

The passageway from the cabin was too narrow to negotiate with the Stokes Litter, so we had to half-walk, half-support our patient out to the stretcher on the foredeck, highlighting yet another weakness in our SAR kit provision. I made a mental note to investigate the possibility of acquiring some eight-handled canvas slings, like those used by the Ambulance Service, to ease the manhandling of casualties round awkward corners.

Fortunately he was none the worse of the manouevre, but even so, I thought it prudent to elevate the foot of the stretcher while we waited to be lifted off. A wee scruffy Frenchman by my side, who looked like the ship's Mate, fussed about, and kept uttering the words—' 'Ttention! 'Ttention!' I thought he was getting the crew to stand to attention as a mark of respect for the Royal Navy, but they just slouched around and let us get on with it. It was only when we got back home that I discovered that what he'd been actually asking me was the state of his captain's blood pressure! The French word being 'Tension'! The follow-up to that minor embarrassment was a compilation of useful medical terms in French, Spanish, Norwegian and German, which I prepared for use in future foreign encounters, and which was subsequently taken up by the Clyde Coastguard.

I went up first, followed by Jerry with the stretcher. Pitreavie confirmed Crosshouse as our destination, subject to our casualty's condition, and I spent the next hour and a half cramped on my knees checking his vital signs every fifteen minutes till we reached the hospital.

The arrival was a bit of a shambles. There was no ambulance to meet us, and the prospect of a long carry to the receiving room did not appeal to me. Luckily, the welcome assistance of four burly Firemen left me holding nothing heavier than the drip bottle—for a pleasant change—as we bustled past crowds of gawping visitors and into Casualty.

'Here's some blood for cross-matching! Do you speak French?' The young lady doctor looked quite bemused till I explained. M. Daubois looked equally bemused, but a lot better.

'Au revoir, monsieur! Bonne chance!' I called, exhibiting my linguistic talents to the full. He acknowledged with a smile and a weak wave of his bandaged hand. What a master of the French language! Moi, Jacques. Roll on next summer vacances. Vive la France! Vive la Dordogne!

Following surgery to repair his artery—and a severed nerve—M. Daubois went happily home to France three days later. It took us a year!

20

7 October 1989

Diving Tragedy

'Vive la France!' I had just penned that final paragraph, sitting in the sun lounge late on a wet, miserable Saturday afternoon, when the bleep went. Helen voiced a vain hope that it would be a false alarm, but I knew this time it would be for real, as my pager had recently been changed at my own request to a different frequency from those of the SAR crew, to try and reduce the unnecessary disturbance to which we had both been increasingly subjected over the years. I dialled Gannet.

'Ops Room here, Sir. Can you come in? We've been tasked to fly a diver with the bends from Oban to Aberdeen for emergency treatment.'

I arrived at the SAR locker room at the same time as my Killick MA, Rod Newman, who was already geared up—and obviously steamed-up about something as well. 'They don't want me! RCC says I'm not trained to cope with diving emergencies. They want a doctor. You've to hurry up and get dressed on the aircraft.'

Sounds like another communication problem, I thought to myself—RCC probably don't know what an MA is. Which was unfortunate, for Rod was probably one of the best qualified LMAs around. A veteran of the Falklands War, his modest claim to fame was that he had put up the first drip on Simon Weston, the badly burned Welsh Guardsman whose courageous fight against terrible disfigurement had been an inspiration to the nation when recently shown on TV. Armed with theatre, intensive care, and other qualifications on top of his standard training, Rod was also a volunteer crew member of Troon lifeboat. Still, there was no time to sympathise, as I rushed out to the warmed-up Sea King simultaneously trying to zip up a flying suit, don a helmet, button a lifejacket, and keep my toes curled-up to stop my unlaced boots from falling off as I ran.

I was hauled unceremoniously on board and we were airborne before I even had time to fasten my seat belt. It was a quarter to six, and the grey dusk was falling fast. The story unfolded as we headed towards Loch Fyne. A professional diver had suddenly taken ill on surfacing from 150 feet somewhere off

Skye, and had been flown immediately by the Stornoway Coastguard Sikorsky 61 to Dunstaffnage, near Oban, where he had been recompressed for several hours in the Marine Research Laboratory's decompression chamber. There had been no improvement. He was deteriorating fast, and RCC had been asked to arrange his transfer to the specialist chamber facilities in Aberdeen.

'That's a helluva distance… it will take us hours. What about Faslane?' I knew there was a chamber at the submarine base, but was not familiar with the degree of specialist care available there for cases of severe decompression sickness.

'Well, that's the good news, Doc!' Lt Vic Gover, the Observer, triumphantly announced. 'It'll be a shorter trip for you, for that's where we are taking him. We've told RCC that Faslane is only half an hour's flying time away, compared with one and a half hours to Aberdeen, and they've just agreed to let us go there.'

I was relieved, not only for the patient's sake, but for my own, as Helen and I were due to motor up to Lairg in Sutherland in the morning, on an autumn inspection visit to the Shin Hydro Scheme with my fellow members of the Secretary of State's Fisheries Committee. We'd both been looking forward to a long quiet weekend away from it all, 'sans enfants', and I mentally cringed at the thought of her reaction to a ten o'clock phonecall—'Darling, I'm stuck overnight in the Thistle Hotel, Aberdeen… see you tomorrow sometime.' End of a pleasant weekend!

Momentarily distracted and disgusted, as we flew north up Loch Fyne, by the giant, derelict, virgin oil platform excavation scarring the shoreline at Portavadie, complete with its dilapidated ghost village of rapidly deteriorating workers' houses—a gross multi-million pound waste of public money from the early speculative days of the oil boom—I sensed a sudden reshuffling of maps up front.

'Can I have the Aberdeen maps?' requested Mark Francey, our Captain. 'That's RCC on again with some doctor from Aberdeen who is insisting that the patient must be transferred to Aberdeen for recompression. I don't know what's going on, but it looks like a long night ahead!'

'How would we get there?' I asked. 'For we'll have to keep under five hundred feet if possible to prevent further decompression.'

'Either up the Great Glen, then round the Moray coast and down to Aberdeen… or through the Stirling Gap and up the East Coast,' replied Gover, 'but I think it will have to be the Great Glen. It'll take us about one and a half hours from Oban.'

By this time we were overflying Loch Melfort yacht marina and beginning our descent towards Connel Bridge and the Dunstaffnage Marine Research Station on Loch Etive. We landed in a field adjacent to the laboratories, and were met by the Auxiliary Coastguard who drove Vic Gover and myself quickly round to the chamber building. Here we were introduced to Dr Muir, an Oban GP experienced in diving medicine who, together with his colleagues Drs Gordon Murchison and Colin Wilson, was in charge of chamber operations. He gave a quick resume of their intensive resuscitative efforts in the chamber over the previous three hours, and shook his head gravely as he gestured towards the oxygen-masked, unconscious patient on the stretcher behind him.

'I don't think the poor chap'll get very far, I'm afraid,' he intoned. 'He's been almost pulseless, with an unrecordable BP since he arrived, and his breathing is beginning to fail.'

In my heart I concurred. Out of the chamber his chances were even slimmer, but our only hope was to try and get him alive to the specialist supersaturation chamber facility in Aberdeen. Loaded aboard the waiting ambulance and during the short two hundred yard journey to the helicopter, his breathing finally stopped. I shouted quickly for the ventilation equipment from the helicopter, but despite sustained attempts to resuscitate him with bag and mask, the ambulance defibrillator tracing registered asystole—and brought our efforts to a sad close.

It was a chastening experience for most of the crew, brought up short in no uncertain manner by a crisis they might easily have had to deal with on their own, if they had been foolhardy enough to shoot off on such a medivac without trained medical help on board.

It also made me acutely aware of the risks to which these professional clam divers expose themselves in search of their livelihood, diving deeper and deeper, up to—and even beyond—the limits of safety for compressed air diving. In the hostile, bitterly cold waters of the Inner Hebrides, at the end of a long hard day, it would only take a moment's miscalculation—an extra ten minutes onto the dive; an extra five metres depth to get at those big clams; or a shorter than usual decompression stop during the final ascent—to precipitate a catastrophic bends attack on surfacing. And being so remote from help, when realistic resuscitation efforts depend on recompression within a few minutes, their chances of survival would almost be non-existent.

Thus I mused, as we flew in darkness down the Firth of Clyde and south across Irvine Bay. 'Where are you taking us, Russ?' A querulous voice broke into my consciousness.

'I'm heading for Prestwick!' came a confident reply from the young Co-Pilot.

'No you're bloody well not! That's Butlin's Wonderwest World straight ahead.'

'Shit! So it is. I thought these were the lights of Barassie. Sorry chaps!'

The conspicuous runway lights of Prestwick Airport were slipping embarrassingly astern on his port quarter by the time he slung the helicopter over on a corrected course for home.

Only a moment's miscalculation!

*   *   *

A postscript to this tragedy was a proposal by diving medicine experts to set up a mobile decompression chamber, lorry-mounted, which could in future be called out to transport similar severe bends cases under recompression to the super-saturation chamber facilities at Aberdeen, rather than attempting such a futile exercise in a helicopter not able to accommodate a mobile 'pot'.

In consultation with the Institute of Naval Medicine at Gosport, I also drew up a reference protocol for transporting diving casualties by helicopter—for use by my Medics and the back-seat crew. RCC would no longer be able to claim they were untrained to care for bent divers.

21

27 January 1990

'It Never Rains But...'

January had been exceptionally mild—and very wet. One deep depression after another had swept middle England, battering the South Coast with severe gales. Scotland had missed the worst of the storms, but not the aftermath of torrential rains drawn in by the moist southerly airstreams.

Weather apart, it had been an equally rough two months for the Practice, coping with a big flu epidemic before Christmas; and after the New Year break, having to wrestle with the complexities and inanities of new administrative chores dreamt up by Whitehall bureaucrats purporting to know more about patient care than doctors. These were due to be imposed on GPs in the form of Kenneth Clarke's 'New Contract', on the first of April. What a sick joke!

The garden was waterlogged, and there seemed little prospect of a few hours' pruning and general tidying up during my weekend on call when the late Friday night Weatherview once again forecast heavy rain on the way. I resigned myself to spending a session on the word processor, cobbling together the final draft of our new compulsory 'Practice Leaflet', and drifted off to sleep counting Kenneth Clarkes jumping off cliffs, chased by angry doctors throwing copies of his 'New Contract' after him!

Somewhere in deepest Nod, my sleep was shattered by an insistent, incessant, unfamiliar noise …the burglar alarm? …the alarm clock? No! It was the bloody SAR bleep. It had been so long since the last time the damn thing had gone off during the night that I had forgotten how horribly intrusive it could be. I grabbed it and my watch simultaneously… Five o'clock.

Still in that disorientated, shaky, half-dazed state so familiar to anyone who has ever been subjected to the trauma of nocturnal rude awakenings, I called Gannet, and hung on for three interminable minutes while a rookie MOD policeman lost my connection to Ops Room and put me through instead to a bewildered Duty Wren in quarters, who was vaguely aware there was a SAR on, but hadn't a clue if I was needed. All this while, I was struggling into my winter-woolly bunny-suit and overalls, and when the bleep went a second time, I knew I was needed.

Hurriedly, I dialled Gannet again, and got another policeman—'Look, I can't wait... my bleep's gone twice... just tell Ops Room I'm on my way!'

As I got to the foot of the stairs, the phone rang in the kitchen. Tripping over assorted Cairn Terriers and kids roused by the commotion, I rushed to answer it. 'Ops Room, Doctor. We've been trying to contact you—there's a SAR on...'

'Don't I bloody know it! I've been trying to get you!' I cut in abruptly, explaining my problem getting through. 'What is it?'

'A woman on Mull in premature labour... for transfer to Glasgow. Could you hurry?'

Too damn right I could hurry. Driving through heavy rain, I was there in ten minutes, to be met at the locker room by MA McNamee.

'Grab me a lifejacket, Liam, while I get into this goon suit.' I could hear the Sea King revving up outside. Liam returned. 'What's the score?' I asked.

'A woman in premature labour, Sir. They want us up there quick. There's an odds-on chance she might deliver in the aircraft.'

'Oh, shit!' Here was a prospect I did not fancy one bit—delivering a baby in the back of a cold, dark, vibrating helicopter in the middle of the night. Only policemen performed those kinds of heroics—in the *Daily Record*—in the back of taxis! Heads down against the rain, we ran for the aircraft.

'Any more details on our patient?' I asked, grabbing my chance during a lull in the multi-channel exchanges between our Captain, Observer, Air Traffic Control and RCC Pitreavie, as we lurched up the Clyde, rocked by a turbulent downdraught from the Arran hills, miles away to our left.

'Nothing yet, Doc,' responded Mark Francey, our Pilot. 'We'll give it half an hour. What's our ETA, Jerry?'

'Oh-six-fifteen,' replied Jerry Scott from the Observer's seat, 'if we get there. The radar's playing us up at the moment. I've been unhappy about it since we left.'

It was a horrible pitch-black night, and we were flying in and out of heavy showers just under a stratus base of a thousand feet when the radar finally packed in at the entrance to Loch Fyne. There was no possibility of going on, and Lt Francey radioed an urgent request to have the back-up Sea King ready on stand-by, as we about-turned for Prestwick.

'Any need to take the Medic this time, Doc?' Francey asked me as we transferred our gear to the heavier stand-by aircraft which contained fully operational sonar gear—unlike the newly-designated SAR Sea King, which had been recently stripped of a thousand pounds of sonar equipment to increase its endurance capabilities.

'We might have weight problems... So if we could leave him behind, we'd manage another two hundred pounds of fuel, and maybe avoid a fifteen minute refuelling delay on our way back.'

'Look, if there is any chance of this lassie delivering in the back of this helicopter, I'll need my Medic!' I forcefully replied.

'Couldn't the back-seat crew give you a hand?' I could see by the petrified looks on the faces behind him that his suggestion was a non-starter!

'No, I'll need all the professional help I can get, and I'd rather have a well-stabilised patient and have to refuel, than a critically-ill one and half-full tanks.'

Well aware of how quickly a prem labour proceeds to delivery, I was dismayed to realise we did not even have a maternity pack on board, with suction, cord clamps, pads etc. We'd have to make do with whatever we could dredge up—and I had visions of using bootlaces to tie the cord! There was a mixed sense of relief, therefore, when ten minutes into the flight we received a signal that the poor lass had delivered on the island, but—panic! panic!—the only hope for the baby's survival was an incubator… Did we have one on board?

An incubator on board? When we didn't even have a proper maternity pack! Not only did we not have an incubator on board, but the last one I had seen in operation was, by a weird coincidence, being used by a paediatric specialist on the Lossie 'Crab' during a medevac from Orkney to Aberdeen, filmed recently as part of an ITV series called 'Rescue'. I ruefully recalled my relieved remark to Helen at the time that at least I'd never had to deal with that sort of problem, thank goodness—and here I was, only two weeks later, right up to my neck in it. That incubator had looked about as complicated to fly as the bloody helicopter!

'Could you arrange for us to pick up an incubator at Vale of Leven?' I heard Mark Francey ask RCC. Affirmative.

As we altered course for the Tail o' the Bank and Dumbarton, my mind was preoccupied with thoughts on oxygen requirements for babies, suction equipment, and how we might secure the incubator against turbulence. We were only two minutes flying time from the Vale when the signal we were dreading came through—'No longer required… patient not travelling… Category Four… return to base.'

The crew was crestfallen, and very subdued on our arrival back at Prestwick, really sick at the thought that our mechanical problems might have contributed to the baby's death.

Two tragic deaths—first the diver, and now a baby—involving the same crew, would do nothing for their morale. To head off any self-recriminations, I telephoned the island GP, who confirmed my own assessment that, sadly, the tiny infant had probably been too premature to have survived anyway. I let the boys know.

*   *   *

But yet, the aftermath of this sad incident, like the diving tragedy, had its positive side. I immediately contacted Ayrshire and Arran Health Board and their neonatal paediatricians to explore the possibility of an incubator being made available locally for a trial on the SAR Sea King. This trial was successful and a protocol was quickly established for the Ayrshire Central Hospital incubator—plus a neonatal specialist team—to be picked up and flown out as and when required. Gratifyingly, within a couple of years it had been used four times.

And in addition, a maternity pack now sits permanently in the SAR Ready Room—just in case!

22

9 November 1990

Manx Tale

'I'll only be a few more minutes, darling! I'll just sign another fifty copies then call it a day.' It was supper-time, and my tea was getting cold. Tomorrow would be a busy day at the Hospice Winter Craft Fair. I had just been down at the Dam Park Hall till nine o'clock, setting up a sales display for *The Dipper an the Three Wee Deils*—a collection of Scots poems and short stories of which I was co-author, the profits from which were destined for Ayrshire Hospice Funds.

'Oh, no, not again!' I could feel a bitter anguish and deep resentment in Helen's voice as a bleeping sound, vainly trying to blend with the stirring of our tea-spoons, shattered the fragile peace of one of the few free evenings we'd had together in recent weeks—although, in fairness, it was herself who had been out gallivanting a lot more than me! I telephoned Gannet.

'Is that you, Boss?' It was Rod Newman, freshly promoted to POMA. 'Are you playing tonight? It's a fishing boat… guy got a nasty leg fracture and is in shock. Can you come in?'

I looked at my watch—just after ten o'clock—would be at least a couple of hours minimum, even if the fishing boat was close at hand. Last night I had been doing a SAR talk to Ardrossan and Saltcoats Rotary Club, and fortunately my Goon Suit was handy in the car boot; so when I reached the SAR Locker Room, I was all kitted up and ready to fly, except for my boots, which I hurriedly pulled on as Rod fetched me a lifejacket.

'I'll brief you as we go out to the aircraft, Boss… The boat's in the Irish Sea, south of the Isle of Man, and the bloke's got a nasty left Tib and Fib and is in a lot of pain. I spoke to the Skipper and asked if he had any morphine… said he had, but didn't know how to use it—or didn't want to! I offered to talk him through it, but he chickened out. Bloody pointless carrying the stuff if you can't use it.'

A flashing torch from the cockpit impatiently beckoned us on board. I peered at my watch as the crew went through their pre-flight checks—ten-thirty—it would be a long night.

'What a grotty, shitty night!' The Scots voice belonged to Alan Findlay, a tall, quiet, young Pilot from Perthshire, whose wife Lesley I had guided through her first pregnancy only a few months previously. 'Well, we've got you up at last, Doc! Were you at a dinner party again tonight?' he continued slyly, getting his wee dig in, reference my moaning to him just a few weeks back that I had not had any callouts since January, due to the new rapid response time. Typically, the very next night I had been dragged away from a dinner party before the starter course, to medevac a head injury from Skye. The ladies had all been mightily impressed by my winter woolly 'bunny-suit' underwear—except Helen of course—but the trip was cancelled just before take-off, and I had managed back just in time for my dessert—or, in the steely eyes of one lady—in time for my just desserts!

This time we were off—into a miserable black night of low stratus cloud, turbulence, and November haze—which forced us to fly low and parallel to the coastline, as far as Loch Ryan. Flying over Stranraer at 800 feet, we kept hitting patches of low cloud, and could only just make out the street-light pattern of the little town below.

Gus Stretton, the Observer, led us over RAF West Freuch on a heading which took us down Luce Bay, past radar images of the remote and unseen Scar Rocks; a wild isolated seabird colony, whose mysterious, romantic, distant, jagged outlines had for years fascinated me as a wee lad on caravan holidays at Port William. Despite frequent trips out with the local lobster fishermen, they had always remained tantalisingly far out of reach. The closest view I ever got of 'The Scaurs' had been through the powerful binoculars of the local Royal Observer Corps when, as twelve-year-olds, we were allowed to join them plane-spotting during their exercises. A middle-of-the-night mercy flight, thirty-five years later, in a Royal Navy helicopter, past these two radar silhouettes, was something I could never have envisaged in my wildest boyhood dreams.

Once over the Irish Sea beyond Burrow Head, the turbulence settled and we flew on smoothly and uneventfully past the north tip of the Isle of Man and down its east coast past Ramsey and Douglas.

'Where exactly are we going?' I ventured.

'Somewhere off the south end of Man, between there and the Lancashire coast,' said Gus. 'I've spoken to the Captain through RCC and he's steaming north east at ten knots and is getting close to the gas rigs off Morecambe Bay.'

'It would be a good idea to lift the casualty off near the rigs,' suggested Al Findlay, 'it would give us good illumination.'

'And then where do we take him?'

'Blackpool.'

'Never ever been to Blackpool… should be plenty of Illuminations there as well!'

'Neither have I. I've always wanted to see what the fuss was about, ever since all the lads at school went on bus trips to see the 'Luminations', except me. I was deprived.'

'Aw, poor soul! We'll see what we can do for you then, Doc.'

Back to business. 'What's our plan of action, then?' Gus Stretton asked the Pilot.

'Well, I think Rod better go down first, and assess the state of the casualty —or do you want to go down first, Doc?'

'I don't mind,' I replied, 'but the PO is better acquainted with the winching procedures and the portable radio than I am, so it would probably be better if he did go down first.'

'OK by me,' said Rod, 'I'll assess him and call the Doc down if I need him—then get Lt Stretton down with the stretcher.'

'I don't want too many winchings—we've already had two hours flying, and I don't want to spend too much time in the hover... How much fuel have we left, Gus?'

'Seventeen hundred pounds, enough for another hour and a half. We'll have to refuel somewhere before the return trip... maybe Manchester or Liverpool... or maybe even from one of these rigs. Hold on! I've got her on radar. Three miles off the outermost rig. Head two-two-five!'

I had just moved for'ard to get myself out of the way of the winching preparations and help the aircraft's trim in the hover, when it turned to starboard and banked, and three huge gas production platforms, lit up like giant candelabras, were suddenly framed in the window by my head.

'I have her visual, Gus. She's a big trawler, about thirty metres. She's still got her trawl booms out—probably to stabilise her... but they'll make good references when we go into the hover.'

LACMN Jim Scott, the Winchman, was at the open rear door, giving precise crisp instructions to the Pilot to manoeuvre the helicopter over the ship's stern, while Rod sat, legs dangling, ready to go. 'Six yards forward... two yards right... Steady! Now winching... thirty, twenty-five, twenty feet to go... three yards forward... one yard right... Steady! Steady! Fifteen, ten feet, five... He's on the deck and clear of the strop.'

The vessel was *The Grove*, of Dublin, and we stood off to port while the POMA disappeared below decks to assess the injured man. Plugged into an intercom which unfortunately could not pick up external transmissions, I was blissfully unaware of what was going on, when suddenly Jim Scott motioned me aft, brandished the strop, and beckoned me to the open door.

Down below me, five crewmen gazed up from the stern deck of the trawler as I swung in mid-air, spinning round and round as I was jerkily lowered towards them, before landing less than elegantly on my backside, but quite happy to be on the right side of the gunwales.

The injured fisherman, a burly lad in his thirties, had been carried by four of his mates out of the cold and into a narrow passageway amidships, where he lay wrapped in quilts, with Rod kneeling beside him. His foot was twisted outwards at an ugly angle, and would obviously have to be straightened and carefully splinted before evacuation. The slightest movement produced excruciating pain.

'Rod! Start him on the Entonox while I draw up some morphine.' The Entonox or 'laughing gas'—that Nitrous Oxide and Oxygen mixture blessed by millions of mums in labour—worked a treat. A few minutes of deep breathing, combined with some I/V morphine, and he was as happy as Larry.

Rod produced a vacuum splint from the grab bag, and after carefully slipping it underneath his legs, I began using the vacuum pump to extract the air and make it rigid. Suddenly the handle came off in my hand. 'Shit! So much for the wonders of bloody modern technology. Have you any triangular bandages?'

Rummaging again in the grab bag, Rod produced an assortment of crumpled bandages; and while we exhorted Bernie our sailor to breathe deeply and think happy thoughts, I managed to lash his legs firmly together.

The next problem was how to manhandle him along the passage and through the narrow doorway on to the stretcher which Gus Stretton had just brought on board. Boy Scout first-aid training again came to the rescue with an old-fashioned blanket lift, by which means his crewmates helped us lug him safely out to the stretcher and along to the after-deck.

'Could you go up first, Doc,' requested Gus, 'then I'll send up the casualty.'

'Oh, Boss, could you manage to take up the grab bag with you?' Rod half-suggested—I thought, in a rather strange, insistent manner.

'Och. You'll manage it fine yourself. There's still some of the gear for you to gather up inside, and we don't want to waste time. I'll get up quickly while you collect the kit.'

Winched aboard, Bernie lay settled and smilingly euphoric, responding with happy nods to our sign language countdown of the fifteen minutes till our arrival at Blackpool Airport. After the engines were shut down on landing, and the rotors finally swung to a halt, he looked up, thanked us, and enquired with a soft Dublin voice—'Hiv ye got te fush?'

Surprised, I jokingly remarked that a Sea King smelt bad enough normally, without the pong of fish to add to it—but thanks for the thought anyway!

As he departed in the waiting ambulance, Rod turned to me, shrugged and grimaced—'Why do you think I wanted you to take up the grab bag, Boss? I needed my hands free—I had it all arranged!'

23

10 March 1991

Fort William

My poor legs were stiff and aching from the much-needed exercise of a half-day walk in the New Cumnock Hills, as I clambered up the lecture room steps a few hours later and sat down behind Craig, in anticipation of what turned out to be an excellent postgraduate lecture on burns. Leaning over, I tapped him on the shoulder. 'I'll take the bleep back now… Thanks for covering me for the afternoon.'

It was out of his hands like the proverbial hot brick, as he complained that it had just gone off ten minutes ago, and when he had phoned Gannet he was told that there was nothing doing.

'That's happened to me twice in the last couple of days. A funny continuous bleep, not like the usual… I've put in a new battery, so it can't be that—it must be a fault.'

The following morning at Gannet, I had no sooner handed it to Jamie, my Killick MA, when the bloody thing went off again, and was duly declared duff by the Ops Room PO. I signed for an authorised replacement from the BT Shop in Ayr the following Saturday morning.

For me and electronic comms equipment, it had not been a good week! On my night on call, the fifth Vodaphone tried out by the Practice in as many weeks had proved just as unreliable as the previous four; and I had also taken a momentous decision to allow a hole to be bored in the wing of my brand new Vauxhall Cavalier, to transfer and re-install, for the seventh time, a crackly, fourteen year-old Pye Westminster ambulance radio, which the engineer informed me was now a museum piece for which no spare parts were available.

Museum piece or not, I was grateful for its availability the following day as, dressed for the garden, I drove Fiona and some of her friends back from a curling session at Ayr Ice Rink. Halfway home, my new bleep sounded, authoritatively and clearly—no fault this time!

'Medic Eleven to Ayr Am Control… Medic Eleven to Ayr Am Control…'

'Ayr Am Control to Medic Eleven… come in please.'

'My SAR Bleep has just gone off. Could you telephone Ops Room at HMS Gannet and find out if they need me?'

As we approached the Fire Station roundabout, the reply came back— 'Medic Eleven. They say they've got a job on and you have to come in.'

It was 12.15 on Mother's Day. Helen would be mega-chuffed! Offloading Alastair and Louisa at the end of their road, I sped home with Fiona, and apologised. It would have been a lovely day for pruning roses! Pulling on my flying overalls over my gardening clothes, I kissed Helen and left.

Jamie McCracken met me at the SAR Cabin.

'I'm not going, Doc. It's a bad head injury at the Belford Hospital, Fort William, for transfer to the Southern General Neurosurgical Unit, and RCC have requested a doctor. I've checked the Red Bag. It's fully stocked up.' We had, at long last, got rid of the useless, antiquated Ship's Doctor's White Box, and replaced it with a properly equipped, custom-built, user-friendly Paramedic's rucsac.

The Sea King was fired up and running when I signalled my intention to come aboard. 'Typical shitty weather!' was the exasperated comment as we flew up the coast under low stratus and through fog banks. It had been an exceptionally mild week, and a warm, moist southerly airstream, cooling as it hit the northern seas, had produced extensive fog right up the east coast for several days. Now it was our turn.

'It might improve as we go further west, but I doubt it,' said Sid Vallance, the Observer. 'The wind will have to pick up a bit first. Is that a flask of coffee within your reach, Gerry… and the biscuits?'

'Is that all you think I've got to do… what do you think I'm here for?' bemoaned Gerry Flannery, the Aircrewman, putting down the chart he had been studying.

'Chief Steward!' I cut in, and a voice from the front remarked it was high time these Sea Kings were fitted with a 'Call Steward' button!

'Thanks, Doc. You're definitely off my Christmas list now. OK Girls, any-one for coffee?' retorted Gerry, as he ambled for'ard clutching the flask and some packets of NAAFI biscuits.

Arran, thrusting her peaks tantalisingly through veils of mist like some exotic limbo-dancer, was left far behind as we approached Ardrishaig and followed the Crinan Canal across to the Sound of Lorne. Visibility im-proved as we traversed the flat isthmus, and I was thrilled as we flew over the rocky outcrop of Dunadd, with the wee whitewashed cottage nestling at its foot.

'If you look down there at 9 o'clock, lads, you'll see Dunadd, where the ancient Kings of Dalriada were crowned after the Scots invaded Kintyre from Ireland in the 5th Century AD. There's a footprint carved in the rock at the top, where the King had to place his foot during the ceremony, or so they say.'

The crew were all English, puir sods, but a wee bit o' auld Scots history widnae gae wrang!

'And see these stone circles… they are Neolithic or Stone Age burial cairns.' It was fascinating to get an aerial view of the spectacular chambered cairns of Kilmartin just a few miles to the north—this whole magical area is steeped in history and prehistory, and endowed with hundreds of very important archeological sites.

The weather closed in again as we overflew the flooded slate quarries of Easdale, skirted Lismore, and hugged the coastline of Appin, past Castle Stalker. We were not wearing our immersion suits, or goon bags, because it was essentially an overland job, and we would never be more than a mile or so from shore. Even so, that water would be bloody cold, I thought, if we landed in it!

The cross-chat was lighthearted as we flew at 400 feet and cut the corner south of the entrance to Loch Leven, heading for Loch Linnhe. Looking down to my left, I was surprised and puzzled to see the Ballachulish Bridge.

'There's Ballachulish Bridge down there—to the left—shouldn't we be on the other side of it?'

'Oh, so it is! Sorry, chaps. Took my eye off the ball for a minute. Should have changed the heading slightly,' came a wee contrite voice from the back.

The steep rocky slopes of the Mamore Range, decapitated by low cloud, menacingly loomed into view directly ahead to the north, a formidable cul-de-sac which emphatically barred any further progress, as Reg Parker our Pilot did a smart right 360 degree loop to take us back out of Loch Leven and into the left hand fork of Loch Linnhe, where we should have been! As he did so, we had a good look up Glencoe, and it was obvious from the grey mists in the valley and low down over the tops that it would be impossible to take our patient by the short route over Rannoch Moor to Crianlarich, and down Loch Lomond to Glasgow. We would have to take the long road round the coast—back the way we had come.

Landing on at Fort William was not without incident either. The landing site was a concrete pad on a piece of waste ground to the north west of the town. Strapped in for landing, we bumped to a standstill to the accompaniment of a volley of expletives over the intercom—'Holy Shite! There's an effing great sheet of polythene been sucked up into the rotors! We'll have to shut down and check it hasn't been pulled through the bloody turbines!'

We all dismounted, and while Gerry Flannery and I went to the road-end to meet the ambulance, Reg and Dave Lambourne clambered over the aircraft to check for any damage. On visual inspection there seemed to be none.

The ambulance arrived, bearing Callum, a plethoric middle-aged man from Moidart, who had sustained a fracture of the base of his skull from that all too familiar Friday night party turn—a somersault down stone stairs. The bleeding from his left ear had stopped, but his conscious level had apparently deteriorated over the past twenty-four hours and it had been thought advisable to have him transferred to specialist care in the Neurosurgical Unit of the Southern General.

He was conscious and communicative at a superficial level in the ambulance, but his family said he had not known who they were that morning—a big change from the night before. With reassuring words that he was safe in our hands, we loaded him on board and strapped in. The engines were fired up and seemed to be running smoothly.

'I don't know if some of that friggin stuff has been sucked into the engines,' said the Captain. 'I'm a bit concerned, for there was some wire attached to it... Prepare for a running landing if the engines are not pulling on take off,' he added ominously.

Is that a euphemism for a crash, I thought to myself, as the rotors picked up speed and the aircraft shuddered with the strain of take-off.

'Engines pulling satisfactorily... lift off at 80% torque.' We relaxed.

For the first three-quarters of an hour as we retraced our path down the coast, Callum was restful—at least as restful as someone can be in the bowels of a noisy helicopter. With his head injury, and the way he was lying, it would have been difficult to fit proper ear muffs, so we bandaged over his bleeding ear, and further protected his hearing with an extra pillow partly covering his head and the dressing. This seemed to work for a while, but as time progressed he grew more agitated, tried to sit up several times, and had to be gently restrained. On top of the inevitable severe headache from his fractured skull, the hundred decibels of noise and juddering vibration from the helicopter must have been well-nigh unbearable.

Fortunately, the cloud ceiling had lifted slightly by the time we reached Ardrishaig, and we were able to cut across the hills from Otter Ferry on Loch Fyne to the head of Loch Striven, and then down Holy Loch and over Ardnadam Pier.

Ardnadam Pier—where my grandfather had been the Piermaster for Glasgow and South Western Steamers before the First World War—which had for the past thirty years been the supply jetty for the US Polaris Submarine Base—and which was now about to slip back into sleepy anonymity as the Americans packed up their Buicks and bombs and headed for home; responding positively to a fast-changing political climate, thankfully much less conducive to a Third World War than when they arrived.

As we flew low up the Clyde past Dumbarton Rock I was busy checking Callum's pulse, and had to grab the stretcher suddenly to prevent myself pitching forward on top of him, as the aircraft unexpectedly swerved to the left and back again.

'Sorry chaps! Shitehawks on the starboard bow. Tide's out and there's a helluva lot of them about. Don't want the engines stuffed with feathers as well as polythene!'

I glanced out the starboard door window at the large expanse of mudflats to the south side of the ship channel, and watched the frantic efforts of a large flock of assorted gulls and wading birds taking their own evasive action as we roared overhead.

The voice of Glasgow Air Traffic Control broke through, clearing our approach to the Southern General, and asking if we would be flying over or under the Erskine Bridge.

'Let's go under, chaps, but look out for shitehawks!'

Sitting in the back, it was a bit of an anticlimax only being able to see the south-bank bridge pillars, and a reflection of the bridge in the water as we ducked underneath, before ascending rapidly to clear the towering high voltage pylons a few hundred yards upriver.

The Southern General lies on the south bank of the Clyde, just upstream of the giant Shieldhall Sewage Works, but fortunately seldom downwind! We circled twice and dropped down on to the landing site, a grassy area beside the grey sandstone of the old hospital buildings, with the modern concrete Neurosurgical Unit only a short distance away.

Callum seemed awfully keen to get out of the open door before we had even landed, and I had to restrain him, half out of his stretcher, as Gerry Flannery, with his back to us and totally oblivious, talked the Pilot down to a safe landing.

His keenness to move on seemed to have impressed the neurosurgeons, as his stay in the Unit was short and uncomplicated, and he was transferred back to Fort William three days later—quietly by road this time—for rehabilitation.

The usual crowd of spectators, nurses, folk in white coats, firemen and assorted Glaswegians, watched as we transferred him to the ambulance and then retired to the privacy of the aircraft to await the return of our stretcher. Some stood around, some kicked the inevitable fitba, and three wee gallus lads tried to see how close they could get to the helicopter without being 'huntit by the Polis'. They circled round the aircraft, slyly reducing their radius as they did so, till I drew Reg's attention.

'Better watch these wee buggers! They'll have your wheels and a couple of rotor blades nicked before you know it, if somebody doesn't get them to hell out of there!' Obligingly, a couple of big Firemen did the needful.

Mission accomplished, we took off, only to land again at Glasgow Airport to refuel. As we waited, a police van drew up and two uniformed officers got out—one brandishing a submachine gun, and the other a camera—and slowly approached the aircraft. 'Airport security must be tight… what the Hell are they up to?'

Suddenly, the man with the machine gun swung round with his back to us, and his mate shot him—with the camera! They then swopped places, while we provided an amused backdrop, sitting at the Sea King door. 'Must think the bloody Iraq War is still on—the pair of posers!' We waved as they jumped back into their van and drove off. 'What did you do in the war, Daddy?'

'Where's the bloody fuel, then?' came an aggrieved voice from up front.

'No problem. It's coming. Gerry's got it under control,' retorted Sid Vallance.

'Aye, he's pissing in the fuel tanks!' I quipped.

Sid laughed, as did the others. 'That's nearer the truth than you think, Doc,' said Reg Parker. 'Did you hear what happened last Saturday?'

'No, tell me.'

'Well, we were over on the east coast on a Navex, and had stopped off at Edinburgh Airport to refuel. With the fuel onboard, Gerry was doing the out-side checks as number two engine was fired, when he noticed steaming hot fluid coming out the side of the aircraft, and, thinking we had a leak, put his fingers to it and sniffed it. Then it stopped. What he didn't know was that Sid had been off-loading his bladder down the comfort tube!' He paused. 'We didn't tell him till he was eating his sandwiches!'

24

13 March 1991

West of Sligo—1

'The problem with Glasgow University…' I grumped to myself as I trudged downstairs laden with two-and-half stones of Colin's medical textbooks, 'is that it's too far away for His Nibs to travel every day, but not half far enough away to stop him from carting up tons of home comforts and sundry junk every other weekend… only for us to have to humph it all back down by the car-load at the end of each term!'

Another precious half-day had been commandeered—to rush up to Glasgow with Helen for the sole purpose of lugging a month's dirty laundry, assorted Anatomy books, radio, TV, stinking grey-white lab coats, and a skeleton, down three flights of stairs from his digs and into the waiting car.

It had to be a quick trip, for we were due back in Ayr by five o'clock for tea, and to get Fiona and friends delivered to the Gaiety Theatre where they were appearing in a highly successful school production of *Oliver*. I was meant to be doing the double taxi run—seven o'clock uplift, with a home run at ten.

While Helen was preparing tea, I slipped down to the surgery about quarter-to-six, to pick up the bleep from Scott who had been covering my absence for the afternoon. At twenty past six, the phone rang.

'It's David Duthie here, Doc.' I recognised the soft Aberdeen voice of the SAR Flight Commander.

'Hello, Dave. What can I do for you?'

'I think we may have a job for you, but thought I'd get your advice first. It's a hundred and fifty miles out in the Atlantic… a Bulk Carrier with a man on board who's vomiting up blood. Do you think this is one the MA can handle, or is it a job for you?'

'Sounds like one for me, Dave.' I felt it would be unfair to land my MA with an acute medical emergency like that.

'You'll be going yourself, Doc—without the Medic, because of the weight factor. There's no hurry to come in… just make your way over.'

Helen was aghast. Two SARs in four days!

'It's a man with a haematemesis, a hundred and fifty miles out in the

Atlantic.' I explained to her. 'We'll probably have to refuel at Machrihanish—like that French fishing boat job—but not as far—that was over a hundred and ninety miles. So we should be home just after midnight.'

At Gannet, the truth was somewhat different. Certainly the ship was 150 miles out, but 150 miles *off the West coast of Ireland*—not Prestwick! My jaw dropped as I absorbed snippets from the plans being discussed all around me in the SAR Cabin—charts and rulers waving, telephones ringing, sandwiches and coffee being prepared.

'It'll be a long night, Doc,' I was informed. 'Probably nearer a three o'clock return than midnight!'

Ian Lindsay, my POMA, arrived down with the drugs pack and key, and a relieved grin, bordering on a smirk, on his face, when he heard where he was not going! I asked him to telephone Helen and keep her posted of our whereabouts, as I knew she would be anxious if I didn't return by midnight.

Reg Parker and Sid Vallance were flying with me again tonight, with Lt Graham Whiles as Co-Pilot and POACMN Paul Lofthouse.

When we took off at 1900 hours, it was already pitch dark, and any chance of twilight visibility was scuppered by low stratus cloud and a thick mist coming in from the sea. It was the same shitty weather we'd had on Sunday, plus the added hazard of flying at night. By the time we were across Ayr Bay, we had already lost sight of the friendly glow of coastal lights, and quickly had to drop down from 400 to 100 feet, in an attempt to get below the cloud ceiling. Any lower and we would have been rowing!

Reg Parker switched on the landing lights, the beams of which simply bounced back at us off the sea fog. Having often driven in bad fog, navigating by the white lines on the road, I had to admire the skill and concentration of the crew as they kept the helicopter on an even keel at one hundred feet in zero visibility. Standing behind the Pilots as a third pair of eyes, I kept one anxious eye on the altimeter, and the other on the artificial horizon!

Well past Pladda and the south tip of Arran, we were still in thick fog; and frantic efforts were being made by Sid Vallance in the Observer's seat to get us an updated forecast from Clyde Coastguard on the weather out to the west, for it would have been foolhardy and near impossible to fly much longer in these conditions.

There was none of the usual relaxed banter and wise-cracking of other SARs—it was total concentration—on instruments, on radar, on radio and on the visibility out front.

Suddenly I thought I saw a pinpoint of light dead ahead, but it disappeared—only to reappear a few seconds later, and it had gone again by the time I drew the lads' attention to it. Finally, to my relief, for I thought I had been imagining things, Graham and Reg got a fix on it too.

'Must be Sanda Lighthouse.'

We flew on past Sanda, and into another bank of fog. Then another pin-point of light appeared at one o'clock, followed by a second at eleven o'clock. Sid, poring over his radar screen, confirmed the first as Mull of Kintyre Light, and the other as Rathlin Island.

As we drew closer, the intensity of the Mull light increased till its search-light beam swept a slow circle through the smoky darkness. It was reassuring now to be able to see both lights at a distance of ten miles, although we still had to fly at a hundred feet to keep below the cloud base.

Rathlin Light loomed closer. It was the north light, and we could also just faintly see the south light peeking above the menacing low black bulk of the island itself, as we approached.

'Best steer well clear and not overfly. Remember, this is a security zone!' instructed Sid from the rear. Reg banked the aircraft to starboard, and we slid past within a few hundred yards of the sheer cliffs, from whose top the north light's reflection glinted and bounced off a calm sea.

'I'm having a job trying to raise Scottish ATC and RCC now,' said Sid, 'before we cross over into Irish Control. Reception is poor.'

Almost on cue, a clear voice came over the radio.

'Rescue One Seven Seven. This is UK Seven Zero Six. Do you read me?'

'UK Seven Zero Six. This is Rescue One Seven Seven. You are loud and clear.'

'Rescue One Seven Seven... UK Seven Zero Six. I have contact with Scot-tish Control. Do you wish me to relay a message?'

Our request for an updated weather forecast was duly relayed and answered by the passenger jet crew, and Sid was subsequently able to pass on our present position, and ETA at Sligo Airport in the Irish Republic, where we intended to refuel. He gratefully thanked our unseen benefactor high overhead who ac-knowledged—'Rescue One Seven Seven. This is UK Seven Zero Six. Glad to have been of assistance. Good luck!'

By this time, the cloud base had risen to around a thousand feet and glowed with the reflected lights of distant Londonderry to the south, as we passed by the entrance to Lough Foyle and skirted Malin Head. Twinkling orange lights pinpointed scattered communities along the Donegal coastline, as the crew discussed the option of a beach landing in case of emergency. It was an essen-tial part of flying training always to have an escape route planned in anticipa-tion of weather problems or an aircraft malfunction on a SAR, and never to hazard the aircraft and crew if there was no way out available. This especially applied to mountain flying, but having previously had the dubious pleasure of three scary trips in and around this troubled land, I felt obliged to point out that this was Donegal, not Northern Ireland, and that there were no safe beaches, anywhere!

'Doc, we've just had an update on the casualty from a Nimrod who's overhead coordinating the rescue. It's an Indian ship, and he is an Indian crew member. He started with a nose bleed yesterday, and today he's been vomiting up fresh blood. His pulse is 94 per minute, and he has stopped being sick.'

'That sounds satisfactory. He seems stable at the moment, for his pulse rate hasn't altered since we set off. I hope to Hell we're not being dragged all this way just to treat somebody who's had a nose bleed and is now puking up some of the blood he's swallowed.' Twenty two years as a GP had imbued me with a certain measure of healthy scepticism as far as so-called 'emergency' call-outs were concerned

'Doc, have you any painkillers?' It was Sid. 'I've had a thumping headache since we took off, and don't feel too hot… my daughter has had a bug over the past few days and I hope I'm not coming down with it!'

'Sorry. Sid. I've nothing milder than morphine! Are you feeling sick or fevered?'

'No. I'm OK that way at present. I should be alright. Just a bit tired.'

We flew on, and half an hour later made contact with Sligo Airport. No one knew what to expect. Would it be like one of those remote Hebridean airstrips where they had to chase the sheep off the runway before you could land? The lights of Sligo had appeared sixteen miles to the east. It looked a sizeable town—but where was the Airport?

Reg Parker asked for a directional heading, and an obliging Irish voice replied, 'Rescue One Seven Seven. This is Sligo Airport. I will switch on the sequential lights to guide you in.'

'Sequential lights'? Our querulous expressions were answered in a few seconds when, like a burst of tracer bullets, a line of strobe lights flashed brilliantly in sequence along the length of the runway fifteen miles away.

'Sligo Airport. This is Rescue One Seven Seven. We have you visual. Your lights are brilliant!' The lads were most impressed, and enthused about what we were later told were the only such set of lights in the British Isles—just recently installed to help approaches like ours from the sea.

We landed on at 2100 hours and refuelled, while a group of curious onlookers observed us from the Airport lounge bar window.

By 2130 we were on our way, straight out into the vastness of the Atlantic Ocean, on a heading of 310 degrees, next stop Newfoundland! It was an inky-black, starless night, and the reassuring lights of Sligo were soon left far behind. Standing behind the Pilots, I felt just a wee shade apprehensive. There was no turning back.

This must be how tiny birds like warblers and robins feel, I thought, as they launch themselves from southern Norway on a starlit night, on their autumn migration across the North Sea, knowing they've four hundred miles to fly before they reach land. And they navigate solely by the stars, and have to rely only on their wing power.

At least we had a radar, a Nimrod overhead, and two powerful jet turbines —though it would be a lot easier for wee birds than for us to land on that pair of trawlers far below, if they got into trouble! A voice from the Nimrod broke reassuringly into my thoughts.

'Rescue One Seven Seven. This is Rescue Eleven. Could you alter your heading to three one six degrees… you are now on course for the ship… dead ahead… sixty miles to run.'

'Thank you Rescue Eleven. We have only a couple of radar contacts, probably fishing boats.' Sid replied.

The Nimrod informed us that there were six fishing boats, in pairs, at eight, eleven and fifteen miles, at 280, 350 and 70 degrees.

'They've got a lot more powerful eyes up there than we have.' There was admiration in Reg Parker's voice. 'Nice to know they're around!'

We throbbed on through the darkness, straining ahead for the first glimpse of the ship's lights. Suddenly, through a gap in the cloud, thrust first the head and shoulders, then the sword belt and sword of Orion. Other stars appeared.

'That's great! We won't need Sid and his radar now… we can navigate properly by the stars!'

'Where's the Pole Star?' asked Graham Whiles.

'Up there,' gestured Reg. 'And there's Taurus, and the Pleiades coming into view… and Jupiter should be visible tonight. Yeah! There it is!'

'Are you heavily into the stars or something?' muttered the jealous voice of a redundant Sid from the back. Then almost immediately he redeemed himself by picking up the first radar contact with the *A P J Anand*, forty miles ahead.

A few minutes later a pinpoint of light appeared, which drew closer with agonising slowness. We should have no problem with winching on to a 450 ft. long bulk carrier—a lot easier than a trawler—they usually had a clear deck the size of a football field. We could probably land the bloody Sea King on her hatch covers! And the wind was only 15 knots, with an eight to ten foot swell.

Confidently we approached, to discover to our horror that the *A P J Anand*, of Calcutta, was not a modern clear-deck bulk carrier, but had four main holds served by two large gantries, from which thick crane hawser-wires angled down at 45 degrees to huge derricks straddling the decks. There was hardly room to swing a cat, far less a Winchman, and even the fo'c'sle was surmounted by a mast and large whip aerial!

To complicate matters further, the wind was from the SW and, as far as we could make out in the darkness, there was a substantial ten to twelve foot swell from the NW, a relic of strong winds the previous day. The ship was steaming south of east, beam on to the wind and rolling heavily in spite of its size in the following swell, with the gantries swaying alarmingly in a wide arc as we circled several times, attempting different approaches.

'It's no bloody use! We'll have to ask him to turn round a hundred and eighty degrees to see if that will help stop the roll.'

'Alpha Tango Sierra November. This is Rescue Helicopter. Do you read me?'

A heavily accented Indian voice affirmed.

'We cannot approach your ship on its present heading because it is rolling badly. Could you please turn your ship round one eight zero degrees and proceed at five knots. Do you understand?'

'Rescue Helicopter. This is Alpha Tango Sierra November. I understand.'

We stood off as the big ship slowly turned in a wide circle.

'I have now changed course to one eight zero degrees at five knots.'

'Oh, shite! He's got it wrong!'

'Alpha Tango Sierra November. This is Rescue Helicopter. I do not wish you to steer one eight zero degrees. I wanted you to turn round one eight zero degrees!'

'Please. I do not understand. You vish me to steer one eight zero degrees. Yes?'

'No! Repeat No! I wanted you to turn round and steer in the opposite direction... two nine zero degree heading at five knots.'

'Ah, yes. Now I understand. A heading of two nine zero degrees at five knots.'

This pantomime had already taken twenty minutes of our limited endurance time, and more time was lost when we found that the ship rolled just as badly on its new heading—the more so when he slowed and stopped dead in the water, at our request.

'Alpha Tango Sierra November. This is Rescue Helicopter. I am sorry your present heading is no use. I am unable to approach the 'H' landing area on your port side. Could you please alter your heading again to zero four five degrees, and proceed at five knots downwind.'

This was probably our best chance. Reg edged the Sea King into position, foot by foot, and twice made an attempt at low level to drop Lofty on board.

There was a sudden flash from the bridge of the ship.

'For Chrissake! Some stupid bastard is taking photographs! Rescue Helicopter to ship! Could you please stop your crew taking photographs!'

'I am sorry. I do not understand.' There was another flash.

'Could you please stop taking photographs. It is distracting the Pilot's attention!'

'Ah! No photographs! I am sorry!'

The sixty-foot high gantries swayed perilously close to our rotorblades. 'This is too risky. Can we try a highline?'

We rose twenty feet above and between the gantries, but the crane cables made it hazardous, and Lofty was hauled back on board for the third time.

'This is too frigging dangerous! I'm not prepared to risk Lofty's life again. We'll have to back off and come again at first light!'

Strapped in my seat for'ard, I had been quietly observing what was going on, and had realised that the crew were desperately tired. It was now 2330 hours. They had been on duty since 0700, and had already put in four and a half hours night flying under the most arduous conditions. We had been over that ship for almost an hour, and it was clear to me, medically, that the lads had pushed themselves to the limits of their endurance. It was also becoming obvious from the time being taken to calculate, reach decisions and take action, that their response time was slowing and their concentration beginning to lapse. That was dangerous. Most flying accidents were caused, not by mechanical failure, but by errors of judgement by the aircrew.

I was quick to give backing to Reg Parker's difficult and anguished decision to put the safety of his crew first, and head for Sligo, in the full knowledge that we were having to leave on board, till morning, a seriously ill man.

'Reg. It might be a good idea if I had a word with the Captain, to give him some advice and support. He sounded a bit apprehensive.'

'Could you, Doc? That would be a help.'

Sid called up the ship and put me through on Channel 16.

'Hello, Captain. This is the Doctor on board Rescue Helicopter. Can you give me an update on your patient's condition?'

I was relieved to hear that the man had not been sick for a couple of hours, and that his pulse was still steady around 94 per minute. What made me more anxious was the information that he had apparently lost over a litre of blood, and had been sweaty and clammy earlier. His severe abdominal pain seemed to have settled.

'You are doing all the right things, Captain.' I reassured him as much as I could. 'Keep giving him sips of iced water, and also keep him lying flat. If he gets sweaty and clammy again, raise his legs up six inches or a foot as this will help his blood pressure.

'I am sorry we must leave you now, but it has been impossible for us to land on, and we are running short of fuel.'

'Thank you, Doctor.' He sounded relieved to have talked to somebody, but added anxiously—'You vill return at first light?'

I promised we would, and put him back to Sid for advice on the course he should steer till morning. Sid instructed him to head for the lee of Downpatrick Point, lying to the south and west of Sligo, which would take him into sheltered waters and out of the prevailing wind.

There was a heartfelt and dreadful feeling of failure and of helplessness as we turned for shore, knowing that our patient might have bled to death by the time we returned.

Nor would we have the cover of our guardian Nimrod for much longer. He reported only one hour's endurance left, and likewise departed for home.

At least he was going home. We could be heading for trouble.

25

14 March 1991

West of Sligo—2

We were now on the horns of a very unpleasant dilemma, faced with two risky options. We had either to try a return to Prestwick, with the prospect of an exhausted crew flying at night through zero-visibility fog for the last sixty miles; or we had to stay overnight in the Irish Republic, in a hostile area close to the Northern Irish Border. (We didn't realise it at the time, but Lord Mountbatten had been murdered only ten miles up the coast, when his boat was blown up by terrorists at Murraghmore.)

A decision had to be made.

'How do you feel about navigating back to Prestwick after refuelling, Sid?' probed Lt Parker. 'We'll have to consider our options.'

'I'm ready to flake out. I couldn't do it. I've still got a thumper of a head-ache, and my concentration's gone. Out there... at the ship... I just couldn't get my mind going and figure out what we were trying to do! I'm desperate for a kip.'

'Well, it looks like we'll all have to kip at Sligo. I'm totally shagged-out myself,' Reg confessed. 'With a few hours sleep, we should be fit enough to pick the guy up at first light.'

We were by now on our final approach to Sligo Airport, guided in by the friendly little leprechauns sprinting up the runway with their torches. Touching down on the main runway, we taxied over to the Terminal Building, where interested spectators again lined the lounge bar windows as we drew up. Reg quickly slewed the aircraft round face on to the windows.

'I think it might be advisable to hide the "Royal Navy" on the tail,' he said quietly.

'Where are we going to sleep?' I asked.

'May be best sleeping on board, with one of us always awake to keep watch,' someone suggested.

'Don't fancy that for a lark—sleeping on top of 4000 lbs of aviation fuel!'

'I think we should contact the Garda,' I ventured, hoping for a nice safe police cell.

'OK, Graham and I will go into the Terminal while Sid supervises refuelling, and call up RCC on the landline… they've probably got something worked out for us.' Watching them disappear inside the airport building, we sat back expectantly, and hungrily rummaged around the foot of a black binliner into which the Co-Pilot had tipped a load of NAAFI biscuits, fruit, and utterly disgusting, inedible Marmite sandwiches—which was all he had managed to scrounge as food for our trip.

The two Pilots returned. 'It's OK, Doc… already been organised… there are men with guns here to look after us… and the Airport staff are knocking up some scran!'

Any 'scran' would have to be better than Marmite sandwiches, I thought to myself—the basic instinct for food overriding that of self-preservation—as we walked self-consciously into the lounge bar to discover that two of the spectators had been Garda Special Branch officers, armed with Israeli-made Uzi submachine guns, slung in leather cases on their shoulders. The RCC must have made a couple of phone calls!

The barmaid was a large, cheerful, middle-aged lady called Sonya, whose unusual Irish accent puzzled me, till she revealed that she was really Danish, although she had lived in Sligo for over thirty years. She rustled us up a couple of rounds of cheese and ham toasties each, and after several cups of tea, we were all feeling much happier.

Although it was after one in the morning, I felt that Helen would sleep better if she knew we were safe on terra-firma, and not somewhere out over the Atlantic. When I rang her on the airport telephone, I could sense the relief in her voice. I didn't mention the armed guards!

We bundled into a couple of unmarked cars and sped off through narrow, winding Irish lanes to a 'safe place' which Terry our minder had told us was five miles inland. As he drove, someone asked him about the safety of the Sea King, to which he replied—'Don't worry! The lads'll take care of it!' At that instant, the awful reality of our predicament hit me, and for one fearful, doubting moment I just hoped that Reg Parker had thoroughly sussed out this guy's I.D.!

However, when he picked up the car radio to check in with Garda HQ, I relaxed—but only momentarily—for on reaching Sligo, he made a sudden right turn and drove through a maze of small side streets—just to avoid stopping at the town centre traffic lights. This was not a joyride.

It was almost two o'clock when we finally arrived at the hotel, and were shown to our single rooms for a few hours' desperately needed sleep. Although there was no one around to witness our arrival except the night porter, I still took the precaution of checking doors and windows before slipping into bed.

Answering the five o'clock call, we dressed quickly and assembled at the entrance, to find a vigilant Terry still guarding the foyer, with his loaded submachine gun by his side. He was obviously taking no chances.

En route back to the Airport, he assured us of the close cooperation between the British and Irish Governments when circumstances such as ours arose—'Because our Government an' your Government would feel most embarrassed if anyting unpleasant happened.'

'Bugger the Government's embarrassment!'—we voiced our thoughts as one—'How about how we'd feel?'

'Ah. Ye'll be alright, lads,' he smiled reassuringly.

'How's that?'

'Because nobody knows ye are here!' A chill ran up my spine.

It was a relief to get back to the Airport, where Keiran, Terry's oppo, had been guarding the helicopter; and even more of a relief to get on board and airborne once more.

The *A P J Anand* had made good speed through the night, and her present position was 54 degrees 30 minutes N, 09 degrees 20 minutes W, just north of Downpatrick Point, and forty miles out from Sligo.

The grey dawn was breaking as we departed, and a thick white mist was rolling up the hillside above steep cliffs to the north of the town. To the west, visibility was clear. With just forty miles to run, a short half hour flight saw us over the ship by 0630 hours.

Unfortunately however, for some reason or other, perhaps trying to anticipate our needs, the Captain had raised one of the massive derricks and swung it out to port, making winching down even more awkward; and Reg had to radio down to ask him to lower it again and swing it over to starboard to clear a safe landing spot. Dwarfed by the giant gantries, tiny figures moved about the deck, manning the winches and guide wires, before the derrick and its giant pulley-block and hook were finally secured out of harm's way on the starboard quarter.

This took over twenty minutes, and despite the advantages of daylight and a much reduced swell, deck references for manoeuvring were not good, and it was seven o'clock before Sid, the stretcher, and finally myself were highlined on board the ship.

A dozen swarthy seamen, well muffled against the cold in heavy jackets, woollen pullovers and gloves, helped us with our gear. I asked to be taken to the sick man, and nearly came a cropper myself as I slipped on an oily patch on the deck as I moved aft. It was a rusty hulk of a ship, flying the Red Ensign, but badly in need of maintenance, and, I noted particularly, a badly corroded step on the stairway leading up to the crew quarters and bridge.

I was ushered into a cramped cabin where, to my surprise and relief, I found my patient, a very dark-skinned Indian in his mid-fifties, sitting up in a chair. Fortunately he had had no further bleeding overnight, not since his initial estimated blood loss of one litre. I got him to lie down on his bunk to examine him. There were no signs of shock, he was not sweating or clammy, his pulse was still 94 per minute, and most importantly, his blood pressure was normal. I reckoned he could probably walk with assistance out to the stretcher, and for the short trip back to Sligo, would not need an I/V infusion.

The Captain appeared at the door and introduced himself. Waving aside our apologies for being unable to lift off his crewman last night, he thanked us for all our efforts. When I told him that the man would be flown to the local hospital in Sligo, he was quite happy and said that the Ship's Agent in London would arrange the paper-work for his repatriation to India.

Sonya was back on toastie duty behind the bar when we arrived back at Sligo and delivered our Mr Bhose to the waiting ambulance. With both aircraft and Aircrew suitably refuelled, we expressed our gratitude and bade farewell to our Garda 'minders' and the Airport Manager and staff.

'Tusen Tak, Sonya!' I thanked her in Danish as we left.

'Du er Velkommen!' she laughingly replied.

The long homeward journey round the Donegal coastline was delightful, in total contrast to the outward trip. Out to sea there were small, scattered, cotton-wool banks of fog, while to starboard stretched mile after mile of stupendous scenery; the heavy swell from a deceptively calm-looking sea boiled over hidden skerries and bursting angrily at the base of deeply-fissured, towering cliffs from which seabirds wheeled and soared in their thousands as we passed overhead. And warm, moist sea air, surging upwards and cooling as it hit the cliffs, formed a thick, heaving blanket of turbulent white mist which rolled up the hillsides from the clifftops as far as the eye could see.

Then we were beyond the rugged cliffs and flying over pretty fishing villages, with their trim little harbours well located and protected in the lee of natural promontories; and over small, deserted offshore islands, whose ruins, lazy-beds and enclosures still remained to tell of a struggle to survive—and a struggle lost.

Then we were over scattered crofts and beautiful long strands of silver sand. It was so attractive, so peaceful, so enticing. And yet, for us, in uniform, so dangerous. An emergency landing here, in the wrong place, could quickly lead to another set of headlines in the national press, and a few more quickly forgotten victims of that darker side of Irish nature—the three hundred year long grudge match between Protestant and Catholic.

Tidal races or not, I felt much safer when the Mull of Kintyre, Southend, and Sanda slipped past to port, and we came under the friendly wing of Prestwick Air Traffic Control once more.

It came as an unpleasant shock therefore, when over the intercom came a terse and bald announcement from Prestwick: 'International Rescue One Seven Seven… Prestwick Control. You are clear to land. Please land on the main

apron at the Terminal Building and proceed to Stand Five where you will report for Customs Clearance!'

'Bloody friggin Hell!' The air was blue.

'What do these stupid bastards think we've been doing for the past seventeen hours at that ship—picking up a load of Cocaine?'

'Will I drop that crate of Bailey's out of the window now?' I quipped, '…
along with the bin-liner full of orange peel and Marmite sandwiches?'

We landed on at 1130, and Sid and Lofty disappeared through the Stand
Five doorway into the Arrivals Lounge. When, after fifteen minutes, they had
not returned, our frustration and anger reached boiling point.

'For God's Sake, Reg, contact the Ops Room and get someone to phone
over and tell these shit-heads to stop mucking us around… Tell them that
we've had ten hours solid flying time—and no bloody sleep for twenty-nine
friggin hours!'

Reg complied, in somewhat more diplomatic language, and shortly afterwards, the back-seat pair returned, extremely annoyed and disgruntled, to tell
us that they'd searched all over the Terminal for Customs Officers, and discovered that they were not even in the building! What's more, when they did
finally contact them by phone, the Customs Men knew nothing about our
arrival—and cared even less!

'It must have been some arsehole in ATC going by the rule book because
we had just flown in from the Republic. "International" Rescue One Seven
Seven… the Bampot!'

'I bet that poor bugger from the ship has an easier time getting back home
to Calcutta!'

26

5/8 August 1991

Islay…and It's Goodbye to Care!

'Wot you doin' in this mornin', Doc?' Matt greeted me with a surprised look as I walked in the Sick Bay door.

I had been on duty all weekend, and, as Sod's Law would have it, had just begun this Monday morning with a seven o'clock visit to a girl with acute asthma. Then breakfast at eight had been interrupted when the Surgery bleeped me for a 'Come quick—he's got chest pain!' call, which turned out to be flu!

And now, at nine o'clock, here I was at Gannet—and the plonkers had forgotten to book my clinic! Although the Base was on summer leave, I had been so busy the previous week that I had felt a need to organise two sessions this week instead of one, to clear the backlog of RAF Air Traffic Controllers' medicals. Matt swore blind that no one had told him, then suddenly remembered that was why the POMA had him typing all those reports which were lying on my desk to be signed!

Apart from the embuggerance factor of a wasted morning, and of piling more medicals onto an already crowded appointment schedule later in the month, I can't say I was unhappy at the prospect of an easy ride after a weekend on call. At one time in the past, the Practice had tried giving the partner who'd done the weekend duty a bit of relief by cancelling his normal Monday surgery. This arrangement had allowed us all, in turn, a pleasant and civilised morning tidying up loose ends and doing revisits, but latterly, with an ever-increasing workload, we found that we could not afford the lost appointments. And so we had gone back to the Monday morning grind, with a grumpy, tired doctor summoning up his last few ounces of patience and goodwill to face the grumpy Monday morning faces of his Monday morning regulars. It was something I was glad to miss today.

Matt had just lifted the phone, at my direction, to re-book some of the outstanding medicals, when his red emergency phone rang.

'Yes! O.K., I'll be right down.' He turned to me. 'There's a job on, Doc. I'll phone up if you're needed. Dunno wot it's about.'

Two minutes later he rang back—could I come down—it was a three-year-old diabetic on Islay who was deteriorating rapidly and had to be flown to Glasgow.

'I've been going there on holiday for twenty years,' I remarked to Harry Blackmore, the Observer, as we clambered on board, 'but I've never been to Islay on a SAR.'

'Well you won't be going this time either, Doc,' he retorted. 'For we're going to Gee-gah!'

Gigha (properly pronounced Gee-ah) was only twenty-five minutes flying time from Prestwick—should the crow fly over Arran—and fortunately the 1000ft stratus level was just high enough to let us sneak through a narrow clearance between cloud and hill at the top of the long glen behind Brodick. A similar hill-hopping exercise took us over the Kintyre peninsula and we were on top of Gigha almost before we knew it. A red Volvo was waiting on the grass landing strip at the south end of the island as we flew in over the tiny pier and a couple of cottages; causing a great stramash among the local hens and sheep who had been quietly pecking and munching and minding their own business.

As we left the aircraft, I was relieved to see an alert three year-old toddler in his mother's arms emerge from the car, accompanied by the comforting ample blue figure of the island's District Nurse.

'What's the problem, Sister?' I yelled above the roar of the engines as the wee lad put his hands over his ears in alarm, and snuggled close to his mum.

'This is wee Gavin McKenzie. He has had a temperature and has been vomiting for the past twenty-four hours,' she replied, '…and has a pulse of a hundred and forty-four per minute. His breath smells of ketones, and his urine is loaded with sugar.'

'Has he had his Insulin?'

She affirmed that he had, the dose having been suitably adjusted after a phone call to Yorkhill Hospital.

Dave Chambers, the Aircrewman, appeared with a couple of ear protectors which he fitted on Gavin and his Mum. Gavin, now looking like a miniature airman—(something like Dave himself at five foot three!)—was quite taken with his new headgear, and settled down happily in the back of the helicopter as we took off—looking with rapt interest through the window at the sea and coast flashing by as we sped up the Sound of Gigha towards West Loch Tarbert.

Shortly afterwards, bored with all the excitement, he fell sound asleep. His pulse had settled, but one look at his chubby, veinless, wee hands as I checked his pulse, reinforced my initial fears that, apart from monitoring his condition, and sucking him out if he had inhaled vomitus, there was precious little else I could have done on board the Sea King to relieve any problems due to dehydration. It would have been impossible to put up an I/V drip. However, his tongue was moist, and he probably was only minimally dehydrated. The problem was potential, rather than actual, and this was why he was being transferred so promptly to Yorkhill for observation.

The weather over Gigha had been bright and clear, so it was disappointing to run into low cloud and rain again on the approach to Glasgow Airport. On arrival, and on cue, young Master Gavin woke up, and was quite unconcerned when I carried him out to the waiting ambulance, though he was a wee bit reluctant to relinquish his flying helmet which he obviously regarded as a legitimate trophy!

'Did you see these poor bloody hens?' said Mark Rowley, the Co-Pilot, as we overflew the hills above Greenock on our way back to Prestwick.

'What? The ones on Gee-gah?'

'Yeah. I don't think they liked flying upside down and backwards, arse to the wind in our downdraught, as we blew them over that wall!' chuckled Cal Brown the Pilot. 'There'll be a lotta free range scrambled eggs all over Gee-gah today.'

Little did Matt and I know that we would be scrambled over Gigha only three days later!

*   *   *

'Is Bob going to the Flower Show tonight?' I called through to Helen as I dumped my bags in a corner of the hall with a sigh of relief that another busy day was over. I would have been home sooner, but 'extras' had been tagged on to the early evening surgery I was doing with the new Trainee, stretching it to nearly six o'clock.

'You've only got quarter of an hour!' she replied from the kitchen. 'Bob was going along at half-past six.' A quick phone call set back our rendezvous at the end of the road to a quarter to seven, and I hurriedly gulped down my tea. Ayr Flower Show was always a marvellous spectacle. The biggest Flower Show in Scotland, and third largest in the UK after Chelsea and Shrewsbury, it was a must for all amateur gardeners, and something I never missed; although I must admit, like many other visitors, I would always spend as much time blethering with folk I hadn't seen for the past year as I did appreciating the magnificent displays of flowers, vegetables, honey, crafts and home-baking.

Savouring the prospect, I set off on schedule to meet Bob, but had only walked a couple of hundred yards down the road when the bleep sounded. Hurrying back as fast as my heavy meal would allow, I breathlessly rang the doorbell.

'What's wrong this time?' asked a surprised Helen.

'The bleep's gone off—but it might just be a duff battery,' I added without much conviction.

I phoned Ops Room.

'Bob Gale here, Doc. Can you come in? We've been scrambled for a guy with a gunshot wound to his chest on Islay.'

Islay at last! Delight at the prospect of a flight out west on such a bonny evening was counterbalanced by a modicum of 'fear an trimmlin' at the prospect of managing a gunshot wound of unknown severity on the flight back to Glasgow. I stripped to my drawers on the front doorstep, and hurriedly donned my flying overalls.

The evening Flower Show and homeward-bound holiday traffic was graciously cooperative as I green-lighted at ninety up the busy bypass, to find the SAR Sea King burning and turning on the tarmac. Gerry Flannery had my lifejacket, goon suit and boots laid out and ready for me, and within a few minutes we were on board and belting out over the Firth at a wind-assisted 120 knots with Lt Bob Gale at the controls.

As we flew, his P2, Lt Andy Baillie, a new face I hadn't seen before, slipped quickly out of the left-hand seat to put on his immersion suit in the confined space next to where Matt Philips and I were sitting, just aft of the cockpit. Pulling the rubber neck seal down over his head, he hurriedly donned the helmet I had been momentarily holding for him.

Before he could get back to his seat, there was a clipped conversation between himself and the pilot, accompanied by a quick scanning of instruments and twisting of knobs. Then he reached down into his flight briefcase and produced a flip-card manual which he began to read out loud.

It was all professional flying jargon to me until he came to the line: 'If "chip" shows again within thirty seconds, continue sortie. If it fails to do so, land as soon as possible'!

'Could you two strap in now!' came an unusually sharp command from Gerry Flannery in the back. Matt and I looked at each other and complied smartly.

Bob Gale banked the aircraft in a 360 degree turn and we began a slow descent and tense ten minute flight back to Prestwick, radioing on ahead for the ground crew to have a replacement Sea King fired up and ready to go as soon as we touched down. I don't know what thoughts were going through Matt's mind, but I was eyeing up the yellow striped emergency handle on the door opposite, and wondering how far I might have to jump!

As we flew in over the airfield, I let out an involuntary, verbal, but fortunately not functional, 'Oh, shit!' as Bob threw us into a violent left hand descending turn, and the ground below rushed up towards us through the side windows at an alarming angle. He obviously knew his aircraft, but as we touched down safely, I reckoned that if it had been me flying this duff helicopter with warning lights flashing, I would have tiptoed in a bit more gingerly… probably going 'Down-bird' at the high tide-mark on Prestwick beach and asking for a tow home!

We quickly transferred the basic minimum of gear required to an adjacent Sea King on the hardstanding while Bob attended to the necessary paperwork, and in five minutes were airborne again.

'Sir!' It was Gerry's voice from the back. 'There's a bloody great panel missing from the roof of this cab, and a helluva draught being blown in from the tail rotor! Is that alright?' We groaned. Surely not a third bloody change of aircraft! Luckily it was only an internal inspection panel in the roof which was missing, and apart from a horrible down-draught which later blew the medical notes out of my hand, it did not hamper our flight.

'Could you get me an update on the casualty?' I requested, now that the drama was past, for I was concerned that our delay might have jeopardised his chances.

'Sure thing, Doc, no problem!' acknowledged Gerry, and handed me up an intercom cable connected to his own radio. I sat silent, taking notes as Edinburgh Rescue literally spelled it out over the air. 'Condition stable... Blood Pressure one-fifty over eighty... Pulse one hundred per minute... Gunshot wound to the left side of chest... may have involved the pericardium... Papa, Echo, Romeo, India, Charlie, Alpha, Romeo, Delta, India, U, M... PERICARDIUM of the heart.'

'D'you get that, Doc?' called Gerry. I acknowledged, explaining to the crew in general that there might be damage to the outer covering of the man's heart; and commented that he sounded surprisingly stable, considering the serious description of his injuries.

'How do you want him flown?' asked Marcus Wilson, the Observer, a tall, bespectacled, bearded lad with more than a touch of the Viking about his appearance.

'We'd better fly low, preferably under five hundred feet, to avoid aggravating any possible pneumothorax,' I replied.

A few minutes elapsed, then the Observer came back—'I've worked out a route, Bob... from the Airport south over Port Ellen and round the south east of Islay; across to West Loch Tarbert; through the Tarbert Gap and across Loch Fyne; over Rothesay and up the Clyde under the Erskine Bridge. OK?'

The Pilot affirmed and continued on course, following the same flight path as we had taken three days before, up over Arran and Kintyre, and down over the southern tip of Gigha.

'Back where we started!' I remarked to Matt. 'D'you think those hens will have started laying yet?'

'You fairly get about, Doc!' laughed Marcus.

'Yes, and I was on Islay three weeks ago on holiday!'

'What a god-forsaken place to come on holiday,' Gerry Flannery commented drily as we began to climb over the bleak windswept hills, moors and lochans to the south of Beinn Bheigeir. 'What do you come here for—the solitude?'

'Believe it or not, Gerry, there are four thousand folk on this island. It's a great place for peace and quiet, walking, bird-watching and fishing... and there are eight distilleries for old soaks like you!'

'Everyone strapped in for landing. I've got the Airport on the nose.' interjected Bob Gale. Two private aircraft were parked beside the otherwise deserted Terminal, one of them an old wartime Grumman Albatross amphibian
belonging to the Laird of one of the island estates. The ambulance was parked
nearby, and a small group of people stood clustered by its rear door.

I hurried across and spoke to the ambulance driver who indicated the open
door, from which emerged an attractive young lady doctor. She smiled and
introduced herself as Dr Buchanan. Behind her, a young man lay on a stretcher,
his bandaged left arm connected to a drip-set, while tell-tale bloodstains be-
spattered the left side of his tee-shirt.

He looked remarkably alert and composed.

'What kind of gunshot wound was it?' I asked.

'I'm not sure,' admitted Dr Buchanan as she handed me a letter for the
Western Infirmary, and his chest X-rays.

A middle-aged man standing quietly beside us, possibly the lad's father,
interjected: 'An air rifle… he was playing with an air rifle.'

'Point two-two?' I asked. He nodded.

That explains a lot, I thought to myself, mightily glad to be relieved of the
responsibility of dealing with half a chest blown away by a shotgun. But this
was still a penetrating chest wound, and a glance at the X-rays indeed confirmed that the .22 waisted pellet was deeply lodged in his chest and lying
against his heart.

We transferred him on to the aircraft stretcher, and as we did so, the doctor
ushered forward a middle-aged lady. 'This is Mrs MacArthur, Jay's mother.
She'll be going with him.'

I could see Gerry spluttering under his breath. No one at RCC had told
him there would be two travelling, and, with the change of aircraft, he had no
drysuit with which to kit her out for the crossing. He was reluctant to allow her
on board till I told him that I'd never yet seen a relative fitted with a drysuit on
all the island SARs I'd done.

While we waited for him to return with headsets for mother and son, I chatted
to Dr Buchanan about our Islay holidays and the SAR work, and asked her why we
had been called on such a fine evening instead of the Air Ambulance plane.

'They couldn't give me an Air Ambulance till eleven o'clock, because it had
been called away to Stornoway,' she replied, 'and I couldn't risk that length of
a delay.'

Five minutes later, we were speeding up the Sound of Jura past Gigha
when I overheard Gerry's Cumbrian voice reporting our position and heading
to Clyde Coastguard.

'Sea King Helicopter Rescue One Seven Seven, with eight persons on board
has just left Eye-lay and is now passing Gee-gah, heading at low level for Tarbert
en route to Glasgow Airport.'

'For Heaven's sake, Gerry,' I complained afterwards, 'if you lot are going to fly up here, at least get the pronunciation right! It's Eye-lah, and Gee-ah!'

'Might be easier if you Scotch used proper spelling, wouldn't it fellahs? Can't even bloody spell up here. Did I get Tarrh-berrht right?' he went on, with a mocking 'burr' in his voice, to a chorus of support from the others.

Within ten minutes of taking off from Islay, we were past Kennacraig and roaring low over Tarbert. 'D'you know,' I informed the lads, 'we've done in ten minutes what usually takes us two hours in MacBrayne's ferry!'

'Which do you prefer, Doc?'

'Depends on the company I'm keeping!' I retorted.

'Suit yourself!'

Since Jay's pulse was normal, and his condition had remained stable throughout the journey, I went for'ard to reassure his mother, and sat beside her pointing out Inverkip, Dunoon and Dumbarton Rock, as we skimmed low up the Clyde. Matt was just doing a final pulse check when I returned to his side for landing. 'What is it?' I asked.

'Eighty-eigh ...'

'Shut up!' came a shout over the intercom. The aircraft suddenly climbed and veered to the right, and I could see the alarm on young Jay's face as he looked from his stretcher through the starboard window to see ground flashing past. Then, just as suddenly, we banked sharply to port before quickly steadying into our runway approach. The land-on and transfer of patient and parent happily proceeded without further incident. Mrs MacArthur, remarkably unperturbed, thanked us all for our assistance.

Visibility was superb as we headed over the Renfrewshire hills towards Ardrossan.

'Isn't Scotland clear today?'

'For once!' someone grumphed from the back.

'Yeah, usually bloody seafog, mist and rain,' moaned another.

'That's it! I've had nothing but insults from you lot today about our weather, our islands, and our spelling! I'm going to insist on an all-Scottish crew next SAR.'

'You'll be lucky!' was the chorus of English voices.

Bob Gale came into the locker room as Gerry and I were changing. 'Any comments on the flight?' he asked.

'Well it was a bumpy ride for the last few miles—for a potentially ill patient,' I said. 'Did you have to take avoiding action or something?'

'Yes. Sorry about that, Doc,' he apologised. 'When I shouted for you to shut up, Glasgow Control were in the middle of telling me that an aircraft was taking off, and to change course. I couldn't see it, so reacted quickly, and then found myself heading straight for a flock of birds, so had to throw it around again.'

Then he added for good measure: 'And just as well we turned back when we did at the beginning, when that indicator chip malfunctioned. They are sometimes prone to do this, but this time it was for real. The mechanics found a loose piece of metal in the gearbox!'

*   *   *

Postscript—In hospital, it was deemed too dangerous to operate to remove the .22 pellet from Jay's chest cavity, but its presence, lodged next to his heart muscle, has caused him no problems, and he still works and lives in Islay.

27

17 November 1991

The Piece

'What do you want in your piece?' Helen called through from the kitchen—'Two gammon rolls and one cheese, or vice-versa? I've put in a slice of that apple tart I made yesterday, a Club and a Milky Way, and an apple and tangerine. Will that do? I'll put it in the fridge.'

'Thanks, Love. That'll be fine.' And a damn-sight more nourishing, I thought, than yon single plastic cup of black coffee which was all the sustenance I'd had for five hours during the last ferry evacuation exercise—on board the *Iona* four years ago in the Sound of Jura… I wasn't going to starve this time!

The Ferrex briefing was at 1000 hours on Sunday morning, but we knew in advance that the Mull Ferry *Hebridean Isle*, with 250 people on board, was due to collide with a benzene-carrying Tanker in the Sound of Mull, near Tobermory.

To be certain of how many oxygen cylinders and I/V infusion sets we could have mustered in fifteen minutes notice for the real thing, I went into Gannet half an hour early and met the SAR Duty MA. This weekend, it just happened to be Jamie McCracken—alias the Ballantrae Barrel—whose capacity for stuffing himself was legendary.

'Have you got a piece made up for yourself, Jamie? It could be a long hungry day out there!'

'Not yet, Boss! But I'll knock together a sandwich or three when we go down to the SAR Shack.'

We checked the available equipment, and reckoned we could have airlifted 10 oxygen cylinders, plus 20-30 infusion sets and fluid replacement bottles. It was just an exercise, and there was no need to physically hump the stuff with us—as long as we could honestly say we would have been able to supply and use that quantity of equipment in treating frontline casualties.

As we approached the SAR Cabin, I was surprised to meet Bob Gale, one of the standby crew Pilots, all kitted up for flying.

'Hullo, Bob.' I greeted him. 'Are you flying too? I thought you were just on standby.'

'Yes, Doc… surprised me too. They've decided to send two aircraft. Dave Duthie is flying Rescue One Seven Eight, with me as Co-Pilot, and you will be coming with us, along with a chap from the Fire Service… Rescue One Seven Seven will be airborne as Duty SAR aircraft, and will divert to join us.'

We dumped the spare SAR gear outside the door, and went upstairs to the Duty Room.

'Look, Jamie, I've been thinking. If by chance we get a real casualty on board the ship, I'll look gey daft if I've nothing to treat him with, so we'd better take down one of the grab-bags—as well as my piece.'

'OK Boss. I'll be flying in the Duty Cab, so I'll come down with our grab-bag.' He grinned. 'I'll hide your piece inside it. Wouldn't look good if the only bit of medical kit you were bringing on board was a box of sandwiches!'

I laughed and agreed.

The Duty Room was crowded as Lt Cdr Dave Duthie, the SARO, expanded the briefing, after the Met Officer had produced a pleasantly favourable weather forecast—light SW winds and sea state one to two, with the prospect of rain from the west in the evening.

We would, as Bob had mentioned, be carrying, and dropping on board, a Senior Fire Officer, Keith Small, who was an official observer.

The Benzene Tanker, to be sunk with four men on board, would be played by the Northern Lighthouses supply ship *Fingal*. After the 'sinking', the *Fingal* was to rise again like a phoenix, and act as a passing rescue vessel to which injured passengers could be airlifted from the *Hebridean Isle*.

RAF Lossie would be sending down a crab Sea King, and the Stornoway Coastguard's big Sikorsky 61 would also be participating—piloted by Al Findlay, with whom I had flown a night-time SAR to the Irish Sea from Gannet twelve months back—just before he left the Navy.

I expressed my pleasure at this piece of news, only to be greeted with a barrage of good-natured grumbles from the aircrews—that big Al had landed on his feet up there right enough—being paid twice as much as Navy Pilots by Bristows', for doing the same bloody job, with a better bloody aircraft!

It was agreed that Rescue (or 'Exercise') 178 would take off immediately on receipt of the callout by RCC at 1100 hours, and that Rescue 177, the Duty Cab, would join in ten minutes later, having been 'by chance' on a training exercise over the Firth of Clyde at the time.

As we set off up the Firth, I stood behind the pilots with Keith Small, pointing out those local landmarks still visible to us on a disappointingly murky, hazy day.

We were overflying Rothesay when RCC came on the air.

'Rescue One Seven Seven… Edinburgh Rescue. Could you divert to Machrihanish? We have a report of a plane with one engine on fire making for the airfield… an Aurora with twelve people on board.'

'Is that gen?' I asked Dave Duthie, 'or is RCC up to one of its ploys as part of the exercise? I remember on the last Ferrex, a couple of the Crabs were diverted to Machrihanish with "engine trouble" and the crews spent their day drinking coffee while the rest of us sweated our guts out!'

'Could be a ploy,' he replied, 'or for real… we dunno yet. What's that up ahead, Bob? Looks like a flare!'

Ahead of us, what looked like a bright headlight hung in the sky against the dark backdrop of a wooded hillside on the far side of a small yacht-studded bay, then slowly spiralled downwards as we altered course to investigate.

Chris Wildish, our Observer, called up Clyde Coastguard to report the flare sighting, and was told it was only part of a local Coastguard exercise and nothing to do with the big one at Oban. With that reassurance, he set us a new heading over Tighnabruaich and the narrows of the Kyles of Bute, and up Loch Striven.

A few minutes later, we heard Rescue 177 inform Edinburgh Rescue that the crippled plane had, in fact, landed at Machrihanish, and that they would now be heading for Oban.

'Well, it was for real after all, Jim.' Dave half-turned round in his Pilot's seat. 'The Aurora is an American reconnaissance plane that carries a crew of twelve, so RCC weren't trying to pull a fast one!'

The words were barely out his mouth, when Oban Coastguard abruptly broke in: 'Rescue One Seven Seven… Oban Coastguard. You are not, repeat not, to enter the exercise airspace… You are not, repeat not, part of this exercise!'

Bob Gale glanced across at Dave with a puzzled look on his face—'Bloody Hell! What's all that about?'

'Sounds as if they're being told they're not being allowed out to play with the big boys. Reg Parker will be bloody annoyed about that.'

'Sod Reg Parker!' I exclaimed. 'What about my bloody piece!'

'What's a piece?' asked Bob Gale.

'His lunch sandwiches! Don't you English know nuffin?'

In the certain knowledge that Rescue 177 was now sulkily heading for home with its tail rotor between its wheels, and my piece in its belly, we pressed on alone, and soon found ourselves in the exercise area near Ardtornish Point, halfway up the Sound of Mull, where we sighted the *Hebridean Isle* lying becalmed, a few hundred yards off the small pier at Lochaline. Its lifeboats and a ten-man liferaft were in the water, and the lighthouse tender *Fingal*, now a rescue ship, was in close attendance.

'Rescue Helicopter… *Hebridean Isle*. We have many injured casualties on board… one very seriously injured requiring immediate evacuation. Have you a doctor on board?'

The affirmative having been given, I tightened the strop round me, clipped the grab-bag onto the winch hook, and was swung out to begin a slow descent to the stern car deck of the *Hebridean Isle*, a hundred feet below. Halfway down, the wire jerked suddenly, and I was left suspended in mid-air in full gaze of a score of assorted observers and crewmen on the ship then, for some unexplained reason, hauled unceremoniously back on board.

I sat with legs dangling over the doorstep, admiring the distant view of Mull for a few minutes, before a tap on the shoulder and a 'thumbs up' from POACMN Pete West sent me down once more to the car deck, from where a crewman led me, peching under the heavy weight of the grab-bag, up several steep companionways to the Forward Lounge past several groups of men in safety helmets, who were just aimlessly standing about.

In the passageway leading to the lounge lay the 'severely injured' man, unconscious, and ominously labelled—'bleeding from right ear'—indicating a possible fracture of the base of his skull. The obvious procedure would be to have him flown immediately to the Neurosurgical Unit at the Southern General in Glasgow. I knew that by taking this decision, I would inevitably cock-up any intended long-term participation by Rescue 178 in the exercise, but there seemed no other choice.

'This guy will have to go off at once to the Southern General!' I announced to the curious group of onlookers. Then, disconcerted by a strange lack of an immediate response, I suddenly realised that there were no officers around to take charge.

'Look, I'll need a runner to act as a go-between with the Bridge… someone to keep them informed which casualties need priority evacuation. Are there any crew members here?'

An anonymous voice in the background sounded out the helpful but vague information—'The crewmen are the ones in the hard hats.'

From a sea of faces sprouting from Board of Trade life-jackets, I picked out one with a hard hat—a young crewman—and asked him to act as a runner and convey my message to the Captain.

Leaving casualty number one to be loaded on a stretcher, I was then faced with a scene of chaos in the main lounge. Bandaged bodies in orange life-jackets lay strewn everywhere—on the floor, in the aisles, and along the bench seats. Others stood or sat in silent groups, and I felt all their eyes staring at me as I entered.

'Right. Could someone point out the most seriously injured!' I demanded, groping in my goon suit pocket for some rolls of coloured insulation tape which I had brought with me to 'triage', or identify, casualties for priority evacuation—Immediate (Red), Urgent (Yellow), Non-urgent (Green), and Dead (White)—in that order.

With no other medic to help me—Jamie would be halfway back to Prestwick by this time—I soon found myself hard-pressed coping with demands from all sides. Check this one, Doctor… unconscious with head and spinal injuries… that one with breathing difficulties… the next with multiple burns… and so on.

They all had small labels pinned to their jackets with details of their injuries; and one guy hurriedly produced a placard which read—'If you have not been rescuscitated in twenty-five minutes you're dead!' I reassured him we had got him in the nick of time, stuck a piece of red tape on his brow, and moved on. To help minimise the risk of some of those prioritised for immediate evacuation being overlooked, I asked for a 'walking wounded' to 'buddy up' with each casualty, and to holler for attention from passing stretcher bearers.

I had been too busy with my sticky tape to pay much attention to the stretcher party's activities, but had to look up incredulously when they decided to stretcher the guy with neck and spinal injuries across the crowded lounge in a short cut to a door opening directly on to the fore deck, which had been designated the helicopter evacuation point.

He was a big, heavy lad, and there was a high risk of some real damage being done to the hands and heads being used as stepping stones, as he was manhandled on a Neil-Robertson stretcher over half a dozen prostrate bodies to this door—only to find the stretcher couldn't get through it, and he had to be brought all the way back again—causing more chaos!

Ten minutes passed, and I still hadn't seen an officer; my 'runner' seemed to have done just that—for I never saw him again! I could only assume that out there on deck someone had taken charge of the evacuation point, and was keeping the Bridge informed of those I was assessing for priority removal.

Progress was painfully slow, as the ship only seemed to have the one Neil-Robertson Stretcher—a wooden slatted canvas contraption like Tutankhamen's corsets—a marvellous device for extricating a single casualty from a confined space, but hopeless for speedy multiple evacuations, as each patient had to be wrapped and strapped into it, and this took up a lot of time. I was glad of the assistance of a few First Aiders among the 'passengers', who used their skills to good effect, and even gladder when someone shouted—'Here's another Doctor!'

Dr Gordon Murchison, the RNLI Doctor, had arrived off the Oban Lifeboat. Great, I thought, we'll get better organised now—for my primary function as the first doctor on the scene—the Site Medical Officer—had been to triage patients for evacuation, not to treat individual cases. I went over, introduced myself, and asked him to 'administer' oxygen to several casualties with breathing difficulties due to smoke inhalation, while I completed triage.

Seconds later, another voice called out—'Is there a Doctor Begg here? Message from the Bridge!'

Good, I thought again, maybe we'll get some action from them at last. 'I'm here!' I shouted and waved my presence.

'You've to go on deck for immediate winching aboard the helicopter, Doc!'

What the Hell's going on now, I muttered under my breath—another exercise ploy?—perhaps to get me out of the action and give Dr Murchison a chance to participate in casualty evacuation. Or maybe my first evacuee had 'collapsed' on board the Sea King, and required the urgent attention of a doctor in transit to SGH, for we had no Medic.

This latter theory was debunked as soon as I emerged from the lounge and found my first critically ill patient still sitting on a deck chair—he hadn't even been winched off the ship! And a sizeable queue was building up behind him.

What the Hell is going on, I wondered, and asked, but no one could tell me anything. Aloft, the Bridge appeared as deserted as the *Marie Celeste*, with not a soul visible on the open starboard wing just above my head.

Rescue 178 hovered expectantly off the starboard bow, but several more minutes elapsed before it finally closed in. Two heads appeared at the open door. I waited, fully expecting Pete West the Winchman to be lowered down, but, surprisingly, it was an empty double strop which slowly dangled its way towards the small eight-foot square patch of deck designated as the winching zone.

I grabbed the strops and gesticulated to ask if they wanted me or my casualty. Impatient fingers from above pointed emphatically at me, so I clipped on the grab-bag, eased myself into the strop, gave a thumbs-up, and was lifted from the ship—banging hard against the side of the Bridge as I rose—the only real contact I'd had with it since coming on board!

Once on board the Sea King, I went forward and plugged into the intercom by the Pilot's seat, still puzzling over my sudden, unceremonious recall. Nor was I any the wiser for the next ten minutes, as Dave Duthie's attention was fully stretched responding to instructions from the Winchman guiding him over the ship to lift off the first two casualties and also, for some reason, Keith Small, the Fire Service observer.

The first casualty hoisted on board got a bit of undeserved stick over the intercom from the Observer, for not moving quick enough once he got on board. I felt like butting in with the comment that the poor sod, though a Territorial, might just conceivably be petrified shitless—having had to strop himself in, and endure a hundred foot lift without the normal reassuring advice and assistance from an Aircrewman down on deck.

Discretion prevailed—there are times, as they say in the Navy, when it is better to 'receive' than 'transmit'—so I kept radio silence till we were well on our way down the Sound of Mull, heading towards Connel Airfield to drop off our casualties, leaving behind Alan Findlay, who had just arrived in Rescue 119—the Stornoway Crab—to do all the donkey work along with the Lossie Crab.

'Why was I called back on board, Dave? Was it part of the exercise?'

'No, Jim. The whole thing has been a bit of a shambles. You were only two minutes on board when we got a signal from RCC to say that Rescue One Seven Seven had gone "downbird" on the Mull of Kintyre, and as relief SAR aircraft we had to abandon the exercise and call you back on board at the double.'

'Some "double"! I only got your message after I'd been on board twenty minutes, and even then you were hanging about for another ten minutes before you came in to pick me up.'

'The communications set-up has not been very good—partly because after the downbird signal, we couldn't send down the Aircrewman after you as we had planned, to coordinate the evacuation via the Bridge; and partly because of radio frequency problems.'

'You can say that again!' I laughed. 'But I suppose that's the main purpose of holding these exercises—to identify problems. And, talking of communications, have you been able to contact One Seven Seven?'

'Not directly. From what we gathered from RCC, they had smoke in the cockpit, and went downbird in a field near Tayinloan. It just had to be in a Vodaphone blackspot, and was five miles from the nearest phone... so they've had their own communication problems—and blistered feet for someone into the bargain.'

A disgruntled crew of Maintainers, kitted out in red immersion suits, was already standing by with repair equipment, ready to be flown out to Kintyre by Rescue 178, when we arrived back at Gannet.

I went home. It was 1430, I'd had enough... and I was starving!

At 1730, the phone rang.

'Hullo, Boss!' It was Jamie. 'What did you have to put tomato in your sandwiches for?'

'Why?'

'Well, I don't like tomato in my piece!'

*   *   *

Jamie no longer needs to scrounge 'pieces' from doctors to survive. A few months after this Ferrex, he came into my room at Sick Bay, and announced that he was putting in his notice as he wanted to leave the Navy to study Law. Knowing in my heart how difficult it could be for students to get into a Law Faculty, and even to get work as lawyers once qualified, I nevertheless admired his courage and wished him well when he eventually gained entry to Law School in London.

Nine years later, when Gerry Flannery arrived back at Gannet from a spell in RAF Nimrods, I was absolutely delighted to hear from him that not only had Jamie achieved a good Law Degree, but he was now practising as a successful Barrister in Birmingham.

28

18 December 1991
'Kartli'

I was dog-tired and could well have stayed in my bed. Throughout the night, Mother Nature's elemental Royal Marine Band had 'Beat the Retreat' from sleep—with a snare-drum rattle of hailstones on the windowpanes, kettle-drum rolls of roof-shaking thunder, and the fluting whistle of gale-force winds round the gable-end of the house. I was restlessly half-awake most of the night; snugly thankful not to have been abroad in such weather. And so it was with some effort that I got up, shaved, and went downstairs for breakfast.

Standing by the hob, listening intently as she stirred the porridge, still in her dressing gown and looking much as I felt, Helen abruptly motioned silence as I began to ask how she had slept.

'Shh! There's something in the Scottish News Headlines about helicopters off Islay... It'll be on again in a minute.' I listened.

'An RAF helicopter from Lossiemouth has been battling in the darkness through gale-force winds off the island of Islay this morning, in an attempt to rescue crewmen from a Russian fishing vessel drifting helplessly with its steering out of action after being struck by a giant wave during the night.

'Several crewmen are feared dead, and a number of injured have already been airlifted to hospital in Northern Ireland. A major rescue operation was mounted after red flares were spotted by a tanker at four-thirty this morning. Other helicopters and ships have joined in the attempt to rescue the fifty crew members reported to be still on board the stricken vessel, and the search continues for some who have taken to the liferafts.'

'What the Hell are the Lossie Crabs doing down on our patch?' Then I remembered.

Last night had been the Gannet Officers' Christmas Ball—as well as the Senior Rates' Christmas Party. Ball or Party, Party or Ball, regardless of rank, were both euphemisms for 'mega-binge'—with a consequent role-reversal—the entire Ship's Company would be 'fleein'—and her helicopters grounded!

RAF Lossie traditionally came down to provide SAR cover on these festive occasions, and the Navy always provided them with reciprocal cover on Battle of Britain Day.

'Bloody typical!' I moaned to Helen. 'The Crabs always get the glory. The biggest rescue operation we've had in years, and it had to happen on the one night the Navy's paralytic! But I wonder why RCC didn't call me in? Mind you, listening to all that hail and thunder during the night, I was quite glad to be snug and warm under the duvet.'

'You can say that again,' said Helen, with feeling—and obvious relief.

I arrived at Gannet at 0830 to find Jamie, not unexpectedly, a bit hung over from last night's revelries, and no sign of the POMA Don Clark.

'Who's the hero, then?' I chaffed. 'Not you, obviously!'

'Don's been away with the Crabs since five o'clock, Boss, and isn't back yet. Two of our Sea Kings have gone as well.'

The Nine o'Clock News gave us an update on the situation. Thirty-two survivors had just been rescued by the Navy Sea Kings and airlifted on to various ships which had rushed to the scene, and others had been flown direct to hospital.

At 1100 hours, Don arrived back, pale, red-eyed, cold and exhausted. We deferred our eager curiosity till he had freshened up with a hot shower, change of clothes, and a steaming mug of tea.

It transpired that, when his bleep went at 0500 hours, although the Navy SAR Cab was grounded, as Duty Medic he was stone-cold sober and available, and was readily accepted by the Crab SAR crew. By flying out with them he reckoned he had saved some Navy pride by making it a 'Joint Services' mission!

The weather had been pretty foul. It was blowing a south-westerly gale with 30-foot seas when they located the *Kartli*, a Bulgarian factory ship, in the darkness, some ten miles south-west of the Rhinns of Islay.

'We arrived over the ship in the pitch-dark, and our searchlights picked out some crew members huddled at the bow. The Pilot manoeuvred the aircraft overhead and the Flight Sergeant Aircrewman lowered a highline to them. I was sitting strapped-in, watching him do this, when suddenly he was catapulted head-first straight out through the open door, and disappeared into the blackness!

'I thought he was a goner… He had been hooked on to the winch wire and highline—which the silly buggers had tied to a rail instead of holding on to it. So when the ship's bow pitched down thirty feet into the next trough, he was yanked down with it. Fortunately for him the line gave at its built-in weak point just below where it is attached to the winch hook, and he was left spinning on the end of the winch wire. He was a lucky man!

'They got the idea next time round, and hand-hauled him onto the ship. But there was no bloody discipline. There was a mad bloody scramble to get off the ship. The first seven up were fully fit, and it was only then that we saw there was a guy left huddled under some blankets! We lowered the stretcher and managed to get him back on board with great difficulty. He was in a bad way, and deeply unconscious. I gave him 100% Oxygen all the way to Ireland.

'We took ten off altogether, including three women and this poor guy, and flew them to Altnagelvin Hospital near Londonderry. I was bloody glad I didn't have to go down myself, I can tell you!'

As if shivering at the thought, Don paused, his hands drawing welcome warmth from the steaming mug in his grasp, and took a long gulp of sweet milky tea.

'The ship must have been hit during the night by a giant rogue wave about seventy feet high, though the seas were a lot less than that when we got there—maybe twenty-five to thirty feet—and they were big enough! The wave stove in the starboard side of the wheelhouse, and it looked as if it had been hit by an Exocet.'

In fact, as was later reported, the wave had done as much damage as an Exocet missile—smashing right through the wheelhouse, killing two crew members, seriously injuring three others, and totally immobilising the ship.

'Why didn't RCC call me in, Don, if there were so many serious casualties?'

'We didn't know that when we lifted off, Doc. The first report we got was of fifty guys gone crazy on a fishing boat… could have been the Campbeltown lads on a pre-Hogmanay ceilidh!

'It was only when we got beyond Arran that info started to come in that there were serious casualties on board—too late for you!' Don continued with his story:

'Anyway, after we dropped off the casualties, we resumed the search and picked up five more from one liferaft, then a single man from another liferaft. He was bloody lucky to be alive. His liferaft had drifted about ten miles and was only a mile off the cliffs at the south end of Islay when we found it. We thought there was no one in it. It was half-full of water, and the poor bloke was only half-dressed, with nothing on his feet, and frozen stiff. Another hour and he would have been dead of hypothermia.'

'What's happening to the others?' asked Jamie.

'As far as I know, they were all airlifted onto the Olna by 819 Sea Kings. I was plugged into the Crab intercom and got the shock of my life when I heard there were two Sea Kings on the scene from Gannet when we came back from Londonderry. After last night, I couldn't think of anyone left at Gannet sober enough to fly them—apart from the cleaners!

'Still, they've kept the Navy's end up, after all. That's the Crabs' job finished now.'

The six casualties brought back by Don and the Lossie Sea King had been landed at Crosshouse Hospital, but we had no information as yet on the future disposal of the thirty or so uninjured survivors. We did not have long to wait.

At 1130 the phone rang.

'Is that you, Jimmy?' It was Dave Duthie, the SAR Flight Commander. 'We've got problems. Eight-One-Nine has been tasked to disembark thirty survivors at Gannet later this afternoon, and they'll also be flying in a body. Could you be here to certify it—and where does it go afterwards?'

I had met with this scenario before, in relation to the body of a dead Fighter Pilot about to be flown up to Gannet from the Solway coast, and was well aware of the legal problems which could arise, with various Sheriffdoms and Procurators Fiscal disputing jurisdiction.

'I'd better ring the Ayr Fiscal's Office to get clarification on this one, Dave, and contact the Police as well.'

'The Police have already been in touch about processing the survivors and setting up a reception centre. Can you come in this afternoon to certify this dead casualty, and do a medical check on the survivors?' Then he added as a sweetener—'I've got a young Dutch lady doctor here who could give you a hand.'

'That sounds very interesting.' I said, happy to rise to the bait. 'How soon do you want me in? It's my half-day anyway, so there's no problem.'

'Early afternoon… We're not quite sure when they're being flown off the Olna.'

A tall, slim, attractive, fair-haired young woman was being madly chatted up by Jamie when I arrived back at Sick Bay just after lunch. She introduced herself as Dr Yvonne Westerhof, now a Surgeon Lieutenant in the Royal Dutch Navy. Having recently left civilian hospital work for something more exciting, she had just arrived in Scotland on a Christmas visit to her boyfriend Mark Rowley, one of our Pilots, only to discover he was hovering over the Atlantic somewhere, lifting survivors off the *Kartli*.

The Briefing Room had been converted into a reception centre by the Police, with a large circle of armchairs positioned round the walls. There was a folding partition at the top end which could effectively divide off one third of the room, and I persuaded the Police to let me utilise it to set up a screening centre where I could check the male, and Yvonne the female survivors, before sending them through for processing by police and immigration officers.

'What are you doing for interpreters?' I asked Jim Brown, the Prestwick Superintendent in charge of Police operations.

'Well, we thought we had it all sewn-up, Doc.' He grimaced ruefully. 'Two guys were supposed to be coming down to Prestwick from the Russian Consulate—but we've just heard that some silly bugger has sent them to Northern Ireland instead! But don't worry! We've arranged other interpreters. They're through the back having coffee. I'll fetch them.'

'That might not be a bad idea, Jim. We can run over a few basic questions I might want to ask them.'

The room was seething with Navy, Customs, Immigration and other personnel, but fortunately no reporters, for the Police had sensibly managed to contain the 'Fifth Estate' outside in the main hallway.

A great hulk of a man, in a Grand Slam sweater, approached and presented himself, accompanied by a petite, dark-haired young woman. He proffered a huge hand. 'I'm Archie. Sent down from the Gorbals, Doc. I don't know what I'm doing here. I only know the Russian Alphabet, and a wee bit out of this phrasebook… Somebody must have told my Super I could speak Russian, so they sent me down here!'

My heart sank. No harm to big Archie, but how the hell was I going to communicate with thirty cold, tired and bewildered Russian sailors, if the best we could muster between us was the Russian Alphabet!

The slim dark-haired girl stepped forward and introduced herself. 'I'm Susan Coontz. I teach Russian at Wellington School.'

This was more like it. Even Archie looked relieved at being let off the hook.

We set to and got a simple protocol organised. Batches of survivors, six or seven per helicopter, would be arriving at staggered intervals. We would collect a group together and ask simply if they felt well or unwell. Those requiring medical attention would be examined one by one behind the screens, and the others taken through to the Police.

Because there had been several fatalities, the whole rigmarole of a formal Fatal Accident Inquiry would have to be set in motion, with each one of the thirty survivors being asked a standard series of questions by the police.

But by now it was almost dark, and there was still no sign of the incoming helicopters. Where were they? The answer was simple and sensible. The Royal Fleet Auxiliary *Olna* was making way as fast as she could steam, round into the lee of the Mull of Kintyre, where, from the sheltered waters of the Kilbrannan Sound, it would be a short and safe helicopter transit to Prestwick.

Soon after dark, there was an expectant hush, as the pulsating throb of a Sea King was heard overhead, and I went out to meet it on the tarmac. It carried a body-bag containing the corpse of a woman crew member who had abandoned ship, but had not made it into a liferaft and, in that cruel December sea, had probably died of hypothermia within a few minutes. Bob Yeomans handed me a bit of crumpled paper. Her death had already been certified by the Surgeon Lieutenant on board the *Olna*, and consequently there was no need for any further input from me. Their other passenger, the ship's Captain, who was suffering from serious leg injuries, had already been dropped off en route, at Crosshouse.

Helicopters now began to arrive at half-hour intervals, offloading six survivors and returning for more. This half-hour gap gave us a breathing space to process each batch before the next arrived.

From the first group, Susan quickly confirmed that there had been a total of only four women on board, that three had been taken to Northern Ireland, and the fourth was now confirmed dead.

'Well, Yvonne. Looks as if you can fall out and polish your medals!' She looked slightly puzzled, then laughed, shook hands and said goodbye, before slipping out for a reunion with her boyfriend.

There was no real need for any medical checks. Although the Russian sailors, ranging in age from young teenagers to elderly men in their sixties, all looked dog-tired and stunned by events, they had all benefitted from their six hours of rest, warmth, dry clothing and food on the *Olna*. Clutching brown paper sacks containing what few pathetic personal belongings they had been able to salvage in their rush to escape, many were now dressed in Service issue blue parkas, denims and plimsolls, courtesy of the Royal Navy. They blinked bewildered eyes as they entered the brightly-lit room, and sat down quietly while Susan asked the appropriate questions. My sole contribution was a friendly gesture with my stethoscope—which triggered swivelled head-shakes and an emphatic and collective 'Niet!' from every group!

As the second batch were shepherded through to be processed, Superintendent Brown slipped up to me—'Eh, Doc… Keep your eye on these brown paper bags will you? If you see one wriggling, let me know. Word has it that they've rescued the ship's cat—and there's about as many Customs men, vets, and public health officials down to deal with this one bloody animal when we find it, as there are dealing with the entire crew!'

'What do you want me to do—open a tin of Whiskas, and grab the first brown bag that makes a dive for it?'

Curiosity finally drove me through to the main section of the Briefing Room. A burly Sergeant was sitting behind a table at the near left-hand corner, recording those who came through, and issuing them with forms to be completed later. Trays of sandwiches, tea and coffee, were being supplied to those men sitting dejectedly round the walls and patiently waiting to have their questionnaires filled in. In their midst, I was delighted to see big Archie, phrase book in hand, helping out a Constable with their answers.

Very few spoke much English, the exception being the only non-Russian on board, a whitehaired middle-aged Bulgarian called Theodor, who was the representative of the ship's Bulgarian owners. He was touchingly emotional in his expressions of thanks to all who had assisted them. I saw Vic Gover, Observer on one of the Sea Kings which had airlifted the crew from the *Kartli* to the *Olna* during the height of the gale, having a long chat with him. He came away quite humbled by what he had learned—and it took a lot to humble Vic!

The *Kartli*, leased by the Bulgarians to the Russians, had been based in Shetland since October 4th, as a Klondyker buying fish from Scottish boats, and had been heading back to her home port in the Black Sea with 750 tonnes of frozen mackerel on board, when the giant wave struck her.

'You know, Jimmy,' Vic confided, 'the only entertainment these poor buggers had on board, was one black and white telly with no sound! A throwback to the bad old days of the Cold War, to prevent any crew member who spoke English from finding out what really was going on in the world.'

By this time, repeated coffee mug refills had begun to overload the bladders of some of the earlier arrivals, and conducted trips to 'The Heads' were organised. As a relieved group of Russians re-entered the room, there was a wide grin on the face of their big police 'minder'.

'Whit's the joke then, Wullie?' someone asked.

'Och, I wis just laughin at the look on yin o thae Russian's faces when I took him intae the bog. He wis staunin haein a pee, an looked up tae see aa thae silhouettes o Russian warships pinned tae the waa in front o him. It took him a wee while for it tae dawn on him whit they were. His jaw drappt, then he turnt roun an gied me a big grin! Must hae thocht it wis a queer British wey o brain-washin—Pilots wattin their shoes!'

One of the other interpreters was a Navy Commander, a three ringer whom I had never seen before, but later learned he was a fluent Russian speaker drafted in from another Base. There was only one group still to be disembarked when Super Brown again came over and asked us to be on the lookout for a guy with a box chained to his wrist. Someone had reckoned he might be a political commissar, carrying some important papers that might be very interesting.

The last flight arrived, and with it our mystery man, carrying a red metal box on whose lid was printed a word which Susan translated as 'Pyrotechnics'—flares, explosives!

There was a flurry of activity as senior-ranking Police and the Russian-speaking Commander swooped on him—only to discover he was the Third Mate, and the mystery box held nothing more explosive than the ship's papers and the crew's passports!

What an anti-climax... for some.

*   *   *

Months later, at the Fatal Accident Inquiry, Sheriff Principal Robert Hay praised and commended the skill and courage of all those who took part in the rescue—the Royal Navy and RAF helicopter pilots and crews; the masters and crews—of the Shell tanker *Drupa* first on the scene, training searchlights on the *Kartli* and calming the frightened crew; of the RFA *Olna* which stood by and took on board thirty-two survivors; and of the Islay Lifeboat which was at sea for ten hours, her radar and navigation useless in thirty-foot waves, and having to rely on helicopter radio transmissions to guide her to the scene.

The *Kartli* was described by James McFarlane, a local fisherman, as being unfortunately in the wrong place at the wrong time—in total darkness, in an area of dangerous overfalls, where the waters of a strong spring tide, thrusting against severe gale force winds, were at that moment battering against underwater cliff faces and being thrown violently upwards as huge fifty-foot high 'stopper' waves. Half-an-hour either way might have made all the difference to the safety of vessel and crew.

The Procurator Fiscal Ian Henderson said it had been *'a textbook search and rescue operation carried out with consummate skill and outstanding courage in most difficult conditions'*; and Sheriff Principal Hay concluded by recording that *'the loss of life might have been substantially greater had it not been for the work of the emergency services. All played vital roles in carrying through to a successful conclusion a difficult and hazardous search and rescue operation at night and in adverse sea and weather conditions.'*

Those commendations were reflected later in the many bravery awards received by the RAF and Royal Navy aircrews involved in the rescue.

29

10 March 1992

'Somewhere in the North Atlantic...'

A spasmodic slam-bang-slam from the flat roof above the surgery slowly and insidiously impinged on my consciousness; a barely perceptible noise which finally became intolerable, as it infiltrated my thought processes, stretched consultation times, and caused me to fall further and further behind with my list.

Overhead, a westerly gale blattered hail and sleet against the skylight window, as scudding black squall clouds turned a March mid-afternoon to gloomy twilight.

I buzzed the front desk. 'Edith, could you check upstairs? I think someone has left that outside landing door open, and it's banging in the wind.' I wasn't being a wimp or a heartless boss, I told myself, sending a poor female member of staff out on to the roof on a day like this—merely being practical—employing some of those managerial skills the Government said all good GPs must learn from their compulsory Practice Management courses. 'Delegation' was the buzz-word... 'Your time is valuable—delegate!'

Edith, duly delegated, buzzed back a few minutes later saying that the door was locked, and that she'd had a quick look outside but could see nothing loose. Duly satisfied, I resumed my long-range plea to Mrs Brown to persevere with her 'Fye-bogle' and porridge for the long term relief of her pent-up motions, while she struggled for twenty minutes behind the screens, lacing up her Spirella, tucking in her multiple layers, and almost certainly pinning her knickers to her vest.

Slam-bang-slam! My pent-up emotions got the better of me. I gently 'ushed' her from the room, cursed inwardly—'If you want a bloody job done, do it yourself!'—grabbed the key from the office and rushed upstairs. The landing door opened with difficulty against the force of the gale, and I was buffetted badly when I emerged on to the flat roof, which the girls were in the habit of using as a 'Sitooterie' on warm summer days.

Warm summer days?

It was the beginning of March, and their white plastic picnic table was still sitting on the roof—since last summer—and slam-bang-slamming against the railings. A definite case for further delegation—to get it downstairs p.d.q.!

Another black squall swooped in over the rooftops from the west, and I was hit by horizontal hail before I had time to regain the shelter of the stair landing. What a day (or night) to be abroad in. Little did I know that out there—'somewhere in the North Atlantic'—a drama was waiting to unfold.

With my mind now clear of rooftop distractions, and reprieved by a merciful lull in telephone interruptions, I managed to wheich through the next half-dozen assorted sore throats, snots, coughs and flus, in jigtime. But as any sportsman on a winning streak learns to his cost, it is fatal to ease off before the final hurdle. Mrs McCurley, third hurdle from home, seemed to sense this, and was relaxing into a long convoluted ramble about her noisy neighbours when, from the region of my left hip, I was saved by the bleep—if not the bell.

I excused myself, and phoned Gannet Ops Room.

'It's a long-range medevac, Doc… Here's Lt Cdr Buckett, Ops Officer, to have a word with you.'

'Hello, Doc! We've just received this signal. I'll read it to you—"Man with peritonsillar abscess and swelling of uvula… now having breathing difficulties"—It's a long one, to a Submarine one hundred and fifty miles out… so we'll take you instead of the Medic.'

I looked at my watch. Five to five. There were only three patients left, so I buzzed big Paul to see if he could tack them on to his list, apologised to Mrs Mac, and sped off, green light flashing, into the rush-hour traffic. Sod's Law. I always seemed to get rush-hour traffic—any hour of the bloody day!

Once on the bypass, I had a foretaste of the weather in store for us, when I had to cut my speed drastically to avoid being buffeted on to the central reservation by strong cross winds.

As I drove through the main gate, I was jolted into action by the sound of engines firing up, and quickly struggled into my goon suit and rushed upstairs to the SAR Shack, expecting to find everyone already onboard. I had just reached the top landing when the engine noise unexpectedly died down, and opened the door to be met with an air of leisurely calm. Fiona McWilliam, my new MAQ, was busy making sandwiches. We now had two girls on the Sick Bay staff doing full SAR flying duties, since Fiona joined Magz Brodie—who herself had made a little bit of Naval history by being the first woman ever to fly aiurcrew on SAR helicopters.

'You're doing a good job, Fi. Just make sure you don't fill them with Marmite!' Memories of Sligo! 'By the way, do you have the SAR Drugs box key?' She fumbled in her pocket and produced the key, attached to a small piece of tattered tape, and I made a mental note to order a more substantial solid plastic label. It would be a disaster if we managed to lose the drugs key at some critical moment during a SAR.

Dave Duthie looked up from his charts. 'Hello there, Jimmy. Another long one for you, I'm afraid… a hundred and fifty miles west of Machrihanish. We'll have to call in there to refuel on the way out. We're stripping the cab of all extra gear to save weight.'

Leading ACMN Richard Fox interjected, 'What do you need to take, Doc? I've already emptied the cab, and all your gear is lying outside on the trolley.'

'Well… I'll need the Grab Bag and the resuscitation kit—and an extra oxygen cylinder just in case this guy's breathing really is bad.' I had a nightmarish vision of having to do some heroic procedure like a cricothyroidotomy to relieve his breathing—something I had never done before, although I was vaguely familiar with the technique.

I checked the Resusc. Kit which Foxie brought upstairs, and couldn't find a Mini-Tracheotomy set in the case. I couldn't go without this vital piece of equipment. There was one in my BASICS Medical Box in the car—so I rushed across to the car park and returned quickly with the Trachi set—and a spare scalpel—in case I had to lance the guy's quinsy throat as well. I'd be kidding myself on I could do brain surgery next—like the Crabs!

Meanwhile, the uncharacteristically slow and leisurely work-up to this SAR continued, in a deceptively casual fashion. It puzzled me. 'What's the delay, Dave?'

'We're just waiting on confirmation. The weather's pretty foul out there, blowing Force Nine, and we'll be flying into the teeth of it for two hundred miles. We won't have much hover time over the Sub, and the transfer may well be tricky.

'The Sub is heading towards us at top speed, so just now we're calculating the optimum time to rendezvous with her to give us maximum time overhead. Got it? If we leave too soon, we have further to travel, and not much fuel left for a difficult hover.'

'It's on! We leave at eighteen hundred hours!' interrupted Doug Fairley, our Canadian Observer, from his seat at the communications console.

I looked at my watch. Five to six! I'd had nothing to eat since a quick sandwich snack at one o'clock. But, considering the weather prospects, I consoled myself that was maybe just as well! Lulled by the slow-time of the last forty minutes, and now fully zipped up in my goon suit, I realised in a panic that, though my stomach was empty, my bladder wasn't! And I now had an added problem of negotiating, for the first time, the horizontal fly zip and rolled-up cod-piece, which were only the first of four clothing barrier layers to be penetrated before relief was to hand!

Although relief occupied three out of the next five minutes, Dave Duthie must have been quite glad I had off-loaded some extra ballast as Rescue 177, burdened with 5200lb of fuel on board, lumbered down the runway like a pregnant pigeon and slowly heaved herself into the grey, menacing, evening sky.

Flying low at 500 feet, into a 44-knot headwind which cut our ground speed down to 50-60 knots, progress was painfully slow as we juddered over spume-streaked waves round the southern tip of Arran. I used the last hour of daylight to double-check oxygen supply and the resuscitation equipment. In two hours time, a blacked-out, pitching, yawing helicopter would be no place to be fumbling around for vital missing gear!

Machrihanish Airbase looked like a giant building site, honeycombed with half-finished excavations for aircraft parking bays. I found myself wondering if work was still in progress, or had it ground to a halt after the recent momentous changes in the USSR which had signalled the end of the Cold War.

By the Control Tower stood three USAF Aurora reconnaissance aircraft. One, unmarked, totally grey and mysterious, fired-up and taxied out as we refuelled.

'Is that our top cover?' I asked Dave.

'No, I've asked RCC for top cover by a Nimrod.'

We resumed our journey, and, almost on cue, over the intercom came—'Rescue Eleven Nimrod airborne… Echo Tango Alpha target area thirty five minutes.' Thirty five minutes from Kinross! We had a hundred and fifty miles still to run from Machrihanish—with an ETA of 2030 hours—at least two hours flying!

Then, ominously, Machrihanish Coastguard broke in with a warning that weather conditions were deteriorating rapidly in the rescue zone.

It was almost dark as we approached Islay, and Doug Fairley took the safe route to the south of Beinn Bheigeir, skirting the coast past Lagavulin and Laphroaig Distilleries, over Port Ellen, and up Traigh Mhor, the Big Strand—a seven mile sweep of silver sand—towards Islay Airport. The heading led over Laggan Point towards Bruichladdich, and I was up front, keen to find out how our Islay holiday friends, the Pearces, were progressing with the building of their new house.

Suddenly Doug's voice crackled—'It's off. RCC have just cancelled!'

'Probably the weather's closing in,' intoned Dave, as he swept the aircraft round in a tight turn over Loch Indaal, just a few miles short of Bruichladdich, thwarting my chance of an aerial recce. 'Let's head for home.'

A couple of minutes later he fired off an expletive and swung the Sea King round 180 degrees back on to its original heading. The Observer had just received a signal from the Flag Officer Scotland and Northern Ireland countermanding RCC and ordering us to press ahead with the mission!

'I wish to hell they'd make up their bloody minds! We've lost ten minutes flying endurance farting about in this bay.'

'Who the hell's in charge of this show?'

'I dunno,' Doug Fairley snapped. 'FOSNI and some of the Top Brass seem to be involved. COMCLYDE have just told RCC that they're not running this one… and I think it's gone up as far as HQ Northwood, with CINCFLEET putting in their ten cents worth.'

Just what is going on, I wondered to myself, as I listened hard, trying to unravel the incomprehensible barrage of Naval acronyms, abbreviations, and jargonese being bandied about by the aircrew, and the fragmented instructions from Captains, Coastguards and Controllers coming over the radio. Gradually it all pieced together. There was a big planned NATO Exercise now underway in the North Atlantic, and our nuclear Submarine was part of the Task Group engaging 'The Enemy'; which was probably why the Top Brass at Northwood were turning purple at the gills—some poor sod of a Rating with a sore throat was buggering up their Exercise!

And they wanted him off their tube come hell or high water, hail, rain or Force Nine. This was now a Royal Navy medevac sortie, and nothing to do with RCC—and our wee Sea King was being detailed to do its duty… 'England expects…'!

However, to give him his due, the poor young RCC Controller across at Pitreavie stuck to his post, and persisted in his duty. Signals were flying thick and fast over his head, and he was obviously only party to a few of them.

'Rescue Eleven… Edinburgh Rescue. Could you please relay your position?'

'Negative!' came a blunt reply from the Nimrod.

'Rescue Eleven… Edinburgh Rescue. Your message was broken. Try again. Please relay your position.'

'Negative! Contact Command HQ by landline for my position!'

The poor sod at Pitreavie, in desperation, asked a third time for the Nimrod's position. The Nimrod commander's reply was curt and clear—'Classified!'

And just to ram home the point, the Navy also put the boot in—'Edinburgh Rescue… This is Captain, COMCLYDE… This is outwith your command. Repeat, outwith your command. You have only been brought in for reference.'

What a way to go on, I thought—this nuclear sub secrecy! Don't they know the Cold War is over? Then it dawned on me that the Nimrod would, in fact, be revealing not only his own position, but that of the Sub and the entire Task Group to their exercise 'Enemy'. It was obviously a very serious game!

Meanwhile, Doug and Dave had been having a serious confab about some problems with 'CBs', and how to avoid them.

'Jeez-oh! Don't tell me we've got truckers, hot-rodders, and radio freaks jamming up the airways now, as well as Captains and Admirals!' I murmured under my breath. But I failed to hear any input from Twin Cam Trev or Mustang Mick.

'Dave! What's this "CB" you're on about?' I finally asked.

'Cumulo-nimbus clouds, Jim. These great bloody squall clouds, or thunder clouds. They can cause a lot of turbulence, and it's better to try and skirt round them if we can.'

Our attentive RCC Controller obviously still had a comprehension problem. Over the intercom came a final plaintive plea to the Nimrod—

'Rescue Eleven... Edinburgh Rescue. Could somebody please tell us what is going on? We're going round in circles with all these conflicting messages from different sources!'

'Going round in circles! If you were sitting up here where I am sitting, you would know what it was like to be going round in circles—LADDIE!'

Rank was being well and truly pulled! This marvellous put-down raised a roar of laughter throughout the cab which, for a few seconds, blanked from our minds our own predicament.

Doug Fairley was getting very worried about a build-up of distant CBs on his radar screen. On a heading of 305 degrees, we were now making 70 knots ground speed against a 35 knot head wind, and had successfully skirted round several large shower clouds. Even on their fringes, the turbulence had been troublesome. Despite the bumpy ride, however, I was feeling quite chirpy and chuffed with myself, having managed to eat four of Fiona's cheese and pickle sandwiches without provoking a 'technicolor yawn' into my kid gloves.

Through the starboard window, during a rare clear spell between squalls, the reassuring flash of Tiree's South Light twenty four miles away to the North gave visual confirmation of the accuracy of Doug's heading. With ninety miles still to run, and anticipating trouble ahead from his radar scan, he called up the Nimrod for an update on weather conditions in the rescue area. Their reply was not encouraging.

'Rescue One Seven Seven... Rescue Eleven. There are several large patches of bad weather on radar. One thirty miles ahead of you, and another fifteen miles short of your target. They are both about twenty miles long and seven miles deep. You will have to go through... there is no way round! Leave you to it... We'll keep an eye on you, Little Buddie!'

' "Little Buddie"! That's nice. These guys really do care about us!'

'They wouldn't like to do our job though,' grunted Dave. '...Think we're bloody mad!'

'They're not the only ones.'

As we forged on through some minor squalls, I could feel a sense of unease gripping the crew as they considered the foul weather we were about to encounter. The usual banter was replaced by a tense concentration, as the two Pilots' thoughts turned to problems of control in severe turbulence, the Observer calculated critical fuel reserves, and the Winchman contemplated the prospect of a horrendously difficult transfer—if we did get through.

It was not to be, however. Just south of Barra Head, and with eighty miles still to run, the signal came through to cancel the mission. The Submarine had surfaced and reported that the weather was too severe to attempt a ship to helicopter transfer. Her Captain had opted to head for the Firth of Clyde and arrange a transfer from the lee of the Mull of Kintyre at first light, as the patient's breathing problems had somewhat improved.

None of us felt inclined to argue with his decision.

Almost immediately, the Nimrod was recalled to base, but to its Captain's eternal credit, and with our grateful appreciation, he refused to leave but hung around to provide top cover for the next thirty minutes till we had reached the safety of the Mull of Kintyre.

The safety, it transpired, was only relative. For the return trip, we were being assisted by a thirty-five-knot tail wind, and I had figured we would make a bee-line straight for Prestwick and be home in twenty minutes. But the CBs raised their ugly heads again, forcing us to detour south almost as far as the Irish coast, then zig-zag back up the Firth of Clyde past Ailsa Craig and over towards Arran before sneaking in behind a squall cloud to reach the Ayrshire coast near Turnberry, and thence back to Gannet. It took us forty-five minutes —but was it all really necessary?

As a hill walker, I reckoned I understood a fair amount about the ferocity of squalls, having been blown off my feet on several occasions. But I weighed only eleven stones—a Sea King weighed in at eleven tonnes! I quizzed Dave and Doug on their reasons for such an ultra-cautious approach.

'Cumulo-nimbus are not like strato-nimbus rain clouds, Jim. They rise to over 20,000 feet, and the violent downdraughts they generate have been known to tear the wings off an airliner. We flew through the edge of one last week in daylight, and the Sea King dropped two hundred feet in a matter of seconds— even at full torque, I could get no lift from the rotors.'

I now understood.

Three days after this graphic description of the immense power of thunderclouds, a Super Puma carrying oil-workers went straight into the sea off Shetland in a squall. Eleven men were lost.

We all understood.

30

25 March 1992

Never Put Off Till Tomorrow…

'Procrastination is the Thief of Time'. This aphorism is writ loud and large on the wall of Colin's bedroom. But despite the intense organisational pressures of second year medical studies at Glasgow, he has never yet quite grasped the concept—at least as far as getting out of his bed before midday during holidays is concerned. Though he still swears he manages to attend all his morning lectures during termtime!

As for myself, recently there seem to have been never enough hours in the day in which to cram all the demands on my professional and spare time; so personal procrastination has had to be simple and pragmatic—no more than a desperate search ahead for any gaps in life's busy schedule in which to slot the mounting backlog of extra-curricular activities.

So it was with the Advanced Trauma and Life Support Course Manual—or ATLS for short. It had arrived in January, just after I had finished two years work on our Family Tree—three hundred years of solid Ayrshire farm and mining stock—and just before I started preparing for the Burns Supper season —with four Immortal Memories lined up. In February there had been a Scots Language broadcast to do for Radio Scotland, followed by a Diving Medicine Course in Portsmouth.

This morning I woke in a panic! Over the past few weeks, I had managed, in that twilight zone of cerebral function between eleven-thirty and midnight, to skim through the ATLS Manual; but felt I had not done it justice, and had retained very little of its contents—with the course due to start tomorrow—26th March.

The last five days had been hopeless. A hectic on-call weekend had left no time for study. Monday night had seen me giving a SAR talk to Ayr Ladies Circle, and tonight, Wednesday, I was due to propose the vote of thanks at Ayr Rotary Club's Fashion Show!

Still, not to worry. I consoled myself that I could cram a second reading of the manual's more salient points this afternoon—my half-day. But I hadn't reckoned on my old friend Sod, and his Naval Oppo—the inevitable Embuggerance Factor!

It was a strange, humid, misty morning as I drove through Monkton. An unusually low cloud base hung less than a hundred feet above the airport. Strange, too, was the all-pervading smell of kerosene hanging in the damp air being drawn in through the car heater fan. Curiously I glanced across at the Airport Terminal. The explanation was readily apparent.

On the apron, and lined up on the taxiways, were four giant matt-olive USAF Starlifters. For a split second I was puzzled. Then it dawned. What I was witnessing was a piece of history, the final chapter in the withdrawal of the US Navy's nuclear submarine fleet from Sandbank, after thirty years in the Holy Loch—no longer would they tread the boards of the old pier at Ardnadam where my grandfather had been Pier Master in 1913. The planes probably contained Navy families' furniture—a sort of transatlantic Pickfords on wings. The Yanks were going home.

'Whit a dreich day for a flittin!' I thought of the old saying, and smiled as my mind conjured up boyhood memories of New Cumnock miners, of open flittings in the pouring rain, on the back of Bill Geddes's coal lorry. Luckier folk could have the luxury of a covered flitting in Lindsay's cattle float—offset by the smell! What a contrast with the computer-checked, custom-built, padded containers being loaded onto these flying pantechnicons, above which the grey mist swirled, scarcely clearing the tops of their huge tails.

'Classical SAR callout weather, too.' I let this unguarded thought cross my mind, and consequently, at 1015, the bleep went!

Fiona had already responded to an alert from the SAR cell, only to discover that RCC were also requesting a doctor to attend the patient, a seventy-five year-old woman on Islay, who had suffered a 'Cardiac Arrest', and who was now being tranferred to hospital in Glasgow. Presumably the mist was too low for the fixed-wing Loganair Air Ambulance.

Flying at four hundred feet, it was a rotten miserable journey, following the same low-level route, south of Arran and through the Machrihanish gap, as we had done in the force nine gale a fortnight past. This time we had low drizzling stratus, not CBs, to hinder progress. Forward visibility was very poor through the swishing windscreen wipers, and as we neared Islay, Marcus Wilson opted for the safe and simple approach—in low over Port Ellen and let the ten-mile straight of the Bowmore road guide us to the airport.

On board the waiting ambulance lay a dignified, alert, white-haired old woman, condition stable, and quite content. As happens so often, the 'cardiac' incident, interpreted by Pitreavie as an 'arrest', had in fact not been an arrest, but something a lot less fatal or dramatic—a 'cardiac arrythmia' or irregular heartbeat which, in this case, had precipitated a degree of breathlessness requiring a spell of hospital care. There was little else for me to do except make sure the old lady was adequately propped up to ease her breathing for the flight to Glasgow; so I made good use of the time to catch up on Islay gossip from the nurse, and to find out what progress had been made with the Pearces' house—the ground had been cleared. In the islands, that's often progress!

And as we talked, the skies cleared—the front carrying the low stratus was drifting slowly away eastwards, and it was an interesting meteorological experience to watch it being replaced by broken cloud at three thousand feet. While this gave Bob Gale, our Pilot, a degree of freedom in deciding his flight path, the old lady's physical condition decreed that she would be better flown at a reasonably low altitude—say 1000 to 1500 feet.

As we flew up the Sound of Jura, the sad sight of the rusting, battered, derelict hulk of the Bulgarian trawler *Kartli*—still fast aground on rocks off one of Gigha's lovely western bays—prompted reminiscences of the rescue, and dry comments on the aftermath:

'I hear some entrepreneur from down south is going to convert her into a floating B and B for tourists.'

'With four hundred and fifty tonnes of stinking mackerel still on board, it would make a better cattery!'

It was a relaxed flight back to Glasgow, enlivened, as we skirted Bute, by Marcus ('It's a fine chimney that!') Wilson's phallic fixation with the tall stack of Inverkip Power Station. We were making good time, and I was contemplating the prospect of a full afternoon's study for the ATLS Course, when suddenly Edinburgh Rescue came on the air with a request for us to refuel at Glasgow—'We may have another job for you!'

After old Mrs Campbell was safely delivered to the waiting ambulance, we hung about outside the aircraft during refuelling, and shared our meagre rations —a packet of Softmints, and a squashed Mars Bar retrieved from the depths of my goon suit pocket—in a desperate attempt to stave off the inevitable hunger pangs of a lost lunch-hour.

Marcus, meanwhile, was busy trying to determine from RCC just exactly what our next job might entail. Finally, as we boarded and strapped in, he announced 'It's a Preggevac, chaps! A woman about thirty-six weeks pregnant, Doc, who has had some bleeding... She's coming down from Benbecula on Rescue One One Nine from Stornoway and we've to meet them half-way, on Tiree, and fetch her back to Glasgow.'

Well, that's buggered up any chance of swotting up trauma care this afternoon, I moaned under my breath—the only consolation being the chance of a rare scenic flight in fair weather conditions out to Tiree.

We short-cut back over the Renfrewshire hills and inevitably overflew Inverkip Power Station.

'Marvellous chimney that—a big one!' came a voice from the back.

'That's a disturbing fixation you've got, Marcus—Stop it! You're a married man… and soon to be a father again!'

Heading west, we traversed Bute and flew up Loch Fyne past Portavadie. Below us, the huge excavation—dug at great public expense twenty years ago as an oil rig construction yard, despite a storm of protest from environmentalists at the desecration of a sensitive and beautiful part of the Firth of Clyde—still lay unused and derelict, having never found a client. The site was now flooded and occupied by a salmon fish farm—the most expensive sheltered anchorage in Britain.

From Ardrishaig, it was a short hop across the isthmus to Crinan. Down to the left, several beautiful luxury yachts, moored in the canal basin, attracted envious comment.

'There's Crinan Hotel… great place for a dirty weekend for yachtsmen.'

'Stop it, Marcus! You're a married man!'

'Yeah, take your wife next time… and the three kids!'

Corrievreckan once again proved disappointing—not a whirlpool to be seen—as the early flood tide slipped undemonstratively through the channel, with only the meekest opposition from a light westerly breeze.

Away to the north west, beyond Iona and the Ross of Mull, my eyes were drawn to what looked like an enormous ship on the horizon. Then it clicked—

'Doesn't Staffa look like a bulk carrier?'

'Yeah, a few million tonnes deadweight, Doc.'

'Anybody here feel hungry?' came a cry from the heart of the stomach of Bob Gale. There was a chorus of affirmatives. 'Marcus, could you try and raise Rescue One One Nine, and see if there's any chance of them picking up a few drinks and snacks for our arrival at Tiree.'

Marcus came back a few seconds later. 'It's all fixed… they're good lads!' Then he informed us: 'We're just passing Conalsay… eight miles at Two One Zero degrees.'

'Conalsay!' I mocked. 'It's Colonsay! You made it sound like Connel Ferry. No wonder you guys get lost so often.'

'We don't get lost, Doc,' protested Bob.

'I seem to remember a certain Pilot flying up Loch Leven instead of Loch Linnhe…'

'Shhhh!'

'Something you're not telling us, Bob?' queried Marcus from the back.

' "What's the Ballachulish Bridge doing down there on our port side?" was all I asked him, Marcus!'

True to its nationally renowned reputation, Tiree's scalloped shoreline of sparkling silver sands lay bathed in glorious sunshine as we skimmed in low towards the airfield and landed on, just a few yards away from the big Stornoway Coastguard Sikorsky 61.

To our surprise, a young woman emerged down the aircraft steps and walked across to ours, accompanied by one of the Coastguard aircrew and a young man, presumably her husband. This wasn't quite the emergency picture we had envisaged. Some one at term, with any degree of bleeding, would have been stretchered and on I/V fluids.

We helped her on board, and ushered her aft towards our prepared stretcher. It would be safer for her to be lying down.

No! She insisted she would rather sit—she had sat all the way down from Benbecula on Rescue 119 and had felt fine. Her notes, in fact, simply confirmed she'd had a slight 'show' and a few contractions the night before, and as she was only a visitor to the island, the local GP had obviously been keen to get her off his patch before she really went into labour!

Against my better judgment, I gave in to her wishes to travel seated, and helped her to buckle up her belt beside me on the for'ard seats. Her husband, a tall young lad with a short back and sides, seemed surprisingly relaxed, and donned a red immersion suit with the minimum of fuss. I scribbled her a note. 'Is your husband RAF?' She read it, smiled and nodded.

It was the last time she smiled on the journey. LACMN Paul Truss came for'ard with some fruit drinks and sundries which our Coastguard friends, true to their word, had acquired for us in Tiree. Gallantly I offered her a drink. She declined. Her pale face got paler, as she withdrew into that 'Am-I-or-am-I-not going to be sick!' trance, experienced or witnessed by most of us at one time or another. She should have been lying down, but she was adamant—and worried me all the way to Glasgow. Next time, I would be bloody adamant as well! From now on all pregnant women would be flying horizontal, on their sides, whether they liked it or not, to head off any problems of sickness, fainting or low blood pressure.

Fortunately, the return flight was high and fast, and in no time at all we were landing on at Glasgow Airport—only fifty minutes—but to our mum-to-be it must have seemed an eternity. Both she and her colour brightened up considerably as soon as she set foot once more on terra firma.

'Right! Straight home and get on with the bloody studying!' I muttered to myself.

Wrong! Bob Gale decided to do a PPI check over the sea off Hunterston Nuclear Power Station.

Bob normally flew his Sea King like a Spitfire. Corners were his speciality. Blue skies would suddenly invert to green fields or red roofs, when he flung his aircraft into tight turns and G-forced our stomachs down our rectums!

But a Power Performance Indicator check really allowed him to let his beard down as he tested the engines to maximum torque, and we dived and twisted through the skies like some demented kite.

Fun for the day over, five hours flying time logged, we landed back at

Prestwick with my half-day gone, and precious little time or energy left for study-revision.

In fear and trepidation, I joined fifteen colleagues next day at the Victoria Infirmary for the dreaded ATLS course. Many were either Consultants or Senior Registrars in Accident and Emergency or Anaesthetics, and the two day course was geared both to teach and terrify. Each lecture invariably ended with the ominous warning—'If you think this is bad, wait till you get the "Moulage" on Saturday!'

The 'Moulage' involved a mock casualty whose perilous clinical state lurched from one crisis to another at the whim of the examiner. Just as one problem was stabilised, another would materialise from the depths of his twisted brain.

My patient was a severely injured pregnant woman, in shock, whom I had the good sense to lie on her left side! I passed.

*   *   *

Passing the ATLS course, I felt, would give me a lot more clinical confidence for the years to come. It was just over five years since I had flown my first SAR —with more gaps than knowledge—and those gaps had slowly and gradually been filled in, as we learned from one job to the next, and adapted our kit and techniques accordingly, where we could.

But poor kit continued to be a major problem. Although the SAR Cell at Gannet had now been up and running as a frontline unit for two and a half years, and had seen a tremendous increase in its workload, on the medical side, we still had no budget for equipment, and were being expected to do our job with second-hand gear begged from old decommissioned ambulances. It was frustrating to know that the new, proven, innovative splints, stretchers, heart monitors and defibrillators, which had been supplied to civilian frontline ambulances and BASICs doctors over the past few years, were probably at least five years away from even being considered for procurement by the Military.

While those first five years had been a novel and fascinating experience, the next five years turned out to be even more challenging, as escalating demands on the services of Rescue 177 placed increasing strain on our inadequate medical resources; and eventually Service bureaucrats were persuaded that patients' lives depend on a good service, and that a good service depends on good equipment.

Stories of the trials and tribulations, tragedies and triumphs of those next five years will be told in the second volume of *Rescue 177*. These include one major setback when the SAR Cabin and its contents, including our new Heartstart defibrillator, were destroyed by fire—resulting shortly afterwards in a twitchy, anxious trip from Tiree to Glasgow with no monitoring equipment, transferring a man who had just survived a cardiac arrest on the island.

Two tragic stories relate graphically to the dangers of helicopter flying. First, the sad loss of a fine Aircrewman, Jim Scott, and the rescue of his three colleagues, when one of Gannet's Sea Kings crashed into the sea off Islay; and second, only a few months later, the Chinook helicopter disaster on Mull of Kintyre, when twenty-nine died. Several stories describe crossings of The Minch in Severe Gale Nine or Storm Force Eleven winds, and testify to the terrifying power of the sea and the skill and endurance of the SAR aircrews. Another tells of a tense hospital transfer, flying a hundred miles in horrendous blizzard conditions with a woman in premature labour, which led eventually to a happy outcome, and great satisfaction for all concerned.

Two unusual and dramatic rescues were later to feature on the BBC '999' series, one involving a Solway fisherman who had lost his leg in a winch accident, and the other involving a man who suffered severe chest pain on top of the Bell Tower at Inveraray.

Further unusual SARs missions were flown—to nuclear submarines. The first, to a British sub off the Mull of Kintyre, led to important revision of certain safety at sea procedures; and the other involved a three-hundred mile trip to rendezvous with a Russian hunter killer submarine off the Orkneys, where we lifted off a young seaman with a ruptured appendix. This incident made history, since it was the first occasion on which Russia had ever requested NATO help in evacuating one of its servicemen—a positive sign of the end of the Cold War.

Throughout this period, my MAs flew as aircrew on almost every mission—around 250 per year—as Gannet quickly became one of the busiest SAR Stations in the UK. Their presence was welcomed and accepted by Aircrewmen and Observers for the medical skills they brought with them and were only too willing to pass on, while learning themselves the basic techniques of cliff and ship winching. This acquisition of medical skills by Aircrewmen was later to become very important as pre-hospital care standards were set higher and higher, and the military SAR authorities began to accept that Inter-Service cooperation and standardisation of training and equipment was the way forward; which would mean, in the long term, Advanced Pre-Hospital Care training for backseat aircrew, and the phasing out of MAs in Navy Sea Kings, as well as myself.

While this book and its companion volume are primarily concerned with the in-flight drama of SAR, I cannot finish without paying tribute to those without whose expertise no aircraft would ever leave the ground. At Gannet, I am constantly aware that the success of SAR relies essentially on a cooperative team effort—not only between aircrew and MAs, but involving, equally, all departments on the Base. From Ops Room to Met. Office, Survival Equipment Section to Pusser's Stores, Flight Maintainers' Workshops to Flight Marshalls on the apron—even the Galley who provide our Bag Rats—we rely totally on their skill and professionalism to see us out and safely back again, and we thank them.

Jackspeak Glossary:
Naval Terms and Acronyms

Admiralty Surgeon and Agent—A civilian doctor who is appointed, in towns all over the country, often ports, to look after any *Jacks* taken ill on home leave, and provide reports to their Ship or Shore base on their fitness to travel. A now defunct relic of the old days of the mighty Navy.

Aircrewman—See *LACMN* and *POACMN*.

arse-up ducks—Any duck, swan or goose.

ASW—Anti-submarine warfare.

ATC—Air Traffic Control.

AWOL—Absent without leave.

Back-seat crew—Always the Observer and Aircrewman, plus an MA or Doctor if carried.

bag and mask—Method of delivering oxygen to a patient's lungs via a mask and an inflatable bag which is gently squeezed.

BASICS—The British Association of Immediate Care Schemes—a voluntary doctors' scheme to provide training and expert pre-hospital medical care at road accidents and major incidents. Founded in the early 1970s by pioneering GPs in England, it has expanded UK-wide, and provides a valuable service, especially in areas remote from major hospitals. Since the 1990s, Ambulance Paramedics now do much of this work.

becket—A strong loop sewn into a piece of safety equipment.

bone dome—Flying helmet.

Bootnecks/Booties—Royal Marines.

bowser—Fuel tanker.

burning and turning—Describes a helicopter with engines firing, blades rotating, and ready for take off.

cab—A shorter name for a helicopter than chopper or helo!

Captain—The title of the Commanding Officer of a Shore Base, or Aircraft. The officer in command may be anything from a Lieutenant to a Commodore. E.g. the Captain at HMS *Gannet*—a Shore Establishment (or Stone Frigate)—held the rank of Commander. On his 'Ship' were one or two Squadrons, each commanded by a CO holding the rank of Lieut. Commander. The Captain of each Sea King might be a Lieutenant, or a

Lieut. Commander—or even a Captain or a Major if the most senior officer on board came from Canada, the USA, or Germany. And he could be either the Pilot or the Observer. All very confusing!

Captain's Table—Formal appearance before the Commanding Officer for promotion or demotion, commendation or court martial, honourable release, or dishonourable discharge.

Casevac—Injured casualty evacuation.

CBs—Cumulonimbus thunder clouds.

Channel 16—The Maritime Distress Safety and Calling Radio Frequency on which Coastguards and all ships maintain a constant listening watch.

Chief—Any CPO.

Chief Tiff—Chief Petty Officer Air Engineering Artificer.

Chinook—Very large twin rotor troop-carrying helicopter.

CINCFLEET—Commander-in-Chief Fleet.

CMP—Civilian Medical Practitioner: the designation of a civilian doctor whether working part-time and alone in a small military unit, or in a full-time post alongside the staff of Service Medical Officers on large Bases.

CO—Commanding Officer.

Cocker's P—The Annual Cocktail Party held in the Wardroom for all those and such as those in the community.

COMClyde—Commodore Clyde. The Senior Officer based in Faslane.

companionway—Entry into a ship's cabin.

CPO—Chief Petty Officer.

CPR—Cardio-pulmonary Resuscitation.

Crab—Navy nickname for anything RAF. The first uniforms issued to the RAF in 1918 came from a cancelled batch ordered by the Tsar of Russia. Their grey/blue colour was similar to that of mercuric oxide jelly or 'crabfat' used at the time to treat body lice—and the name stuck.

Destroyer—Fast escort warship used mainly for the air defence of a convoy or fleet.

dispatch harness—Heavy webbing belt attached to the Winchman and the roof of a Sea King to prevent him falling out of the aircraft's open door when directing a winching.

dit—A story or account of an incident or event.

Doc—Nickname for the MA in charge of a Sick Bay on board a ship without a doctor. On a big ship, the Doctor would be the Quack, and the MA the Doc. On SAR sorties, I was referred to as Doc, and, on one memorable occasion, my POMA became 'Baby Doc'.

dockyard omelette/pizza—The visual aftermath of a vigorous *huey*.

Doppler—The forward, sideways, and upwards motion-sensing equipment within the aircraft.

downbird—A helicopter which has made a precautionary or emergency landing, and requires attention from the Maintainers.

Drills—Six monthly Pool or Wet Drills practising with inflatable one man and ten man dinghies in Ayr Baths; and also Abandon Aircraft Drills in the hangar. In addition there were yearly Sea Drills in the Firth of Clyde, swimming to and boarding a ten man liferaft, then a one man dinghy from which the occupant was winched up into a Sea King.

Dunker—The dreaded helicopter underwater escape training tank at Yeovilton, in which all Aircrew have to pass their Dunker Drills every two years to keep in date.

dunking—Dipping the aircraft sonar in the sea to listen for submarines.

embuggerance factor—An extra little something sent to try us, and make our day!

endurance—The number of hours a Sea King can remain airborne without having to refuel. Normally around four and a half hours. See *range*.

ETA—Estimated time of arrival.

FAA—Fleet Air Arm.

Faslane—UK Northern Naval Base, Firth of Clyde—HMNB (Clyde).

Ferrex—Rescue exercise involving a ferry.

fin—The conning tower of a submarine.

First Lieutenant—See *XO*.

flash-up—Start aircraft engines.

F/Med 4—The Tri-Service patient's Medical Record folder.

FONAC—Flag Officer Naval Air Command (now changed to Flag Officer Maritime Air—*FOMA*).

FOSNI—Flag Officer Scotland and Northern Ireland.

Frigate—Fast warship used mainly in an anti-submarine role.

goffered—Swamped by a big wave.

goon bag/suit—Supposedly dry cotton ventile immersion survival suit with rubber neck and wrist seals.

heads-up—A briefing or early warning of a potential problem.

helo—Helicopter.

HIFR—Helicopter inflight refueling procedure.

highline transfer—A winching done from a great height, involving first the lowering of a sandbag on a thin line attached to the winch hook, which is held from below to control the movement of the person on the end of the winchwire, or the stretcher.

HMS Gannet—Several Royal Navy warships bore this name before it was finally bestowed on an ASW Helicopter Base. HMS *Gannet* moved to Prestwick from Northern Ireland in 1971, following the onset of 'The Troubles', and occupied the site of the former wartime and post war US Air Force Base on the northern perimeter of Prestwick Airport, till it was decommissioned in March 2003. As from April 2003, the name lives on as *HMS Gannet SAR Flight*, with its three designated SAR Sea Kings.

huey—A noisy retch, or *technicolour yawn.*

hunter-killer—A class of nuclear submarine whose function is to seek out and destroy enemy submarines or ships—as distinct from the 'Bombers' equipped with ballistic nuclear missiles.

ICU—Intensive Care Unit in a major hospital.

Jack—Shortened version of Jack Tar—generic name for all Royal Navy sailors.

Jimmy—The XO or First Lieutenant of a ship.

jolly—A carefree jaunt in a helicopter.

Jossman—The Master-at-Arms.

jump seat—The bulkhead seat at the front of a Sea King, just behind the Pilots, and close to the front entrance door.

Killick—Any Leading Hand.

knot—Nautical Mile—approx 2000 yards. Thus, a 30 knot wind = 34 mph.

LACMN—Leading Aircrewman. Usually trained Sonar Operators on Anti-submarine Sea Kings. Some are also trained as SAR Divers. Now all designated SAR Aircrewmen have to undertake advanced paramedical training to equip them to deal with most inflight emergencies. See *POACMN.*

lightweight stretcher—Anything but! A rugged tubular metal basket stretcher used in the transfer of casualties to the helo.

LMA—Leading Medical Assistant.

Lynx—The small twin-engined helicopter carried by Frigates and Destroyers.

MA—Medical Assistant. Till recently, *MAQs* were female MAs, separately governed by QUARNNS (Queen Alexandra Royal Naval Nursing Service). Trained to man and administer Sick Bays on Ship and Shore Bases, MAs look after all medical records, pharmacy, immunisation programmes, First Aid training courses, and emergency packs. They are given training in basic diagnostic skills, and allowed to prescribe a limited number of basic drugs. MAs are also highly skilled in pre-hospital emergency care. See *LMA* and *POMA.*

Maintainers—Aircraft engineering ground crew.

Master-at-Arms—The MAA is in charge of Base policing and discipline, together with his team of Regulators.

Medevac—Evacuation of a medical case—usually a transfer from a lowland or highlands and islands country cottage hospital, to a major city hospital.

MRT—Mountain Rescue Team.

Navex—Navigational exercise.

Neil-Robertson Stretcher—A wrap-round slatted rescue stretcher with multiple straps which can be used for vertical stretchering of a casualty from a confined space, e.g. a submarine.

Nimrod—RAF long-range ASW jet aircraft based on the design of the old

Comet passenger jet. From RAF Kinloss they provide *top cover* support for exposed, long-distance helicopter SARs.

Northwood—CINCFLEET HQ.

Observer—The Navigator and operational tactician of the Sea King, who is in charge of flight operations and communications. Is also cross-trained with the Aircrewman to operate the winch, or go down the wire himself. Observers now undergo extended medical training to equip them for their SAR role.

Oggie—Native of Cornwall.

OOD—Officer of the Day or Duty Officer.

oppo—A sailor's buddy or mate.

OPSO/OIC Ops—The Operations Officer.

Ops Room—Operations room.

ovies—Flying or Maintainers' overalls.

paraffin budgie—A helicopter—which always smells of paraffin!

Perishers—Final 'pass or perish' course for potential Royal Navy Submarine Commanding Officers, usually conducted in the waters of the Scottish Sea Exercise Areas.

Pilot, Left-hand—The Co-pilot or P2, who occupies the left-hand seat in a Sea King, shares the flying, and also keeps tabs on fuel levels and instruments while the P1 is in the hover over a casualty.

Pilot, Right-hand—The P1 Pilot who will fly the Sea King during a rescue, because the cargo door from which the Winchman gives his directions is situated on the right side of the aircraft.

playmate—One of a pair of helicopters on an exercise together.

PLB—Personal Locator Beacon—attached to a PLP and giving out a signal for searching aircraft.

PLP—Personal Life Preserver—put more simply, an inflatable lifejacket.

PO—Petty Officer.

POACMN—Petty Officer Aircrewman.

POMA—Petty Officer Medical Assistant. NCO usually in charge of a Sick Bay on board a Frigate or Destroyer, where there is no Doctor on board. Larger ships will have full medical facilities with Doctors, operating theatres, and wards.

PO(SE)—Petty Officer Survival Equipment.

pot—Hyperbaric recompression chamber.

Preggevac—Transfer of a pregnant patient to hospital.

PSP—Personal Survival Pack: a yellow plastic case containing an inflatable one-man dinghy and other survival aids, on which Sea King aircrew sit, attached by straps, during flight, and which is supposed to go out of the aircraft window with them during an escape from a sinking helo.

Pusser—Describes anything to do with the Navy, especially anything of inferior quality, e.g. kit issue. Derives from the old Purser—the Paymaster or Supply Officer.

Quack—A Navy Doctor.

RAF Kinloss—United Kingdom's Rescue Coordination Centre, and home of the RAF Nimrod force.

RAF Lossie—RAF Lossiemouth, home of the Crab Sea King SAR Flight.

range—Maximum number of miles radius from Base that a Sea King can travel, hover over casualty, and return safely on a full tank of fuel. Normally around 200-250 mile radius, or 400-500 mile round trip. The maximum fuel load is about 5200lb, or 520 gallons of kerosene, and the fuel consumption is about 1 mile per gallon! This range can be considerably extended by means of refuelling stops.

rat-arsed—Blind drunk.

rat-bags—Packed meals.

RCC—Rescue Coordination Centre. Now there is only one Centre for the UK, based at RAF Kinloss, covering an area from the Faroes to the Bay of Biscay and half of the North Sea. Prior to 1997 there were two centres, one at Plymouth, Cornwall for the Southern sector, and the other at Pitreavie, Fife, known as 'Edinburgh Rescue', which covered the Northern Sector.

Reggie—Regulator—or 'Crusher'—member of the MAA's team.

RFA—Royal Fleet Auxiliary—supply ships for the Royal Navy.

RNAS—Royal Navy Air Station.

RNLI—Royal National Lifeboat Institution.

RNR—Royal Naval Reserve. Officers and Ratings who have left the Service have the opportunity to join the Reserve for a specified time, and usually spend 2-3 weeks per year on service duties.

RTA—Road Traffic Accident.

SAR—Search and Rescue.

SAR Cell—The name given to the unit within 819 Sqn, HMS *Gannet*, which undertook SAR duties, and which was superseded by the *SAR Flight* in April 2003 when HMS *Gannet* was decommissioned.

SAR Crew—Pilot, Co-pilot and Observer, who are all Officers, and an Aircrewman who is an NCO. Till recently, HMS Gannet Sea Kings also flew with an MA as aircrew, and also a Doctor when his services were required. From 2003, the extended-trained Aircrewmen will replace the MAs who are being phased out.

SAR Flight—Dedicated Search and Rescue Unit, comprising perhaps three specially equipped Sea King helicopters with back-seat crews specially trained for mountain, sea, and medical casualties. All backed up by a full team of aircraft maintainers, SE Section, Stores, Admin, etc.

SARO—Search and Rescue Officer. The Lieut. Commander in charge of

SAR operations in a SAR Flight.

Sea King—Built by Westlands to an original Sikorski design, this twin-engined helicopter has had an ASW role for the Royal Navy and a Commando carrier role for the Royal Marines for over thirty years. A smaller cousin of the Coastguard's Sikorski 61, it is also the designated SAR aircraft for both the Royal Navy and RAF.

SE Section—Survival Equipment Section, whose job is to inspect and maintain all items of survival kit, and supervise all aircrew survival training.

shitehawks—Usually seagulls.

shout—A SAR callout.

SNLR—Services no longer required. Dishonourable discharge.

SOBS—Senior Observer of a Squadron.

SPLOT—Senior Pilot of a Squadron.

Squadron—819 Squadron, Fleet Air Arm, based at HMS *Gannet*, RNAS Prestwick, initially comprised nine ASW Sea King helicopters, with a Ship's Company of around 350 personnel. Later, an extra one, then two, designated SAR aircraft were added to the Squadron assets.

STASS—Short Term Air Supply System: a small cylinder of compressed air attached to a PLP, giving an extra 1-2 minutes underwater breathing time for aircrew escaping from a sinking helicopter.

Stokes Litter—See *lightweight stretcher.*

stone frigate—A Royal Navy Shore Establishment such as HMS *Gannet*.

stoofed—An aircraft crash.

strop—Heavy webbing loop with sliding toggle passed under the armpits and used to winch people to or from a helicopter. Just don't raise your arms!

Subby—Sub-lieutenant.

technicolour yawn—A spectacular vomit.

tits-up—Broken down and useless.

top cover—Support from 6 miles high, given by RAF Nimrods skilled at locating stricken ships, dropping liferafts, and providing weather, locational guidance, and communications relay, for searching SAR helos on long-range missions.

tube—ASW aircrew nickname for a submarine.

VF—Ventricular Fibrillation. A terminal heart flutter following a cardiac arrest, which can be converted back to a normal rhythm using a Defibrillator.

Wafu—Service nickname for anyone associated with the FAA—supposed to stand for 'wet and flippin useless'

Watch Bill—Schedule of the whole Ship's Company, detailing the general working routine of the ship, each man's place of work, special sea duties, etc.

wet—A brew, a mug of tea.

Wessex—Replaced in 1988 by the Sea King as the Royal Navy and RAF rescue helicopter, mainly because of lack of range, radar, and a second pilot. Some are still used as workhorses by the RAF.

Winchman—The Aircrewman or Observer in charge of winch operations from the rear door of the Sea King, directing the Pilot via the intercom.

Wren—Member of the Women's Royal Naval Service, formerly the organisational backbone of the old Navy. Now disbanded in favour of an equal opportunities Service (almost) where women can now serve at sea in front-line ships and aircraft, and there is meant to be no obvious distinction between the sexes—except the obvious!

WO—Warrant Officer.

XO—The Jimmy, Executive Officer, or First Lieutenant of a ship—Second in Command to the Captain of a Ship or Shore Establishment.

yawing—An unpleasant sideways movement of aircraft or boat.